A John Catt Publication

Empowering Learning

The Importance of Being Experiential

Malcolm Pritchard

First Published 2017

by John Catt Educational Ltd,
12 Deben Mill Business Centre, Old Maltings Approach,
Melton, Woodbridge IP12 1BL

Tel: +44 (0) 1394 389850 Fax: +44 (0) 1394 386893
Email: enquiries@johncatt.com
Website: www.johncatt.com

ISBN: 978 1 909 717 98 5

Set and designed by John Catt Educational Limited

Table of Contents

To Marjorie for my being,
to Jane for my thinking,
and to Holly for the experience.

Preface

What is wrong with us? The question, or a variant, of which there are many, is asked, often without any rhetorical intent, countless times each day. The question comes from a troubled place within the deep well of humanity that lies at the core of our being. The original premise for this book – *What is wrong with education and how can we fix it?* – is one such variant. It is a question that lies quietly slumbering in each paradigm-shifting reformation of education; it also screams with mindless anger in each terror-inducing failure of education that besieges our humanity.

We are troubled, but cannot understand the reason for our disquiet. We journey to the stars, yet have forgotten our roots. We seek safety at home and shun the terrifying wonder of discovery. We celebrate the virtues and triumphs of our own; we fear the vices and decadence of others. We purify consensus, suppress diversity, marginalise dissent, and forget our shared humanity. We assert our rights to rule a planet, while neglecting our stewardship to care for it. We desert alliances in anger, in frustration we elect leaders who reflect the worst of human nature, and seek refuge in the fantasy of an imaginary past. Our voice is drowning in noise of our own creation. We feel lost.

Intuitively, we do know at least part of the answer: arouse the somnolent, harness angry energy to create, respect the other voice, draw order from complexity, remember our humanity, act with courage, and find wisdom in everyday experience. Being, we must know; knowing, we must do.

It would be an act of ultimate hubris to assert that the ideas expressed in the following pages will answer these questions and in so doing set humanity on the higher path many seek. It would be a denial of a quiet personal truth, however, to conceal the fact that these questions, among others, have stalked the mind of the writer with enduring persistence and have therefore contributed in no small way to the ideas explored herein.

The book is a reflection of a personal journey to find something useful, perhaps precious, in the largely unexamined experiences that fill our hours and minds. It will most likely not answer any of the questions posed above to the satisfaction of many. It will not generate a new wave of innovation in learning for the next generation. It may, however, suggest an unanticipated detour from the well-trodden pathways of institutional education for just a few. And it is with naïve hope that I trust it may change the mind of just one.

Introduction

Chapter 1: An Overview of Experiential Learning

All learning is ultimately experiential, but not all experiences result in learning. From birth, we experience, and from birth we learn. Learning marks every phase of our lives, and shapes our every action. We learn consciously, deliberately, and methodically; we also learn intuitively, instinctively, and experientially. We learn in company and in isolation. It is our most powerful tool for survival and progress. We are innately curious about our surroundings and our surroundings have a propensity to inflict salutary lessons, often unbidden. We learn to be more careful as a result.

This book is about learning, and more particularly about learning through and from experience. Learning is a process of developmental change, from one state to another. Experience is the mechanism by which such development is initiated, enacted, and reviewed. These terms will be explored in more detail in the following chapters. Together, they inform the three fundamental dimensions or properties of the human experience: *being, knowing,* and *doing.*

Being is an ontological state in which we construct our individual and collective identities that together reflect the socio-cultural 'I'; this embodies our social status, culture, values, beliefs, and attitudes. *Knowing* is a cognitive state of understanding and meaning making constructed by the individual within a social reality. *Doing* is the behavioural extension of our being and knowing: it is the observable manifestation of who we are and what we know. Our being, knowing, and doing are inherently social: we do not exist 'alone'. Thus, learning is an experiential process of change that informs our being, knowing, and doing. To put this in a visual context, the following diagram offers one way of connecting these ideas:

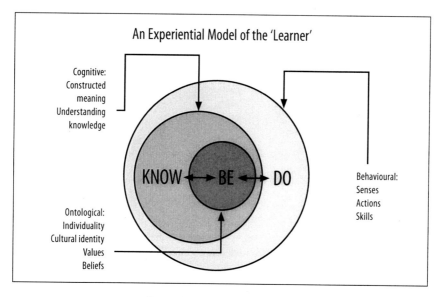

Figure 1: *An Experiential Model of the Learner*

At this point, the reader might be forgiven for thinking that these statements are gross simplifications of complex ideas. To an extent, that would be a fair judgement. However, the paradox of the human condition is that it is both breathtakingly simple and absurdly complex. We come into existence without any particular effort on our part; we are nurtured biologically and socially by others until we can sustain our lives independently; we seek out others to pass on our genes through biological replication; and we then reach the end of our lifespan, however short or long, and take no further direct role in human affairs. This simple biological progression becomes absurdly complex when we try to make sense of the journey. Learning facilitates the biological journey: we learn to walk and feed ourselves for example. Learning also drives the search for understanding; it arises from an innate hunger to know and understand. And, paradoxically, as we experience and learn, increasingly broad vistas of human ignorance become more brightly illuminated, we come to understand that the more we learn, the less we 'know'. This idea was captured neatly some thousands of years ago by Confucius: *Wisdom is found in knowing what we know and knowing what we don't know* (1983).

Notwithstanding the paradox of 'learned' ignorance, learning is widely accepted to be so important to humanity that considerable time and effort is devoted towards its practice across nations and cultures, formalizing and even institutionalizing it in many different ways. Formal learning is constructed to develop shared cultural values that shape actions and attitudes and to develop skills and knowledge that may have some social utility. It is also intended to assist individuals in making sense of the world in a way that is unique to the learner. Through our learning experiences we develop what Jerome Bruner describes as a 'logical calculus' of the world – essentially a working mental model of the way things are (1997). As we develop this working model, we use it to make decisions or take advice about who we are (being), our understanding (knowing), and the way we do things (doing). Our education is a journey expressed with an elegant brevity by the Chinese saying: 先做人后做事 – Become human first and then act on your humanity.

Learning is a ubiquitous constant in the human experience, but it does have its dedicated time and space where it is formally institutionalised in a process generally termed 'education'. Education, particularly in the critical formative years of pre-adult, school-based education, provides the context for much of the content of this book. In later chapters, the institutional dimension of the practice of teaching and learning, chiefly in schools, will be explored with specific reference to experience. In these introductory remarks, however, it is important to make some general remarks about institutional learning and its practitioners, the teachers.

Great institutions of learning have something in common that goes beyond their organisational principles and philosophies, inspiring guiding statements, effective management, collaborative faculty teams, engaged learners, and committed parents: their greatness is both achieved and reflected in the rich experience of each learner through each and every interaction within the learning community, every day of the year. The experiences of all learners, moment by moment, hour by hour, day by day, serve to build, but also reflect, the reality of great schools. The extent to which 'experience' in this sense is recognised, acknowledged, and incorporated into courses of learning is highly variable. A discussion of the operationalization of experience in schools forms the practical focus of the later chapters.

Great schools have great teachers and great learners. The ideal is found in the balance between being open to learn from anyone at any time and contributing to the learning of others through sharing, understanding and experience. The most effective learners are also great teachers; the most inspiring teachers are also highly accomplished, practicing learners. As will be explored in more depth, we can pretty much learn from anyone – provided we are paying attention.

Experiential learning, which is the core focus of this book, appears to have a life of its own in the field of education; it is seen as different to other forms of learning. We can easily find examples of learning that is called 'experiential' in many primary and secondary curricula, but its integration into mainstream learning in those curricula is often fragmented, underutilised, marginalised, and at worst ineffective. Experiential learning may be found deeply embedded in the value systems of some schools, whereas in others, it is banished to the educational periphery of fun-filled holiday camping programs, diverting 'change of scenery' excursions, and sundry co-curricular activities outside of the formal school timetable. Its location within the life of a school does say a lot about the educational values of the institution.

Experiential learning tends to be marginalised by some educators who see 'learning by doing' as a poor substitute for solidly quantifiable, theory-driven, content-rich, assessment-verified education. Indeed, some educators give little thought to the underlying theory of experiential learning, why it differs from mainstream or semantic learning, and how students might benefit most from learning experientially. It is seen as a minor punctuation mark, or perhaps a parenthesis, in the educational narrative.

If this seems to paint a rather dark and dispiriting picture of experiential learning, there is considerable cause for cautiously optimistic hope for better things ahead. Thoughtfully designed and imaginatively implemented, experiential learning can be the most durable, memorable and life-altering learning undertaken by learners in any education system. The extent to which it might become an enduring and defining learning experience depends on the design and setting of the experience itself, the way in which its challenges are posed and activities implemented, and its sensitive integration into the mainstream curriculum, both prior and post program.

Figure 2: Watching the Sunrise, Michael Leunig (1974)

Experiential learning offers some authentic respite from the artificiality of the controlled classroom learning environment and embraces the 'real world' beyond the school gates. It reaches beyond the carefully crafted benchmarks of classroom assessment and high-stakes external examinations to address the questions of life that for most learners who emerge from systems of highly regimented education remain largely unanswered. It is risky, messy, at times chaotic, difficult to plan, even more difficult to implement consistently, and produces results that are in a very real sense highly subjective and learner driven. After all, it is the learner's own experience, not that of the teacher. It also meets a pressing need that is posed, paraphrased, and restated by every adult who engages with the graduates of our educational institutions: "Why don't schools teach skills and knowledge that we can really use in the adult world?" If this seems to resonate, please read on.

The book and its limitations

So what exactly is this book about?

Its title appears to imply that it has something to do with experience and possibly learning. There is a great deal of literature that purports to be about learning, but which in fact is about something else. In some cases, the literature deals with a particular set of policies, practices, and procedures in use in an educational context or 'system', but which fails to illuminate how we come to understand our world. Much of the literature deals with the human predisposition to quantify and compare things that are considered to be important: this reflects the idea that if we spend time on it, we should measure it and keep score. By keeping score, we can compare one thing with another, assuming that the score is calculated using the same method and under identical circumstances. A higher score means 'better' in some way. This forgivable predisposition becomes complicated when we attempt to understand learning by comparing one learner with another, or comparing entire cultures and countries with others using mechanisms that are exceedingly ill-equipped or ill-suited to the task. To make matters worse, we then see the expenditure of enormous time and effort to reshape formal education in ways that appear to be consistent with conclusions drawn from the aforesaid deeply flawed measuring process.

There is an urgency, somewhat politically motivated, to prepare learners for the challenges of the future, while at the same time returning to traditional core learning competencies and values. Education is seen as both the cause and the cure for the ills of society. Education is therefore on notice to 'lift its game'. For example, in recent years in the United States a rich and complex national literature has emerged from the development and implementation of the Common Core State Standards Initiative, known as the 'Common Core'. A similarly vast body of literature exists about initiatives such as No Child Left Behind and Race to the Top. Vast in scale and perilous to navigate, the publishing industry surrounding just these two 'educational' initiatives appears to be primarily concerned with learning, but in fact is largely concerned with the political economy of institutional education, teaching standards, teacher accountability, and the socio-economic outcomes of formal education. There is a clear assumption that there will be movement in a particular direction (no one is to be left behind) and competition with someone (we are in a race). Whether the direction of movement is the 'right' one for the future, or the choice of competitor is appropriate as a relevant and reasonable benchmark, is perhaps not explored with any clarity or sense of purpose. It is a fascinating and complex literature, but it sadly sheds little light on the nature of learning.

Similar academic debates rage across much of what we might call the 'developed world', where books and articles dissecting with forensic precision the limitations, shortcomings and failures of institutional and state sponsored education abound. International 'league tables' are now compiled based on international studies, such as the Organisation for Economic Cooperation and Development (OECD) Program for International Student Assessment (PISA), Trends in International Mathematics and Science Studies (TIMSS), and the Progress in International Reading Literacy Study (PIRLS), all of which appear to permit some degree of direct comparison between the educational attainments of students attending schools in participating nations. These comparisons have gained a high degree of academic authority, public recognition, and accordingly, have generated enormous political traction. Educational administrations around the world have mobilized task forces of their brightest and best academics and career administrators, armed with deep pockets and powerful mandates, to lift national standards by emulating the apparent academic superiority of anyone at the top of the table: the Finns, the Koreans, the Singaporeans, or the Shanghainese. It is a thinly disguised *race* to the top of the world through education. We have launched a global 'Educational Arms Race'.

These standardized international assessments of numeracy and literacy, only possible in the Information Age, have created mountainous repositories of data that offer fascinating insights into national pride, international politics, educational funding models and cultural insecurities. Have we gained any insights into learning, however? The unkind observer might even draw the conclusion that the international benchmark-testing phenomenon says a great deal about the superficiality of what we appear to value and perhaps how we fail to learn, but that is the topic for another book.

The argument advanced here is that we err in focusing too much attention on the all too narrow assessment of learning, which seeks to maximise test results through the mastery of a very limited, and limiting set of testing instruments. We might be tempted to ask, somewhat rhetorically, are these tests important? Do they measure anything that is useful for life or even subsequent learning? Do we emerge with a clearer understanding of how and why we learn?

By way of practical example, if learning is the focus in the average 112 state mandated tests undertaken by American children during their years of primary and secondary education, the results appear not to have been particularly useful in boosting the national standing of the United States in testing regimes such as PISA. They have, however, generated an industry dedicated to the development, production, and administration of these tests (Zernike, 2015). A key symbiont is the tutoring industry, now a global phenomenon, which prepares candidates for standardised tests. The recent announcement by the US Government that seeks to limit the formal curriculum time devoted to test preparation to no more than 2% only serves to highlight the extent to which quantification of observable learning outcomes has become entrenched in educational thinking in one part of the world: many other nations are on the same journey (Zernike, 2015).

A fundamental premise of this book is that enhancing the quality of education is best achieved through studying the hugely complex process of learning itself, rather than accumulating a relatively narrow set of easily quantifiable testing data. The complexity and limitless variability of human development cannot be reduced to a statistical growth profile, no matter how sophisticated. One does not grow roses by measuring them.

Education confers prestige on nations that rise to the top of international comparisons and individuals who excel at those tests constructed to inform debate about comparative international education. The stakes are indeed high for some. Countries that test well are seen as highly literate, educated, civilized, knowledge-rich and cultured. They are invited to join the world's leading forums and power structures that seek to shape the future of humanity. Those individuals who test well, find easy access to precious educational resources, such as tertiary education at world ranked institutions, access to prestigious and highly lucrative careers beyond, and by extension, the power conferred by their earned status.

This brings us to one of the core motivations for writing a book about experiential learning. If we could adopt an intelligent approach to learning that develops resilient, confident, resourceful, competent learners, capable of doing well in both school-based assessments and life beyond school, and without dismantling and rebuilding the great institutions of learning globally, then the world might just begin to sit up and take notice.

There is a catch, however. Schools and teachers are generally not well prepared in both principle and practice to tap into the power of experiential learning. This is due in part to our under-developed understanding of why experiential learning is different to other forms of learning, why it might offer unique and educationally desirable outcomes to learners, and how to go about putting it into practice.

Happily, experiential learning is not theoretically complicated, aligns well with our broader understanding of how humans learn, complements other approaches to learning, and is largely free of any form of testing beyond participation in the experience itself. It appears infrequently in the literature dealing with institutional education; it defies any attempt to rank outcomes on the basis of experientiality; it is not the focus of any international benchmark comparison; and, as such, it is largely apolitical. Even in the world of academia, experiential learning attracts little academic attention. To invoke a modern metaphor, it is a 'stealth' technology in the educational firmament, flying somewhat unmarked under and through the radar of administrative accountability. Unnoticed, unremarkable, and perhaps a little unfashionable, experiential learning can perhaps be approached in a relatively straightforward manner: what you see is what you get. It is with some degree of confidence and tentative hope therefore that this book seeks to offer some respite to the highly politicized literature of mainstream education and focus its attention on understanding learning through experience. It is aimed at teachers, parents, researchers, and most importantly, *learners*.

Some working definitions

At this point, some may experience a growing disquiet over the rather epistemologically awkward and as yet unaddressed question of *learning* versus *learning experientially*: is there a difference and, if so, does it matter? The foregoing paragraphs may seem to take this difference as a given. This is, however, an essential question that this book seeks to explore. A basic premise, to be justified in a more satisfactory manner in due course, assumes that there is a divide separating mainstream *institutional* or *semantic* learning from 'real world' *experiential learning* that is philosophical, theoretical and practical. Whether this divide is sufficiently remarkable as to warrant the publication of this book is a question that must be answered by the reader.

Experience is a term much discussed in the literature of education, psychology, philosophy, and science. Indeed, books of considerable scholarship and erudition have been written about what it is and what it isn't.

For our purposes, *experience* might be defined in the following terms:

> *The totality of the ways in which humans sense the world and make sense of what they perceive* (Miller & Boud, 1996, p.8).

Or,

> *...the connection between our minds and the sensory stimuli provided through our contact with the surrounding environment* (Mowrer & Klein, 2001, pp. 1-2).

Put simply, experience might be described as the sensory *bridge* between the human mind and the external world.

In this book, the term *experiential learning* has been adopted as a general all-embracing term with which to identify models of learning based primarily on experience. There is little evidence in the literature to indicate any discernible difference between what is intended by the terms *experiential learning* and *experiential education* in the specific senses used, save for the obvious semantic intention differentiating *education* from *learning*. *Education* refers in a formal sense to matters of educational policy, institutions, courses of study and associated qualifications, all with a strong organisational dimension, whereas *learning* is seen as an activity within an educational context focusing on the actions and outcomes for the individual learner (Itin, 1999). With the exception of direct quotations, the former term – *experiential learning* – is adopted throughout this book as the preferred term, having its focus on the learner.

Experiential learning is discussed in more detail in Chapter 3 and a more comprehensive definition is offered in Chapter 6. For now, experiential learning might be described as:

> *The process which takes...experience and transforms it in ways which lead to new possibilities, which may involve changes in actions, ways of viewing the world or relationships* (Miller & Boud, 1996, p.8).

This is what occurs when the brain is stimulated through contact with the experienced world and that experiential stimulation results in new knowledge and changed behaviour or attitudes (Mowrer & Klein, 2001, pp. 1-2).

Book Structure

This book is divided into three parts. In Part I, we will seek to explore several key questions concerning the nature of learning, experience, and experiential learning: what it is and why it is important.

In Part II, we will explore the practice of experiential learning: how experiential learning might be designed and implemented in a school or classroom. It is aimed at practitioners who might be interested in putting some of the ideas raised in this book into practice. The substance of Part II is largely the product of the generosity of colleagues working in different parts of the world who have contributed enormously to the author's understanding of experiential learning. Some of the evidence discussed in Part II was gathered by the author during doctoral research into experiential learning programs and practice in Asia and Australia over a period of 15 years (Pritchard, 2010).

In Part III, we will briefly examine the wider implications of adopting a more experiential approach to learning and the questions that, as yet, remain largely unexplored.

For those readers interested in learning more about the research that underpins some of the content of this book, an electronic version of the author's doctoral research is available at the time of writing at the following on-line URL: hdl.handle.net/11343/35988.

Ultimately, the book aspires to explore and map the territory between learning theory and experiential practice and in so doing change the lives of learners through understanding and harnessing the educational power of experience.

Part I: Experience as Learning

Chapter 2: A Brief Overview of Learning Theory

The first step in the journey to understanding experiential learning is to review what is known about human learning in a more general sense, and from there explore the connections that we might make with learning from experience in more detail.

There are those who claim that humankind's capacity to learn from and reflect on experience is the sole reason for our apparent mastery of the planet. Humanity's impact on the planet is undeniable. The sum total of human experience and 'wisdom' has generated activity so profoundly transformative of our planet that we have named a geological age in our 'honour': the *Anthropocene* (Crutzen & Stoemer, 2000). As a species, we have clearly learned a few things from experience. The net result of what we have learned has taken us beyond meeting our immediate physical and social needs into the realms of the gods. Indeed, one might go so far as to say that human experience has shaken our world to its very core.

It would be sensible to assume that the profound, planetary-wide impact of human activity arises from a well-developed and universally shared understanding of how we got here in the first place. Perhaps a little alarmingly, the proliferation of theories about learning seem to bring us no closer to developing what Einstein might have termed a 'unified theory' of learning. In our formal institutions of learning, the waxing and waning of explanatory theories of human development, the ebb and flow of what constitutes 'best practice' in education at a given point in time, show no sign of abating. We seem to be no closer to agreeing with any certainty as to exactly what learning is and how it might be managed to maximum effect.

There are many plausible reasons for this uncertain state of affairs. Human thought and development are hugely complex, perplexingly context dependent, and inherently unpredictable. Employing human thought to understand human thought and defining it in self-referential terms is always going to be a risky philosophical proposition. Humanity generates physical and metaphysical phenomena of apparently inexhaustible variability that reflect an intriguing alchemy of molecular biology, organic chemistry, neurology, psychology, physics, not to mention philosophy, culture, spirituality, and sociology. The term 'alchemy' here is used quite deliberately. Physically, we are a collection of commonplace natural elements, transformed by a process that borders on the miraculous, developing into something quite extraordinary. Given the mind-stretching variation in the human outcomes of this miraculous developmental process, one might be forgiven for despairing at its apparent capriciousness.

We have not been idle in seeking to inject a greater degree of certainty into the learning enterprise. Research into the ways in which humans learn and how to nurture or organise such learning into an efficient and effective social and economic undertaking has shaped and reshaped human institutions at an accelerating pace since the advent of the Industrial Revolution. We have moved from the mimicry of masters, to filling empty vessels, observing 'black-box' behaviour, shaping social interaction, to the constructivism and cognitive revolution of the late 20th century. The interval between educational paradigm shifts has shrunken markedly in the past 100 years or so. Approaching the turn of the millennium, the field of education has embraced an increasingly broad range of established and emerging disciplines, such as neuroscience, genetics, psychology, and ethnology aiming each time to illuminate the neurological, psychological, sociological and cultural processes associated with learning that are generally not directly observable.

In searching for answers, we have observed our surroundings in an attempt to discover more about learning from apparently analogous processes in other species. We have considered how animals adapt and 'learn' from experiences in an attempt to understand our own learning. Köhler's chimpanzees (1930, pp. 155-156), Guthrie and Horton's puzzle-box cats (Guthrie & Horton, 1946), and Epstein's pigeons (1984) have, in a collateral sense, given us some fascinating 'insights' with respect to learning. We have learned that animals observe, mimic, and test solutions when solving problems, largely on the basis of what we might term animal experience, albeit with varying degrees of success and with varying degrees of external stimulus, prompting, or training. The concept of 'mind' and our capacity to empathize or even feel vicariously the experiences of others, pain for example, seems to set humanity apart.

There is still much to be learned about learning beyond observable phenomena, however. When it comes to deciding whether we are the product of nature or nurture, there is perhaps more to be gained by reflecting on Schrodinger's Cat rather than observing actual lower-order beasts; it is an unknowable and tightly interconnected mystery. The famous animal experiments cited above certainly revealed some interesting things about adaptation. By extension, we may have gained some confirmatory insights into human cognition, but there remains a great deal that is unknown and currently unknowable about the precise processes that regulate and control human consciousness, what drives and shapes human development, and how we acquire new skills and knowledge (M. Cole & Hatano, 2007, pp. 113-115).

Current evidence regarding animal learning from apparent 'insight' still supports the contention that, in contrast to the imitative/adaptive learning observed in other animal species, only humans seek to *understand* the world as they experience it. And based on this experience of the world, only humans seek to learn in a systematic and sustained way to create new knowledge and make meaning about the world (Bruner, 1997, pp. 63-71; M. Cole & Hatano, 2007, pp. 113-115; Jonassen, 2009, pp. 13-25; Richardson, 2000, pp. 1-4, 122-123). Kohler's chimpanzees solved an immediate problem of accessing bananas, but did not demonstrate any observable interest in why the problem existed in the first place.

Uniquely, we seek to gain a greater understanding of the world through learning. We do not seek to solve problems alone, but to make meaning, sometimes about the problems themselves. Increasingly, we have taken this search for meaning to a higher level. Metacognitively, we have sought to understand the nature of the search itself, as both a process and a target for improvement. This requires a deeper understanding of learning itself.

In order to go a little deeper, we need to look at the theories that attempt to describe the learning process, of which there are many. In fact, there are different, competing paradigms of learning theories. The position offered by the famous American educational philosopher and pragmatist, John Dewey, simplified things to just two metacategories:

> *The history of educational theory is marked by opposition between the idea that education is development from within and that it is formation from without* (1997 [1938], p. 17).

Nature versus nurture indeed. For Dewey, our learning is either innate, emerging from an internal process, or inculcated through deliberate shaping by external influences. Or perhaps it is both?

The traditional view of learning is that it is an external process that 'forms' or shapes the learner in a particular way to achieve an intended outcome. It has many guises, but it is essentially a process by which knowledge is 'transmitted' or shared from one person to another. This is sometimes known as the *empty vessel* model or the *transmission* model (Confrey, 1995, p. 203), in which new knowledge is transmitted from an expert teacher to a novice student (R. Mayer, 2005, p. 12).

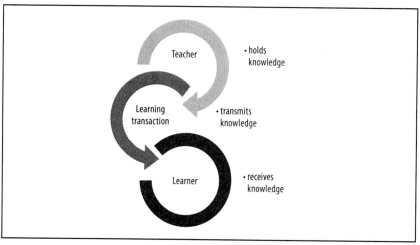

Figure 3: *Transmission Model of Learning*

The transmission model assumes that the learner is a *tabula rasa* – a blank slate – waiting for the wisdom of the elders to be inscribed upon it. It is an inherently conservative view of learning, in which the sum total of knowledge possessed by one generation is passed on to the next generation. The viability of each generation is thus dependent on filling the empty spaces in our memories with the facts and wisdom learned by those who went before.

The metaphor of knowledge transference from the knowledgeable master to the ignorant acolyte is powerful in its simplicity. It is also practical in its apparent explanatory power of learning, simply because it appears to describe what actually takes place when learning occurs. It certainly serves a purpose because it does appear to offer an approximation of the learning process for the external observer: the 'teacher' possesses knowledge, and through 'teaching' the learner, the learner demonstrates acquisition of the teacher's knowledge and thus transfer appears to have taken place.

This is a highly comforting explanation. It reassures those of us who care about such things that education will ensure wisdom is handed down from each generation to the next and that civilisation will be preserved. We will not be at risk of the peril stated so memorably by George Santayana:

> (W)hen experience is not retained, as among savages, infancy is perpetual. Those who cannot remember the past are condemned to repeat it (Santayana, 1980 [1905], p. 284).

There are, however, some awkward aspects about this highly practical and enduring way of thinking about learning. It avoids the obvious question about new knowledge and the place of creativity. Furthermore, a key theoretical difficulty with the transmission model is its silence on what takes place in the mind of the learner. Simply, it seems to ignore learner agency completely.

Transmission describes an observable outcome without offering any enlightenment as to the process that produced the outcome. The mechanism by which we acquire knowledge remains unclear, the mind of the learner is a 'black box' into which we cannot see. In our thirst to understand, this state of affairs is problematic. This is also precisely the dilemma that led the behaviourist school of psychology to abandon attempts to peer inside the mind and instead focused attention on external manifestations of what goes on inside the mind: human behaviour. It was assumed that if it could be observed, it could be measured, analysed, and perhaps understood.

When learning, what is observable seems simple enough: knowledge is encoded in some way (a system of semiotic symbols that hold meaning for someone who can interpret the symbols); we can perhaps see it, if it is represented visually in written or pictographic form; we can hear it, if it is represented aurally through sounds. The learner then encounters this knowledge-encoded artefact in a way that results in the learner being able to recall and demonstrate in some way that they now 'know' something in a form that more or less replicates or represents its original form or configuration when possessed by the teacher.

In fact, what actually happens in the mind of the learner between the encounter and the demonstration of 'knowing' is a mystery: an irrelevant mystery for the 'transmissionists', an unknowable mystery for the behaviourists (who were largely interested in externally observed behaviours), and a challenge for anyone else who really wants to understand how learning actually takes place. The missing piece of the puzzle is the precise mechanism by which the learner actually acquires, creates, or constructs new knowledge.

Based on research into human cognition, the transmission view is now largely discredited as an accurate theory of how the brain actually learns (Ernest, 1995). Researchers also began to consider other aspects of the learning phenomenon, such as memory. Is learning therefore just about memory? If so, then how does new knowledge find its way into our memories? Other questions arose about memory, however, such as, "Why are memories so varied, inconsistent, even unreliable?"

When considering other explanations about learning, one of the most troubling aspects of the simple process of transmission, that people tend to remember things – sights, sounds, words, tastes, feelings – in slightly different ways, offers a clue to the revolutionary theory about thinking and learning that started in the 1950s and still dominates much educational thinking in the early 21st century. These differences, sometimes imperceptible, sometimes profound, point to the fact that people seem to 'know' or remember things in slightly different ways. We might ascribe these differences to imperfect memory or imperfect learning, but the differences seem to exist across all learners, in all contexts.

In seeking to understand the underlying reasons for these small changes, researchers had to move from external 'objectively' observed phenomena into the largely untapped and seemingly unknowable world of what was actually going on in the minds of learners. At first, this appears to be a rather daunting challenge. At the very least, research ethics prevent us from dissecting human subjects to observe 'thinking' in a real-time physiological sense. Furthermore, the thing we wish to observe in action – the brain – is the very instrument we need to use to undertake the observation. Using the brain to examine the brain is, of course, methodologically difficult. Thus a full understanding of the workings of the human mind remains tantalisingly hidden from scientific scrutiny, despite the apparently inexorable march of technological progress, which offers increasingly accurate and detailed imagery of neural activity. We just cannot quite see (yet!) what is happening inside the 'black box' of the mind.

Findings about human perception emerging from the so-called 'Cognitive Revolution' in psychology, encouraged educators to embrace this idea that we make or 'construct' our knowledge in ways that are highly individualistic, idiosyncratic, subjective and experiential. This new way of thinking about how we learn suggested that we 'invent' our understanding of the world around us (von Foerster, 1973). In contrast to the long-standing view that we could be dispassionate and unbiased observers of a fixed reality, the idea that we 'make up' much of what we perceived of the world around us was novel in a number of ways, one of which was that it abandoned the long-cherished notion of

27

objectivity. Instead, von Foerster asserted the inherent subjectivity of human agency when observing:

> *Objectivity is the delusion that an observation could be made without an observer (von Foerster cited in von Glasersfeld, 1996).*

Constructivism is the name given to the theory that describes this process of individual invention or interpretation of the surrounding world. Interestingly, the basic idea of constructivism has a long history in western thinking. The Greek philosopher Heraclitus (535 BC – 475 BC), famous for reminding us that the dynamic flow of time and life means that we will never step into the same river twice, is cited as one of the original sources of constructivist ideas (Mahoney, 2003, pp. 212-213; Pegues, 2007, pp. 316-317). The Italian philosopher Giambattista Vico (1668-1744) offered an insight, unusual for its time, suggesting that we cannot reconstruct the past exactly as it was, because we cannot avoid framing and understanding our recollections in terms of the concepts we have in the present (von Glasersfeld, 1996). As we build our understanding of the world from infancy through to adulthood, we tend to add our own interpretations, embellishments, and perspective; we also leave things out or remove things that we see as irrelevant. In the 1930s, the French thinker, Gaston Bachelard, took this a step further, declaring that *everything* is constructed (Bachelard, 2002 [1938]).

Regardless of its provenance, the idea that each of us *constructs* an individual understanding of reality, based on our perceptions, is both powerful and illuminating. We find that our fixed past is inextricably bound to our subjective present and we have a degree of agency in constructing our future. This idea has taken root deeply in our thinking about cognition and learning. Accordingly, constructivism is seen by some as the dominant paradigm in Western contemporary educational philosophy (R. Mayer, 2004, p. 14).

What does this mean for our understanding of learning? In fact, constructivism changes everything. We now must move from content as the focus of learning to the learner as the central element. If it is the learner that does the constructing, then we need to make sure that the builder (learner) has access to the best materials, but is also trained to construct.

No longer a passive recipient, the individual learner is now seen as an active participant in *constructing* a personal and 'viable' version of the external, objective 'real' world based on experience and perception. This idea of 'viability' is important because it highlights the notion that each of us tries to make sense of the world in a way that allows us to go about our business in a relatively stable state of mind. We do this through interacting with our surrounding environment, our families, friends, society at large, and the myriad knowledge artefacts that we might encounter (Tobin & Tippins, 1993, p. 3; von Glasersfeld, 1995, pp. 7-8). Knowledge no longer consists of discrete pieces of information transmitted from person to person. From birth, we use previously constructed, experientially-based understandings to construct new understandings when we encounter something novel or unexpected (Ernest, 1995, p. 470).

Perhaps a little ironically, this theory that suggests we construct our own unique understanding of the world is somewhat proven by the fact that there is no single, agreed description of constructivism: there are many forms of constructivism and little agreement as to which represents the core of constructivism (Ernest, 1995, pp. 459-470).

For the sake of simplicity and brevity, but also with some considerable academic justification, this book considers the two most highly influential theories or schools of thought in the world of constructivism, proposed by the leading educational theorists of the 20th century: Jean Piaget and Lev Vygotsky. This discussion also lays a foundation for the development of a description of experiential learning in the next chapter.

Piagetian Constructivism

One of the pioneers of constructivism as a coherent and developed theory, Jean Piaget (1896-1980) is seen by many as one of the greatest educationalists of the 20th Century (von Glasersfeld, 1995, pp. 4-5; 1996, p. 13). Much of the contemporary literature dealing with the topic of childhood development and education owes a debt to Piaget's thinking. Teacher training programs around the world invoke the name of Piaget when describing how children learn.

Piaget's key idea, one that still shapes our thinking about childhood development today, is that from birth, children pass through a set of common *logical stages* on the way to adulthood (Bruner, 1992; Inhelder & Piaget, 1958, pp. 1-2; Piaget, 1952). Piaget states that we all pass through each of the four stages – *Sensorimotor, Preoperational, Concrete Operational,* and *Formal Operational* – in the same order and, roughly, in the same time frame (Flavell, 1963; Piaget, 1952, p. 4).

According to the Piagetian model, human interaction with the world is largely governed by an integrated network of logical actions (or 'operations') that mediate between the *mind of self* and the outside world (Bornstein & Bruner; Bruner, 1997; Piaget, 1952). Through these operations our minds constantly test and compare our internal model of 'how the world works' with what we can see, hear, feel, taste, and smell through our senses. When we encounter something new that is not part of our internal model or perhaps contradicts it in some way, we adjust our inner model.

Thus, as learners we do not 'discover' new knowledge, we replicate it, but in a unique, personalised way that reflects our previously constructed model of the world and our associated experiences (Bruner, 1997, p. 66). Putting this in another way, Piagetian constructivism sees knowing as an on-going adaptation to the external world (von Glasersfeld, 1995, p. 7).

This offers us a very elegant and compelling explanation of human development. We habitually pass our days in a quiet, happy, and stable state of mind in what we might call 'equilibrium'. When something unexpected happens and our stable state of equilibrium is upset, we become unsettled: this is what Piaget described technically as *disequilibration*, in which a state of conflict emerges between our inner world and our external perceptions (Bornstein & Bruner; Bruner, 1997; Piaget, 1952, pp. 4-5; Piaget & Garcia, 1991). In another school of thinking, this might also be called a cognitive *dissonance* or cognitive *gap*. In this somewhat uncomfortable state of mind, we respond by attempting to bring things back into balance (Bornstein & Bruner, 1989; Bruner, 1997; Piaget & Garcia, 1991). Infants enter the world without a settled, stable state and are therefore in a constant state of disequilibration. The innate capacity of infants to respond and adapt to this situation is constrained by their physical and mental state of development, hence the notion of stages as a developmental model.

According to the Piagetian model, there are two responses that can happen as a result of disequilibration: we can either incorporate or absorb the unexpected into our existing world view by a process called *assimilation*; or we can change our world view by creating a new model of thinking through a process called *accommodation* (Piaget, 1952, p. 6).

Assimilation is seen more frequently in education. It reflects incremental change, in which something is added to our existing understanding of the world (Furth, 1987, pp. 67-69). *Accommodation*, on the other hand, occurs when we encounter something truly novel. In such cases, we cannot just assimilate the novel encounter into existing or prior understandings; we are forced to accommodate through creating a new view of the world (Harlow, Cummings, & Abersturi, 2006, p. 45).

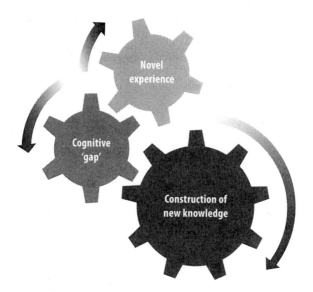

Figure 4: *A 'question' of cognitive dissonance*

Both assimilation and accommodation result in the creation of knowledge. For Piaget, *knowledge* is a reconstitution of reality, but not reality itself (quoted in Bringuier, 1980, p. 64). However, Piagetian constructivists hold that we never actually 'acquire' knowledge in the external world; we reconstruct our version of knowledge through what Jerome Bruner described as a *logical calculus* (Bruner, 1997, p. 66). Because each person's specific set of experiences and encounters are unique, each person's logical calculus will also be unique.

Piagetian constructivism offered a startlingly novel and intuitively insightful view of human development, but it was not without its critics. Some felt that the invariant stage structure was excessively rigid; others felt that it focused too much on individual learners and thus downplayed the role of adults and other learners in the learning process (Bruner, 1996, p. 20; Dennen, 2004, p. 816). The surrounding social or cultural context in which learning takes place was not an area of particular focus or interest for Piaget; children also seemed to display a remarkable degree of autonomy (Bruner, 1992, p. 230; Moore, 2000, pp. 11-13). For teachers, Piaget and his supporters had little to say about the pedagogical implications of the model (Moore, 2000, p. 13).

It was the question of how learners interact with others – intersubjectivity – that attracted the most criticism for Piaget's theories (M. Cole & Wertsch, 1996; M. Freeman, 1987, pp. 25-27). While Piaget adjusted his position somewhat in later years, acknowledging the influence of social factors on the cognitive development of children (1962), this remains a key criticism (Bruner, 1997; M. Cole & Wertsch, 1996; Tudge & Rogoff, 1989; Vygotsky, 1986 [1934]).

Vygotskian Social Constructivism

The other branch of constructivism to be considered here has a number of slightly different names, but the most commonly used term is *social constructivism*. Social constructivism retains the essential notion of learners constructing their own understanding of the world, but it claims that learning is mediated through interaction with others, such as parents, teachers and peers (Hickey, 1997, p. 175).

Emerging largely in reaction to a perceived lack of attention paid to social mediation in Piaget's theory, social constructivism offers an alternative model of human development in which the interconnectedness of all human elements of society is seen as central to our understanding of the learning process (Ernest, 1995, p. 480; Vygotsky, 1986 [1934], p. 34, Trans. A. Kozulin; Vygotsky & Luria, 1993 [1930], Trans. M. Cole).

In social constructivism, new knowledge is first manifested through social interaction prior to internalisation or 'assimilation'. Indeed, interaction between people as the core element of learning is the essence of the social constructivist model. In social constructivism, as individuals, even when alone, we are always seen as a part of an on-going network of social interactions, or *conversations* (Ernest, 1995, p. 480).

Acknowledged pioneer and chief architect of social constructivism, the Soviet-era psychologist from Belarus, Lev Vygotsky (1896-1934), based his own theory of human development on the idea that as social beings, humans do not learn without some form of interaction with other humans, either directly through social interaction (person to person), or indirectly through semiotic mediation (person to sign/symbol). Semiotic mediation may use any form of signs or symbols, such as spoken and written language, pictures, diagrams and charts (Tharp & Gallimore, 1988, p. 19). For social constructivists, even when we are reading a book or admiring a picture, we are 'interacting' with the creator of the sign or symbol, albeit in an asynchronous way.

In a frequently quoted passage from one of Vygotsky's most admired and influential works, *The Mind in Society,* he asserted that learning will always take place on two levels or 'planes', first on the social plane and only then on the individual plane (Amin & Valsiner, p. 87; Vygotsky, 1978, p. 57). For Vygotsky and his followers, the social nature of human activity is the fundamental point of departure for explaining the process by which we construct new knowledge, from earliest childhood through to adulthood. The essence of Vygotsky's theory of learning can be reduced to this one idea: *through others, we become ourselves* (1987, p. 105).

According to Vygotskian theory, at its most basic level, learning is an instinctive and adaptive process, a ubiquitous survival strategy adopted by humans and other species (Vygotsky & Luria, 1993 [1930]). Through learning, humans, as socialized beings, naturally develop the means of recognising and dealing with the threats posed by the outside world through interacting with others, such as parents and peers (Vygotsky & Luria, 1993 [1930]).

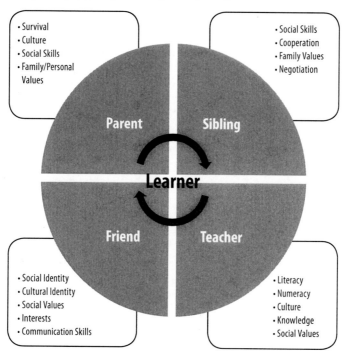

Figure 5: *Formation of self: learning through social interaction*

At a more advanced level, our learning takes place through the medium of language, which results in *deep transformations,* when as infants we are progressively, if somewhat haltingly and tentatively, connected into the social and cultural environment into which we are born (Vygotsky & Luria, 1993 [1930], p. 171). As individuals, we are connected together to form social groups that rely on semiotic mediation to form bonds through time and space, and these bonds ultimately form social communities (Vygotsky, 1986 [1934], p. 7). From a Vygotskian perspective, the understanding of the world we seek through learning can only be achieved through the experience of social interaction.

Vygotsky set aside the classical Piagetian notion that development occurs through the staged maturation of our pre-existing higher mental functions, and instead claimed that our higher cognitive functions actually emerge through the interpersonal functioning of more elementary or 'primitive' human cognitive functions (Wells, 1999, p. 101). Interestingly, some have observed that much of this early and low-level interpersonal functioning, and specifically language, which leads to the development of higher mental functions, occurs in social settings that are not designed to be specifically educational in structure or purpose (Wells, 1999, p. 101).

The role of language-based personal interaction is central to social constructivism. For humans, language acts as the medium through which social interaction takes place. It also provides the very building blocks, the means by which our 'inner speech', the internal monologue that each of us routinely conducts, is structured (Daniels, 1996, p. 10). In every sense, language shapes the way we think and interact with others (Wells, 1999, p. 101).

Our ability to create and master semiotic tools, such as language, is *the* critical step in our development as social beings. Where do these semiotic tools come from? Vygotsky noted the importance of interaction between people in developing language, with sign and gesture emerging in infanthood as the precursors of verbal language (Vygotsky, 1978, p. 56). Through gesture, pre-verbal infants learn to communicate basic needs to parents or carers. This is a powerful survival tool for us when newborn, as we have very few tools or means at our disposal to meet our needs. We are reliant on others. When we use hand or other body movements and gestures and an adult responds, we learn the power of gesture (M. Freeman, 1987). As our needs become increasingly complex, we learn to master sounds, initially through experimental vocalization in response to parent language. Within the limitations imposed by the physical development of our speech organs and our primitive muscle control, our first, tentative, experimental sounds have in fact already taken on the phonemic shape of our 'mother' tongue, thus demonstrating the impact of social interaction and environment on our early development (Bruner, 2004).

The infant-mother phase of learning warrants a moment of reflection, as it has a powerful influence on how we go about learning in subsequent years. It also serves as strong evidence to support Vygotsky's focus on the social nature of learning. Much has been written about the intense bond between mother and child, a bond that commences in-utero and typically extends to the early years of infancy and beyond. This binary *duocentricity* between mother and infant, in which the helplessness of the infant provokes an instinctual, caring, nurturing response from the mother, creates the perfect relationship and context to promote communication between the two (M. Freeman, 1987). It is the very lack of infant independence, combined with the maternal instinct to nurture, that creates the ideal conditions for socialising interactions between parent and child.

Paraphrasing one of Vygotsky's famous quotes, we might say, at least initially, that it is through our *mothers* that we become ourselves (1987, p. 105).

The importance of the *other* in the development of self is important in social constructivism, as we cannot develop into our adult selves without the mediating influence of contact with other members of our surrounding community. It is through the influence and interaction with those significant 'others' – parents, family, neighbours, teachers – that we construct our own understanding of our parent culture (Vygotsky, 1978). As we grow, we participate in *doing* and *making*, gradually extending our mastery of semiotic tools to link us and ultimately bind us to the wider community; these semiotic tools shape and facilitate our links to the world of objects and the world of people (Wells, 1999, p. 47). This emphasis on the role of adult influence in the development of the child offers a clear point of distinction between social constructivism and other constructivist theories (Gredler & Green, 2002).

While the scope and nature of learning is facilitated by the physical and psychological development of children, they remain highly active participants in their own development. Their egocentric needs adjust and adapt to the prevailing social reality (1986 [1934], p. 37). The extent to which the minds of our children are shaped by their own internal forces and motivations, however, is also specifically challenged by Vygotsky. He directly contradicted Piaget's claim that *things do not shape a child's mind* (1986 [1934], p. 39). In fact, according to Vygotsky, in realistic situations when the egocentric speech of a child is connected to *practical* activity, the development of the mind is quite strongly shaped by external forces (1986 [1934], p. 39).

In making this important connection between inner development and outward reality, Vygotsky underlined the primacy of *experience* as the way we encounter, interpret, and assimilate our external reality. Experience is the critical step in learning; it is a powerful force in shaping the inner structure of the developing mind. Vygotsky defined this experienced contact with reality as neither passively reflected in the perceptions of individuals, nor as an abstract contemplation in isolation; in every sense, Vygotsky believed that our experience of reality arises from our active engagement with it (Vygotsky, 1978, p. 40).

Taking elements of Piaget's pioneering work on constructivism, Vygotsky sought to transcend the individualistic focus of the former to embrace what he saw as the social reality of the human condition. Vygotsky's ideas have proven to be powerful theoretically and offer enormous potential in the field of education to provide organising principles for formal learning in a broad sense. Since accurate translations became available in English in the 1970s, Vygotsky has enjoyed widespread popularity and influence in western educational circles. It is therefore somewhat unusual that Vygotsky's recorded works have provided little practical guidance to educators on classroom practice – with one major exception: the Zone of Proximal Development (Wells, 1999, p. 102).

Zone of Proximal Development

No account of Vygotsky's work, no matter how short, would be complete without some reference to what has been described as Vygotsky's greatest contribution to our understanding of the process of learning (Wells, 1999, p. 25): the *Zone of Proximal Development* (ZPD). Jerome Bruner, one of the pre-eminent educational thinkers of the second half of the 20th century, hailed the ZPD as a *theory of development*, a *theory of cultural transmission* and a *theory of education*, all at the same time (Bruner, 1987, pp. 1-2). The ZPD concept describes the gap or 'distance' between what we can do independently and what we can do with some degree of assistance from or through another person (Vygotsky, 1978, pp. 84-86).

As learners in any setting, we are operating in our ZPD if we have stepped outside of our 'comfort zone' of prior accomplishments and embraced a task or challenge that requires some form of help, sometimes known as 'scaffolding', a frequently used term in educational circles that, I should hasten to add, was never invoked by Vygotsky himself. Scaffolding as an educational concept is perhaps most closely associated with the theoretical work of Jerome Bruner (1966 & 1976). While scaffolding typically refers to adult assistance, the help may not come from someone physically present. It may take the form of an instruction manual or textbook, for example. While the scaffold supports, it also sets limits and constraints on the learning undertaken (Bruner, 1966, pp. 158-159).

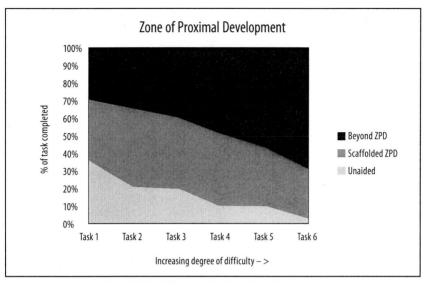

Figure 6: *Multi-task illustration of the Zone of Proximal Development*

Scaffolding of learning through external support is closely associated with the operationalisation of the ZPD (Wood et al., 1976). The management of scaffolding in practice, however, has proven to be pedagogically challenging. Recent criticism of scaffolding as a pedagogical concept, notes its centrality within constructivist thinking, but also asserts that the work to develop a set of testable principles to guide the implementation of scaffolding remains an unfinished task for educational theorists (Kirschner, Sweller, & Clark, 2006; Tobias & Duffy, 2009, p. 5).

We all have our own 'zone' that will stay with us throughout all stages of life, although the nature of the task and the degree of difficulty we can manage independently will be totally dynamic (Tharp & Gallimore, 1988; Wells, 1999, pp. 24-25). In a given activity, while engaged in a complex set of tasks, it is possible that we might be working at a number of different levels with respect to our ZPD. Where we are exercising a skill already mastered, we may be acting as a 'scaffold' support for another learner, while at the same time, receiving the assistance of someone else more experienced in a given task. The bi-directional nature of mediation in a learning setting might mean that a group of learners participating in a task under the supervision of a teacher may, in fact, be assisting the teacher in the development of competence in a teaching or supervising task in his or her own ZPD (Wells, 1999, pp. 40-41).

Individual differences impact on the extent to which scaffolding assistance might boost performance of a skill. For example, two students of similar chronological age, but with differing mental ages, as demonstrated through the degree of aided competency necessary to complete a task, will have different ZPD profiles (Vygotsky, 1978, pp. 85-86). This particular feature of the ZPD concept demonstrates that the gap between actual and aided competency differs from person to person (Vygotsky, 1978).

Returning to the centrality of social interaction, both direct and indirect, as the mechanism driving learning, Vygotsky's general law of development is that all higher mental functions ultimately develop from interaction between individuals. This idea stands in direct opposition to the notion proposed by Piaget (1978, p. 90). Thus Vygotskian learning is generated through interaction between the learner and another agency, not purely from within.

In contrast to the Piagetian view of learning as an internal process, and one that lags behind physical or cognitive development in the individual, good learning occurs ahead of demonstrated or actual competence in a task, rather than following the achievement of competence (Vygotsky, 1978, p. 89). Using the analogy of *budding* flowers, Vygotsky stated that the idea of ZPD applied to competencies that are in the process of maturation, but have not yet developed the *fruit* of independent competence (1978, p. 86).

The notion of ZPD has been criticised by Chaiklin as one of the most misunderstood and misused concepts in contemporary education (2003, pp. 40-41). The implementation of the ZPD concept as a pedagogical tool requires that a learning task is not multifaceted and multilayered and that its level of difficulty falls neatly into the two boundaries of the ZPD: a student's demonstrated competence on the one hand and the furthermost limit of assisted competence on the other. Of course, learning tasks are rarely singular and undifferentiated in nature. Furthermore, what constitutes scaffolding or assistance in the sense intended by Vygotsky is open to debate (Chaiklin, 2003). For some, the notion of the ZPD does not require the physical presence of a mediator, hence text, for example, can also act as a mediating influence within the ZPD concept (Daniels, 2001, p. 64). Others believe that human agency may assist learning, even when not present: Gredler & Shields (2004, p. 21) cite the example of the child undertaking a homework task away from the classroom, yet still under the tutelage of the teacher.

The learner's age, current stage of development, and current abilities are identified as a potential limit to the latitude for assisted completion of a task by an individual (Wells, 1999). The effective implementation of the ZPD concept in the classroom is heavily dependent on an interaction between the individual learner's level of development and the form of instructional practice adopted in the classroom (1985, pp. 70-71). It is possible that by varying the nature of instructional practice, access to the developmental phenomena associated with the ZPD concept may also be affected. Affective domain factors such as learner motivation may therefore impact on the extent to which adult mediation is successful in the completion of a task carried out within the ZPD. A final observation is that the notion of ZPD lacks a mechanism to guide the collection of empirical data demonstrating the consequences of adopting different forms of ZPD intervention at both an individual and class level (Daniels, 2001, p. 64).

Of Knowing and Knowledge

In constructivist theories of learning, the end product of learning is the creation of knowledge or the making of meaning, which may also give rise to behavioural or attitudinal changes in the learner. What we know shapes our behaviour. The knowledge we create through learning may lead to the creation of knowledge artefacts or semiotic tools that embody the created knowledge and which may in turn result in others creating their own tools and artefacts (Wells, 1999, p. 89).

We do need to make a clear and vitally important distinction between knowledge itself and the artefact that merely represents the knowledge. As the creation of knowledge from an artefact is the product of our subjective interpretation and misinterpretation, knowledge artefacts and semiotic tools should not be confused with knowledge itself. These artefacts are *representations*, they do not contain knowledge (Wells, 1999, pp. 73-77). A book, for example, is an artefact that contains symbols, which for a reader who can decode or interpret the symbols may carry meaning. If we cannot read or interpret the symbols, however, the book carries no inherent meaning.

For social constructivists, knowledge has both an individual and a social dimension. Knowing is an intentional activity undertaken by the individual, but within a social context; the individual constructs knowledge, but does not *know alone* (Leontiev, 1981). Even without the immediate presence of another person, our knowledge construction has a social dimension, as it relies on experiences and understandings constructed through previous social interaction (Wells, 1999, p. 79). Knowledge itself cannot be separated from the actions of representing and making of meaning (Wells, 1999, pp. 73-79). Knowledge is passed across generations and geographical distance through acts of reinvention and rediscovery. Previous paths of reasoning and imagination are explored anew by successive generations and other communities through acts of knowledge creation (Popper & Eccles, 1997; Wells, 1999, pp. 76-79).

In making meaning and creating knowledge artefacts, it is important to remember that the products of our thinking remain open to modification, revision, and evolutionary change. Learners exert their own influence, however subtle, over the symbols and tools manipulated in the learning process (Vygotsky, 1978, pp. 74-75). For example, it is this bidirectional influence that creates the mechanism for the evolutionary changes in languages.

It is the act of knowledge making, rather than the physical artefacts created, that defines constructivist knowledge (Wells, 1999, p. 86). Knowledge artefacts may act as representations or carriers of *previous reasoning* (Pea, 1993, p. 53), but individuals must still re-learn previous knowledge through their own active participation in meaning making in a contemporary setting (Wells, 1999, pp. 78-79).

This notion of active and current knowledge creation raises a further question: when an artefact no longer carries any semiotic significance for a community, is the knowledge that created the artefact lost (Wells, 1999, p. 86)? If there are no living individuals capable of interpreting or making knowledge from an artefact, does the original knowledge that led to the creation of the artefact still exist? As knowledge cannot be transmitted or acquired without understanding and intentional participation, without intentional acts of meaning making, knowledge is *inert* (Wells, 1999, p. 86).

The role of semiotic tools in mediating the actions of past, current, and future generations is, for Vygotsky and his followers, the *central fact* in human psychology (M. Cole & Wertsch, 1996, p. 251). Tools and artefacts do not just support mental functions, but in fact play an essential role in the shaping and transformation of human mental functions (M. Cole & Wertsch, 1996). Ultimately, all higher mental functions are merely internalized social relationships.

The concept of *mind* therefore extends beyond the proximal limitations of the physical senses to be shaped by the mediating tools and the cultural and physical setting in which the tools are created (M. Cole & Wertsch, 1996, p. 252). The growing interconnectedness of individuals facilitated through technical media, such as the internet, for example, provides an illustration of this concept. Indeed, through on-line activity, the creation of virtual electronic personas and their attendant artefacts leads to a blurring of the point at which the individual might be said to end.

Vygotsky sought to avoid what he perceived as an implicit dualism in Piaget's description of the inner self and the 'others' with which the self interacts. He did this by bringing the two states together in a form of natural conflict in which the outer social state conquers or overpowers the inner world of the child as a part of the maturation process (1986 [1934], pp. 48-51).

Peer to Peer Learning

Of course, social interaction of the type described by Vygotsky was silent on the roles of the individuals interacting. There is an implicit assumption that in a learning context, learners interact with teachers. One of the intriguing possibilities opened up for theoretical consideration as a result of Vygostky's ideas of social constructivism is that of peer-to-peer learning. Pre-constructivist ideas of learning centred on the notion that teachers acted as the providers of knowledge and accordingly controlled the learning process. Piaget helped us see the individual learner in a clearer light, but again placed the stages of development in a context in which competent adults formed an essential part of the process. Even Vygotsky, the champion of socially mediated learning, did not find much to say about learning from peers.

However, as more work has been done on the precise nature of knowledge construction, the idea that at least some of this might be attributable to peer interaction has progressively gained more attention (Wells, 1999, p. 304). There is substantial evidence of the benefits of peer-centred social interaction in the process of learning under some circumstances (1999, p. 45). The age at which peer collaboration confers maximum benefit to the student, however, remains the subject of debate (Hogan & Tudge, 1999, p. 48).

What is clear for our understanding of the learning process is that we can learn from anyone, not just the designated teacher.

The Learning Paradox

In viewing learning through the lens of constructivism, there is an important philosophical question, known as the learning paradox, that demands some attention at this point. According to this paradox, in order to acquire a novel external cognitive 'structure' (for the sake of the discussion, let us refer to this as a new idea), it must be received and accommodated within an existing internal cognitive structure. How do learners therefore acquire and assimilate novel concepts, for which they have no experiential or semantic referent? How do we create new cognitive structures when the theory seems to suggest that we work within, through, or around our existing cognitive structures and understandings?

While 'thinking outside the square' is something of a cliché, it does in fact illustrate quite neatly the learning paradox. The square represents the sum total of what we have experienced and what we know. Because our 'knowing' is constructed within that 'square' of understanding, it presents something of a logical puzzle that we might somehow step outside the frame of reference through which we experience everything. How can we think outside the square if we have never been there and have no known way of getting there?

The examples of history, however, show us that once someone of extraordinary originality or creativity has breached the walls of the 'square' and ventured beyond, the shared cognitive mindscape changes to accommodate the new way of thinking. We might call this a Kuhnian paradigm shift (1996), but what is the precise mechanism by which it occurs? How do we step outside the framework of what we know to build new understandings? Is it purposeful or random?

This is a problem at least as old as Plato and has been more recently articulated in the debate over Piagetian constructivism (Fodor, 1980, p. 149). There are various physical metaphors to describe this apparent paradox: seeing a new colour for the first time, for example. Daniels, citing Vygotsky, creatively illustrates this idea in terms of learning to swim: one must have had some experience of water and swimming in order to succeed (Daniels, 2001, p. 35). It is an unprecedented change of state: something unexpected enables us to step outside of ourselves and plunge into uncharted and seemingly unknowable waters.

For cognitive structures that fall within the realm of the shared experience of a social grouping, Vygotsky's idea of socially mediated transference of learning resolves the paradox for individual neophyte members. Experienced, knowledgeable adults facilitate the construction of knowledge for new learners. This solution still doesn't identify the source of truly novel ideas that lie beyond the realm of a community's shared knowledge. What is the mechanism for innovation and change?

For novel ideas at a societal level, the learning paradox creates difficulties, as discovery of a truly new idea should transcend all previous individual and shared experience. If new ideas are sufficiently infrequent, perhaps they could be described as a form of cognitive mutation leading to a psychological Kuhnian paradigm shift, in which an intuitive leap of perception acts as the mechanism by which a new realm of thinking is opened up and accommodated (Kuhn, 1996).

Others might explain the emergence of genuine novelty in terms of sudden and inherently unpredictable changes to dynamic systems that permit accommodation (Boom, 2004, p. 84). Predictive adaptation through a generative form of cognitive self-organisation, termed *connectionism* is also cited as a plausible explanation (Bereiter, 2000). This is where one idea suggests a connection with another, leading to novel insight. Everyday experience provides inspiration through the application of metaphors that support emergent intuition. Through our experience, we apply knowledge we have learned in another context to a new situation, sensing that it may be applicable in some unknown manner. Eventually, this leads to the collection of empirical evidence to support or disprove the original imaginative leap (J. P. Smith, diSessa, & Roschelle, 1993).

There is merit in all of these explanations, but the learning paradox might best be understood through the application of an evolutionary metaphor to the field of metacognition, in which these intuitive, imaginative leaps are frequently attempted in human endeavour, but are rarely successful or fruitful in leading to viable and sustainable cognitive structures in their own right. Human response to experientially-driven stimuli is one of the key mechanisms driving this process.

Criticisms of Constructivism in Theory

In constructivism, we seem to have arrived at a happy state of complete understanding of learning. Well, perhaps not. The sceptics and opponents of constructivism are legion and their objections collectively pose a significant challenge to any uncritical acceptance of constructivist learning theory. While much space could be given to a detailed critique of the work of Vygotsky and Piaget, this task is well beyond the scope of this book. For the sake of completeness, however, it is worthwhile reflecting briefly on some of the perceived shortcomings of constructivism.

For example, the emergence of social constructivism marks a bifurcation in the epistemological orientation of constructivism, between the social and individual construction of knowledge (Liu & Matthews, 2005, pp. 386-387).

Some critics of Vygotsky would like to see a stronger focus on the individual construction of knowledge (Karpov, 2003, p. 66); others claim that autonomous agency in learning has not been fully accounted for in Vygotsky's writings (Piaget, 1962). Individual construction of knowledge is also emphasised in Brunerian learning through acts of *discovery* that are exclusively the property of the individual learner (Bruner, 2006, pp. 57-58).

Due to the temporal, social, and geographical limitations of the context and age in which Vygotsky worked, the impact of class, ethnicity, setting and gender on the course and nature of individual development is an important dimension of Vygotsky's work that is incomplete (Wells, 1999, p. 39). In particular, in a multi-cultural or multi-class society, the impact of language, environment, family structure and social status, may have an enormous impact on our ability to master the process of knowledge construction through decoding and encoding semiotic symbols and associated knowledge artefacts (Wells, 1999, p. 40).

Differentiation between different kinds of social mediation is also seen as a weakness in Vygotskian constructivism, as all sources of social interaction are seen as equal, regardless of institutional setting, cultural context, socio-economic factors, or history (J. V. Wertsch, Toma, & Hiatt, 1995, p. 164).

The structure of the Vygotskian model of development contains an element of implied intergenerational conformity that appears to emphasise cultural replication, without allowing for the creativity or dissent of the individual learner (Wells, 1999, p. 41). Strict replication is an inherently unidirectional process that does not accord with the phenomenon of social or cultural change we observe in the implicit bi-directionality of development in Vygotsky's account (Vygotsky, 1987, pp. 105-106; Wells, 1999, p. 41). The interaction between the subject and the mediated object does allow for the possibility of change in both the subject and the object. Indeed, Wells (1999, pp. 40-41) sees this type of mutually interactive evolutionary change as an unavoidable consequence of mediation.

The nature and progression of human development, a feature of Piagetian constructivism, is not fully explained in Vygotsky's writings (J. V. Wertsch, 1985). For one critic, this created the impression that Vygotsky believed learning and development to be the same thing, leading to the erroneous conclusion that development is limited only by opportunity to learn (J. V. Wertsch, 1985, p. 73). Echoing Piagetian developmental stages, Wertsch (1985) asserted that development actually proceeds according to its own internal dynamic, independent of external factors.

Vygotsky's ideas have had a powerful influence on our understanding of the place of the individual in the social formation of knowledge. However, Vygotsky had little opportunity to take his research into the realms of practical application in the classroom; he was largely silent on how teachers might apply his ideas (Daniels, 2001; Karpov, 2003; Wells, 1999).

There are different kinds of social constructivism, and the differences, although minor, appear to be irreconcilable. The result of this is that there is very little agreement on anything, with the possible exception of the general acceptance of knowledge as a social product that is individually constructed (Ernest, 1995, p. 459; Floden & Prawat, 1994, p. 37; Gallego, 2001, p. 318). For some, despite the large volume of related writings, social constructivism is not sufficiently grounded in theory in either the educational or the psychological field. One of the main reasons for this is its positioning at the intersection of cognitive psychology and sociology, a slightly awkward location that renders it cross-disciplinary in nature and subject to the theoretical fads and fashions of two discrete fields of knowledge (J. V. Wertsch et al., 1995, p. 159). This has led to the establishment of somewhat ill-defined theoretical boundaries for social constructivism, and has therefore contributed to its development into a very broad collection of theoretical models, with many sub-categories and definitions. Social constructivism has thus become associated with a wide range of pedagogical approaches, such as the cognitive apprenticeship, reciprocal teaching, intentional teaching, and communities of learners (Hickey, 1997, p. 176).

Criticisms of Constructivism in Practice

Moving from the realms of theory to the classroom, as the dominant theoretical paradigm in western educational writings, constructivist ideas and influences are commonplace in discussions of educational theory. We might therefore expect to see constructivism as the undisputed source of inspiration for pedagogical practice. Constructivism as a way of teaching, however, remains problematic. As in theory, so too in practice; there are many *constructivisms* (Ernest, 1995, pp. 459-470), leading to what one critic describes as *rampant sectarianism* among constructivists (Phillips, 1995, p. 5), which in turn results in many myths, misconceptions, and misunderstandings about constructivism (Harlow et al., 2006; Hyslop-Margison & Strobel, 2008). It has also resulted in a wide and varied range of teaching practices being lumped together in a form of theoretical portmanteau known as constructivism.

The most influential criticisms of constructivism focus on the perceived shortcomings of student-centred implementation and pedagogical practice that minimises teacher intervention in learning (Kirschner et al., 2006). Part of the problem is that the term *constructivism* itself has lost some of its specificity, as it now reflects many different things: a philosophy, a methodology, a pedagogy, an epistemology (Harlow et al., 2006, p. 41), or even *powerful folktales* (Phillips, 1995, p. 5). Increasingly, it is a term that is coming to mean whatever people construe it to mean.

The single most persistent criticism of constructivism is that it is hard to put into practice in a school (Baines & Stanley, 2001; Kirschner et al., 2006). Constructivists have been accused of advocating an approach to learning that is not adequately grounded in theory, impractical and largely unproven as an effective mode of learning (Baines & Stanley, 2001, p. 695; Land & Hannafin, 2000, p. 1). For some, constructivism is philosophically strong, but pedagogically weak, reflecting a gap between theory and practice (Tobias & Duffy, 2009, p. 4).

While constructivism remains the dominant theoretical paradigm in the field of education and teacher training is largely informed by constructivist ideas (Hausfather, 2001), much of what is done in practice appears to be more consistent with what some might call the oversimplified thinking of behaviourism, largely concerned with cause and effect and, particularly, observable results (von Glasersfeld, 1995, pp. 4-5). In many classrooms around the world, the institutional organisation of learning, reflected in timetabling, discrete subject delivery, and testing regimes, seem to work against the adoption of constructivist theories of learning in the mainstream school setting (Hackmann, 2004, p. 697).

For some critical observers of institutional education, constructivism, while espoused in theory, is largely replaced by practice that reflects the *transmission* mode of education (Mok, 2003, p. 2; Parkinson, 2003, pp. 230, 236; Perkinson, 1984, p. 165). Administrative policies in schools tend to emphasise the more *visible achievements* of individuals, focusing on competencies and knowledge recall that are easily tested, measured and often disconnected from the learner's own experience of reality and the processes of personally relevant knowledge construction (Scardamalia & Bereiter, 1994, p. 268).

What of the leaders of learning in an educational setting – the teachers? One fairly sharp criticism of constructivism at a practical level is its apparent devaluing of teacher expertise that some observers have asserted lies at the heart of student-centred constructivist pedagogy (Baines & Stanley, 2001, p. 695; Chrenka, 2002; Kirschner et al., 2006). If the learner is at the centre of learning, where does the teacher stand in practical terms? Learner autonomy is a powerful idea that promises all manner of efficiencies and positive engagement. Flipped classrooms, for example, sit nicely with the idea of learner agency and individual construction of learning. Who, we might ask, designs, launches, and flips the classroom? The learner constructs, but the teacher constructs the setting, the context, and provides the stimulation and scaffolding in which the learning takes place.

As a learner-centric epistemological theory, constructivism logically places the teacher in a role that is different to that found in more traditionally didactic settings; the role of the constructivist teacher remains a topic of protracted historical and contemporary debate (Chrenka, 2002; Dewey, 1997 [1938]; Kirschner et al., 2006). In the constructivist classroom, the teacher is a visible presence who scaffolds learner inquiry (Chrenka, 2002), acting as a co-learner and equal member of a learning community who shapes the course of study (Dewey, 1997 [1938], pp. 57-58). The teacher provides a supportive and well managed environment in which students explore their individuality of experience (Dewey, 1997 [1938], p. 58). Dewey, anticipating the future evolution in the role of the classroom teacher predicted:

> *When education is based upon experience and educative experience is seen to be a social process...The teacher loses the position of external boss or dictator but takes on that of leader of group activities* (pp. 57-58).

This notion of the teacher relinquishing control of the learning process is a key criticism of constructivism in practice (Kirschner et al., 2006), as it is equated with leaving learners to their own devices. Furthermore, in contrast to the constructivist criticism of traditional pedagogy which asserts that there is an emphasis on the right answer, critics of constructivism despair that there appears to be no right answers at all (Chrenka, 2002).

Some of these criticisms are aimed at particular forms of constructivist practice (Baines & Stanley, 2001; Kirschner et al., 2006), where constructivism has been adopted in name to suit institutional or governmental agendas. However, without sufficient understanding of the profound pedagogical and epistemological implications for classroom practice, constructivism risks being reduced to little more than a set of hollow slogans and policies that are educationally ineffective (Hyslop-Margison & Strobel, 2008, pp. 72-73). One explanation of the perceived *failure* of constructivism as a pedagogical practice is the lack of a supporting body of practice-based knowledge (Baines & Stanley, 2001).

Constructivism is therefore not a single epistemological theory, but a collection of theoretical positions, frustratingly dichotomised in the writings along several different axes: for example, the individual-social divide, the novice-expert divide, and the adult-peer divide. The divergent theoretical positions between the social and individual approaches to knowledge construction are the most numerous, thus creating a new dualism, precisely what the pioneers of constructivism set out to avoid in eradicating the subjective mind-objective reality dualism (Liu & Matthews, 2005, pp. 386-387). In one way, it might be seen as a victim of its own theoretical and practical syncretism: invoked by many, owned by none.

From this brief overview of constructivist learning theory, it can be seen that constructivism is theoretically diverse, terminologically imprecise, and difficult to implement in practice. What constructivists do agree on is the centrality of knowledge construction based on personal experience in the process of learning. The *construction* or *building* metaphor is the unifying feature of constructivism (Ernest, 1995, p. 461). Building on the model of individual cognition in Piagetian constructivism, the theories of the social constructivists, pioneered by Vygotsky, provide a robust advocacy for socially mediated cognition in knowledge creation.

Summary of Key Concepts of Learning

Through our growing understanding of cognition and social mediation as the core elements of the interactive relationship between learners and knowledge artefacts, how the learning process is understood has undergone a profound paradigmatic shift. Learners are no longer perceived as passive recipients of facts in an intellectually inert transmission process, but as constructors of their own knowledge. This theory of learning is known as constructivism. Constructivism is currently the dominant theoretical paradigm in education in which learning is not a process of knowledge transfer from teacher to learner, but a process in which learners actively *construct* their viable version of knowledge, making meaning from their own experience of the world (von Glasersfeld, 1995; Wells, 1999). Constructivists hold divergent views on the role of social mediation in learning: some believe that knowledge is individually constructed (Piaget, 1952), whereas others assert that it is socially constructed (Vygotsky, 1978, 1986 [1934]).

In constructivism, cognitive equilibrium reflects a dynamic balance between the experienced world and the constructed inner model (Piaget, 1952). Disequilibration occurs when a novel experience disrupts this stable cognitive state and triggers learning (Dewey, 1997 [1938]; Piaget, 1952; Seiffert & Hutchins, 1992). Constructivist learning recognises two cognitive processes, *assimilation* and *accommodation*, that re-establish cognitive equilibrium through incorporation of the novel experience into existing cognitive structures (Piaget, 1952).

Ideally, this new experience should sit just beyond the learner's comfort zone, but not beyond the breaking point of abject failure and confusion. With some form of assistance or support, the learner should be able to handle a new experience and grow in confidence, skill, and knowledge as a result. This point of balance between 'can' and 'cannot' was first described by Vygotsky and is known as the 'Zone of Proximal Development' or ZPD. Put simply, the ZPD is the gap between what we can do unaided and what we can potentially accomplish with help of some sort (Vygotsky, 1978).

Help, or mediation, is most typically sourced through a more experienced member of the community, most likely a teacher, but also possibly a more experienced peer, or a member of the community encountered in the course of a learning activity; mediation may also be provided through an agency not immediately present, like a guidebook. This assistance is almost universally known in teaching circles as *scaffolding*, a commonly used term in experiential learning (Bornstein & Bruner, 1989, p. 60; Wood, Bruner, & Ross, 1976).

Due to its highly individualistic nature, constructivism is difficult to put into practice in schools and in particular poses some challenges for the teacher, who no longer deals with a discrete, unified body of knowledge, but a plethora of interpretations and partly constructed understandings authored by learners.

Chapter 3: Theoretical Foundations of Experiential Learning

Experiential Learning: Why Do We Need a Theory?

Readers of this book have all learned throughout their lives both semantically and experientially. As literate, social beings, we have all experienced learning in a sustained and systematic fashion. We have learned from and through others, we have learned through our own reflections on things that have happened to us, things we have heard, seen, experienced: we can therefore claim to have a very good, personal, *experiential*, understanding of learning, albeit our own. We have a less experientially-informed understanding of how others learn.

As described in the second chapter, the shift from the long-standing, traditional 'empty vessel' metaphor (used to describe the process of content transfer from the knowledgeable to the ignorant) to the socially-mediated constructivist model that emerged from the cognitive revolution of the 20th century marks a substantial change in how we think about learning and how we manage it as an essential social endeavour. This paradigm shift is still the topic of much debate. There are many who understand the thinking behind constructivism, but cling to the notion of students as 'empty vessels' because it is well-entrenched, it is a simple physical metaphor that mirrors many other aspects of human activity (such as commercial transactions), and also because it still seems to hold some power to describe aspects of learning. We are not empty vessels, but as learners we seem to be treated as such.

Experiential learning seems to be relatively straightforward and enjoyable, and as such appears to offer some respite for the theory weary veterans of the classroom and staffroom and terminologically confused parents. Experience is something we all share. Learning from our experience, "learning something by just doing it", seems a comfortingly straightforward and politically neutral summary for the layperson and educational practitioner alike.

In fact, experiential learning is relatively simple and its simplicity reflects an important truth. Experiential learning needs to be simple because our lives depend on it. Experiential learning is the survival mechanism that is kicked into action with our first crying breath at birth. Because of its ubiquity and simplicity, however, it tends to be overlooked as a 'given' element of the collection of human skills, abilities, capacities, and potentials that each learner brings to the formal or institutional part of learning, typically commencing with kindergarten. We do, we learn, we change, and life goes on. Why does this need a theory?

According to the OECD (2014), the average child undergoing compulsory and post-compulsory schooling around the world will receive an average of 10,000 hours of formal instruction prior to graduation. Perhaps coincidentally, this number was also made famous by Malcolm Gladwell (2008), who asserted that we require 10,000 hours to acquire mastery in any field of endeavour. While it seems like a lot of time to spend in class, the crowding of the curriculum, caused in part by the exponential growth in the volume of human knowledge, imposes a discipline of efficiency and effectiveness on all that is done in the name of formal education. If we are successful in this drive to make better use of the time, we have achieved something meaningful.

The flipside, and one that perhaps reflects the experience of many undergoing formal education, is that if we labour in the pursuit of the mirage of content mastery by attempting to insert an exponentially expanding amount of knowledge content into the fixed chronological vessel of the academic year the end result is frustration and despair.

If time is of the essence (it is), and 10,000 hours seems far too short a time to equip anyone with the skills, attitudes, and knowledge needed for life in the 21st century (it is), we certainly need to understand how and why experience contributes to learning so that we can ensure learners derive the maximum benefit from their learning experiences, both intended and incidental. Our lives in the broader sense seem to rely on getting this right.

Returning to an important point discussed in Chapter 2, learning is triggered by the new and the unknown. When we encounter something unexpected or novel that does not accord with our previous experience, or we find a gap in our understanding when we face the 'unknown' we experience what might be termed the learning 'question' or 'problem'. This cognitive dissonance or 'gap' is the driving force for all learning, whether conscious or unconscious. It might be said that we are at our best as learners when we are seeking answers to our own questions, seeking to eliminate our own cognitive gaps. The place of the 'question' in learning is therefore of paramount importance.

Creating experiences that are novel and which create questions about the world and its ways lies at the heart of experiential learning. The French constructivist, Bachelard, put this proposition most elegantly:

> *Before all else, we have to be able to pose problems...problems do not pose themselves...All knowledge is an answer to a question. If there has been no question, there can be no scientific knowledge. Nothing is self-evident. Nothing is given. Everything is constructed* (Bachelard, 2002 [1938]).

In fact, it might be conjectured that educators and learners should spend far more time creating thoughtful *questions* that generate genuine inquiry than focusing on mastery of answers to questions already posed, as suggested by one critic of traditional educational practices:

> *To fulfill the cultural desire for certainty, the conventional practices of schooling often discourage playful curiosity and experimentation and insist on the existence of the one right answer* (Chrenka, 2002).

If our schools are encouraging mastery of answers to questions already asked, presumably arising from the experience of others, we create two major problems: we create a 'right answer' focus in education that is at variance with the world beyond school; we also run the risk of ignoring the experience of the learner and imposing the experiences of others, regardless of relevance.

We might accept that using already answered questions as a basis for an education is logically sound. Where we are dealing with 'known knowns', a learner's response can be easily compared to what is accepted generally as the right answer. Where this becomes problematic is where this safe, comparative approach becomes the sole focus of our education system. In fact, we should be preparing learners for life in a world of problems that have no solutions, problems that are difficult to define, resistant to known solution-seeking approaches, problems that are inherently *wicked* (Rittel & Webber, 1973).

Donald Schön, echoing his own concerns about a system of education that focuses on finding answers to known problems, offered a compelling metaphor to urge us to refocus education on problems that are ill-defined, complex, and of enormous concern to humanity:

In the varied topography of professional practice, there is a high, hard ground overlooking a swamp. On the hard ground, manageable problems lend themselves to solution through the application of research-based theory and techniques. In the swampy lowlands, messy, confusing problems defy technical solutions...in the swamp lie the problems of greatest human concern (1987).

If we descend from the neat, well-ordered college on high, hard ground into Schön's swamp to find messy and confusing problems, we do leave the world of certainty and right answers, albeit contrived and controlled, and enter a complex world of high risk and low certainty. Schon's swamp is the heartland of human experience and the ideal experiential learning environment. As we take this journey, we need to reflect on the nature of the questions we explore as a part of a complete education and assess the extent to which they are the worthy adversaries of intelligent, adult human endeavour. This is a journey in search of the key questions of humanity that need to be answered, the problems of global scale and complexity that are truly worthy of our attention.

A theory of experiential learning is essential to help us make this transition.

An Educational Definition of Experience

As promised in Chapter 1, the first step in examining experiential learning from a theoretical perspective is the task of defining *experience,* which as it turns out, is no simple task. The inherently subjective and interpretive nature of experience makes it complex to define (Fox, 2008). In the field of philosophy, experience is often defined phenomenologically (Cooper, 1993, pp. 3-5) in terms of *consciousness* of the world (Husserl, 1983 [1913]-b, p. xix). The phenomenological *world* is the sum-total of *objects* of possible experience (Husserl, 1983 [1913]-a, p. 6). For our purpose, with its focus on learning and learners, this is not an entirely helpful working definition.

Perhaps a more accessible definition, with direct connection to our own lived experience, is the following from the field of cognitive science, which states that experience is:

(T)he sum total of impressions and other input from our sensory network that connects the brain, and particularly the memory, to the perceived world beyond the individual (Jarvis, Holford, & Griffin, 2003).

We all receive sensory input of varying types in the (seemingly) incessant 'flow' of consciousness that is a defining quality of *Homo sapiens.* Put simply, experience connects our minds through this sensory flow to the perceived surrounding world. Curiously, we can also experience vicariously, feeling in a virtual sense the pain or distress of others around us (Vandenbroucke et al.,

2013). Thus, we have the unusual capacity to project the experiential world created by our minds beyond our immediate sensory connections; we are free to imagine things that are not as if they were.

While we often do not understand what we experience, particularly if there is no pre-existing frame of reference, through exposure and processing of the sensory stimulation collected through experience, our minds construct working models or *analogues* of the world to accommodate or assimilate our perceptions (Bruner, 1997; Piaget, 1952). These models are one of the products of the learning process. We call on them frequently and unconsciously to compare current sensory input with previous experiences stored in memory to make sense of things (Luckner & Nadler, 1997, p. xvi).

This chapter and in fact the entire book is primarily concerned with experiential learning or *educational* experience. It is important to draw a distinction between experience as the sensory flow of stimuli to the mind and experience of a slightly more focused variety that generates learning. Not all experience leads to learning, although all human activity yields experience (Dewey, 1998 [1897], pp. 231-233; A. Kolb & Kolb, 2008, p. 2).

Much of human experience is routine and unremarkable, where individuals make *as if* assumptions on the basis of the perceived immutability of daily reality: *presumption is the typical response to everyday experience* (Jarvis et al., 2003, p. 61). We are immersed in a moment-by-moment flow of sensations that may not necessarily connect directly to learning. Other responses to experience include *non-consideration,* where experience is ignored, or *rejection,* where an individual makes an active choice not to learn from an experience (Jarvis et al., 2003, pp. 61-62). In this study, references to experience are intended to reflect those experiences that explicitly or implicitly lead to learning.

An Historical Overview of Experience in Learning

As a shared element of human existence, experience and its connection to learning have been on the collective minds of great thinkers for a long time.

Historically, there are many views on learning and its relationship to experience. While the view of learning as a process of *transmission* of knowledge from teacher to student, or a form of societal *initiation,* dates back to ancient Greece (Perkinson, 1984, p.164), learning based on direct experience and action has an equally distinguished historical provenance in the ancient world.

Philosophers from the great ancient civilisations of the Eastern and Western hemispheres, such as Aristotle and Confucius, have wrestled with the nature and utility of experience (Henson, 2003, p.6; F. Mayer, 1960, p.99). Aristotle, for example, in the Nicomachean Ethics, masterfully stated the paradox about learning from experience:

> *For the things we have to learn before we can do them, we learn by doing them* (Aristotle, 1908 [350BC], Book II, Trans. W.D. Ross).

In *The Republic*, Plato articulated a theory of education that places experience as the primary instrument of education, where the trials of experience in the real world (the *cave*) complete a student's education in preparation for service to the community (Barker, 1959; Plato, 1952, Book VII, 540, Trans. B. Jowett).

At the beginning of the Age of Enlightenment, John Locke detailed his views on education in *An Essay on Human Understanding*, asserting that *all reason and knowledge have but one source: **experience*** (Locke, 1952 [1689], p.122, emphasis in original). In Locke's view, experience is the means by which individuals develop more abstract forms of cognition, specifically reasoning.

Immanuel Kant, in exploring the boundaries of knowledge and reason, and the difficulties associated with *a priori* reasoning, agrees that our cognition, knowledge and experience are inseparably linked (Kant, 1996, pp. 44-52, 752-753, Trans. W. Pluhar; Kitcher, 1996, p. xxviii). The idea of education as a process of individual *growth* emerging from experience first appeared in the writings of Jean Jacques Rousseau (Perkinson, 1984, p.164):

> *The gift of education...comes to us from nature, from men, or from things. The inner growth of our organs and faculties is the education of nature, the use we learn to make of this growth is the education of men, what we gain by our experience of our surroundings is the education of things (Rousseau, 1957 [1762], p. 6).*

Significantly, Rousseau focused his attention not on education as a process of initiation for neophytes or transmission of knowledge from teacher to student, but as a process in which the student is at the centre, growing through participation in the experience. He also recognised the importance of interaction with the learning setting – the *surroundings* – in education (Duffy & Cunningham, 2001; Rousseau, 1957 [1762], p. 6). The importance of the setting and context in which learning takes place will be explored in more detail in a later chapter.

In the 20th century, many schools of philosophical thought sought to understand our experience of the world and its relationship to learning. William James developed the notion of *radical empiricism* (1912), responding to what he perceived as a failure to ground rationalism in daily human experience. James suggested that the totality of our experience is *quasi-chaos* (1912, p. 65), with the individual as the nucleus of those experiences. There are two forms of knowledge emerging from our experience: *perceptual* and *conceptual*; our experiences provide *percepts* which form the foundation on which abstract concepts, values, and beliefs about the world are constructed (Baker, Jensen, & Kolb, 2002; James, 1912, pp. 65-67). James' work was significant because it sought to explore experience beyond our immediate sensory perceptions.

Based on the experimental work of Pavlov, and pioneered by Thorndike, Watson, and Skinner, Behaviourism was the dominant theoretical paradigm in education throughout much of the 20th century that focused attention on observable human responses to experience (Amsel, 1989, pp. 3, 15-19; Skinner, 1950; von Glasersfeld, 1995, p. 4). Behaviourism is a philosophically materialist school of thought that overcomes the problems of the Cartesian physical/body-spirit/mind duality by ignoring anything that is immaterial and focusing on what is 'real'.

Powerful in its capacity to eliminate unobservable and essentially unknowable metaphysical considerations from philosophical debate, behaviourists focused our attention on what could be observed; everything else was deemed to be irrelevant. Educationally, behaviourists see learning as experiential reinforcement, or patterning, based on stimulus and response, or *training for performance* (von Glasersfeld, 1995, p. 4). While seen by some as essentially *mechanistic*, behaviourist thinking remains a highly influential force in education (Gibboney, 2006). Indeed, one might be forgiven for thinking that certain forms of institutionalised testing are strongly reflective of behaviourist thinking.

One of the pioneers of the modern student-centred focus in education, Carl Rogers placed particular emphasis on individual experience as a direct result of his client-centred practice as a therapist (1969, 1983). Objecting to the dominant teacher-centric pedagogy of the time, with its focus on transmission as excessively authoritarian, Rogers saw the student as the logical centre and focus of learning (Perkinson, 1984, p. 151; Rogers, 1969, pp. 4-5; 1983, pp. 188-189). This shift in focus was an important step in the evolution of contemporary ideas about student-centred learning that also valued individual experience. Rogers, echoing Dewey, saw the teacher's relationship with each student as one of facilitation of individual learning, assisting self-discovery, rather than didactic instruction (Dewey, 1997 [1938]; Perkinson, 1984, p. 151).

The emergence of educational ideas in the 20th century that moved away from content transmission, metaphysics, teacher-centric didacticism towards a focus on observable behaviour and individual experience, radically changed the landscape for planning and executing programs of learning. If the learner was at the centre of learning, not the teacher, then the location in which learning took place was clearly up for renegotiation. These ideas also created an environment in which the fundamental motivations for the design and practice of learning programs could be re-examined.

Kurt Hahn was one of the key figures behind the emergence of 20th century experiential learning (Hahn, 1960; Hattie, Marsh, Neill, & Richards, 1997, p. 44). Hahn pioneered an unusual approach to learning that focused on outdoor adventure and survival. Arising from Hahn's belief that many fatalities in World War Two were the result of a flawed educational system that failed to provide learners with the resources to cope when faced with challenges, *Outward Bound* offered a challenging program of experiential learning in which the inner resources of students were tapped to endure physical and emotional testing in an outdoors setting (Outward Bound International, 2004). Hahn's ideas of learning through experience were also put into practice through other programs of learning through community service, such as Round Square and The Duke of Edinburgh's Award (Round Square, 2010; The Duke of Edinburgh's Award, 2011). It also informed the learning philosophies on which Gordonstoun and the 15 United World Colleges were founded (UWC International, 2015).

This form of learning through basic survival and coping with physical challenges resonated with a basic and ancient human survival instinct that is often masked or supressed in the manicured and tightly crafted institutions of learning today. Hahn's notion of learning stems from his graffiti-inspired leitmotiv: *there is more in you than you think* (Outward Bound International, 2004). It suggests that there are inner reserves and potentials awaiting release by the right set of circumstances and experiences. This idea forms an important part of our journey to understand how experience connects with learning.

Deweyan Experiential Learning

Learning through experience has a long and storied history. However, one figure, the early 20th century American educationalist John Dewey (1859-1952), stands out as the chief architect and leading advocate of experiential learning in the modern era and no account of experiential learning would be complete without a detailed examination of his ideas. John Dewey's ideas remain a unique combination of pragmatic constructivism and learning through experience (Beard & Wilson, 2002, p. 15; Henson, 2003; Pegues, 2007). Philosophically, Dewey sought to interpret the world as he saw it, making sense of the reality of human experience as it appeared to be. The Cartesian duality of the inner mind and the outer world was something rejected by Dewey as impractical

(McDermid, 2015). The world exists and our concrete everyday experience provides the only evidence we need: if something works, then it is held to be true, but only to a point, until something better emerges.

Dewey's views on education, and its connection with personal experience, retain a highly influential place in theories of learning and his ideas continue to resonate with relevance in contemporary debates on issues such as the role of the individual and society in cognitive development (W. Garrison, 2003; Gibboney, 2006). Indeed, some even suggest that much of the current debate on education has not moved much beyond the progressive reforms proposed by Dewey (Dewey, 1909; W. Garrison, 2003).

Those who take the time to read Dewey's writings closely are rewarded with exposure to his visionary ideas on learning and educational reform, which focus on how best to structure and implement a system of education that meets the needs of contemporary society (Dewey, 1909, p. 11). A noted pragmatist philosophically, Dewey proposed the idea that experience is the most effective way of teaching to achieve the greatest degree of social utility (Hoberman & Mailick, 1994, p. 19; Khalil, 2004, pp. 7-8). Dewey strongly advocated for a strong alignment between the needs of society and the outcomes of formal education. He advocated for a student learning experience that reflected the values and practices of the wider community: *Apart from participation in social life, the school has no moral end nor aim* (Dewey, 1909, p. 11).

Deweyan pragmatism is captured most succinctly in his statement: *Things are what they are experienced to be* (Dewey, 1998 [1905], p. 116). This draws a clear distinction between *reactive* experience induced by external stimuli and deliberate, constructed understanding based on planned and intentional experience (Dewey, 1998 [1905], p. 117; Khalil, 2004, pp. 99-100). This *knowing* experience, for Dewey, is the *organising force* of all learning (W. Garrison, 2003).

Dewey's definition of experiential education made a clear connection between one experience and a subsequent experience:

> *(It is) that reconstruction or reorganization of experience which adds to the meaning of experience, and which increases ability to direct the course of subsequent experience* (Dewey, 1921, pp. 89-90).

Thus, Dewey provided us with a very useful way of distinguishing between different kinds of experience: it makes the clear distinction noted earlier between the ubiquitous type of unremarkable, routine daily experience, found in the flow of sensory stimulation each of us receives, and the novel, cognitive dissonance inducing experiences that lead to some form of change or 'learning'. Routine experience does not necessarily lead to learning, as it rests on the immutability of the experienced world and as such informs the formation of habits based on assumptions and routine (Miettinen, 2006, p. 252). The type of experience that is educationally interesting occurs when our routines are disrupted in some way by an experience that causes these habits to fail; the resulting uncertainty gives rise to reflective thought and learning. This type of experience forms the central focus of this book.

Experience is not passive or static and it is not isolated from other experiences, past, present, or future. For Dewey, the educational merit of any given experience is measured by its *continuity* with future experience, the way in which it connects with subsequent experience and its capacity to shape or generate future behaviour (Dewey, 1997 [1938]; Luckner & Nadler, 1997, p. xvi). A novel experience is broken down, analysed and reconstituted through the process of learning that is both reflective and adaptive so as to influence future experiences, using previous experience as a framework; (1921, p. 163):

> To "learn from experience" is to make a backward and forward connection between what we do to things and what we enjoy or suffer from things in consequence (Dewey, 1921, p. 164).

In this sense, the individual acts within the experience and is in turn acted upon by the experience. This is the Deweyan experiential equivalent of Piaget's cognitive disequilibration, which is then followed by assimilation or accommodation.

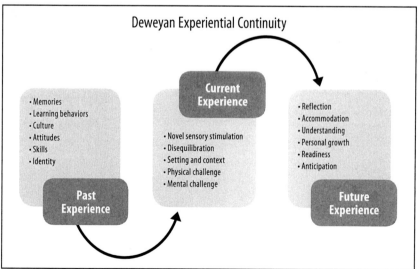

Figure 7: *Deweyan Experiential Continuity*

How does past and current experience then connect with future experience? Experiential learning is not an instinctual reaction to a set of novel stimuli. It is the thoughtful and considered response to a novel situation. According to Dewey, thinking about an experience – *reflection* – is the essential step in learning experientially:

> *Thought or reflection...is the discernment of the relation between what we try to do and what happens in consequence. No experience having a meaning is possible without some element of thought* (Dewey, 1921, p. 169).

Reflection is the considered, purposeful conjecture that follows the experience of uncertainty, incompletion, and doubt. Dewey distinguished clearly between different forms of reflection, from immediate trial and error, to more intentional and considered long-term reflection (Dewey, 1921, pp. 173-176). Ideally, reflection based on experience should lead to tentative conclusions that are then tested in the real world. We can never truly escape from trial and error arising from experience, as reflection connects past experience through the present to the future (Dewey, 1929, p. 109). While reflection is seen by some as an interruption to the sensory flow of an experience (Quay, 2003), reflection can also be an experience in thinking, complete with its own processes and outcomes (Dewey, 1921, p. 176; Quay, 2003).

Another defining characteristic of Deweyan experiential learning is that *action* follows reflection where action is the operationalization of reflection. It serves to separate presumptive, habitual acceptance of the routine from genuine learning experiences; the former requires no action, whereas the latter implies uncertainty (cognitive dissonance) and a responsibility to respond in a rational way:

> *Reflection is the acceptance of responsibility for future actions arising out of an experience* (Dewey, 1921, p. 171).

Educational experience ideally should *arouse curiosity, strengthen initiative and build purpose* (Dewey, 1997 [1938], p. 38). Through its continuity with future experience, it should continue to exert a powerful motivating force well beyond its initial impact.

Does this mean then that in order to learn, we only need to experience? In fact, Dewey sounded a warning against the uncritical acceptance of all experience as appropriate for educational purposes:

> *The belief that all genuine education comes about through experience does not mean that all experiences are genuinely or equally educative. Experience and education cannot be directly equated to each other* (1997 [1938], p. 25).

Thus, only certain kinds of experiences are suitable for learning.

This of course raises the rather complex question of how we might go about selecting or designing educationally appropriate experiences. Any such selection would necessarily reflect or serve to inform the underlying values and philosophies of an educational program and the community it serves, either by intention or by default. Dewey was quite clear on what the community needed in his lifetime. He judged that not all experiences were desirable: some experiences were perceived to be mis-educative, distorting growth and leading the learner to disintegration and dissipation (Dewey, 1997 [1938], pp. 25-6; Lutterman-Aguilar & Gingerich, 2002).

In addressing the difficulty in determining an appropriate organising set of values and principles to inform the task of formulating an experience-based curriculum, Dewey sought to articulate an approach based on the utilisation of social factors that govern experience to distinguish between desirable and mis-educative experience (1997 [1938], p. 21). Perhaps responding to William James' notion of experience as *quasi-chaos*, Dewey believed that experiences, no matter how intrinsically interesting, if lacking a coherent, underlying structure binding them to an educational and social outcome, would give rise to a disintegrated and unconnected curriculum (1997 [1938], p. 26; James, 1912, p. 65).

This need for structural coherence between design and outcome, however, raises at least one potential problem for us. It brings us rather close to seeing experience as just another delivery system for the transmission of content. If learners construct their own understandings anyway, regardless of coherent intent, then James' quasi-chaos might be a closer representation of reality.

While not a key discernible theme for Dewey, the underlying constructivist nature of learning is given tacit acknowledgement through what he referred to as *collateral learning*, which we might equate to the notion of the 'hidden' curriculum (1997 [1938], p. 48). Collateral learning acknowledged that the actual learning achieved by learners might be significantly different to that intended by the supervising teacher. If learners potentially walk away from a learning experience with a set of largely unintentional or *collateral* learning outcomes, we find ourselves back at the somewhat vexed question of purpose, design, and outcome. True to his pragmatic roots, Dewey invoked the notion of personal growth to benefit to society, both planned and unintentional, as the ultimate litmus test of any desirable learning experience (1997 [1938], p. 56).

Learner motivation provided a clear demarcation between what Dewey referred to as the *traditional* style of education and the experience-based model of learning articulated in his writing (1997 [1938], p. 26). This is not to say that learners in 'traditional' learning programs don't have experiences or are automatically unmotivated. It was Dewey's contention, however, that the experiences of students engaged in this type of learning were marked by routine and certainty and that this led to a gradual diminution of motivation (Dewey, 1997 [1938], pp. 26-27). Dewey's experiential ideal was the design of learning programs that motivate students to raise challenging questions that in turn lead to authentic learning for the ultimate benefit of the community (1997 [1938], p. 26; O'Brien, 2002, p. 22).

As a contemporary of both Vygotsky and Piaget, Dewey was keenly aware of the tensions between the theories of learning that pitted individual cognitive construction against the socially-mediated formation of knowledge (1997 [1938], p. 17). Dewey was unequivocal in his identification of learning as a *social enterprise* (1909, pp. 11-12; 1997 [1938], p. 56). In critiquing the individual developmental model proposed by Piaget, Dewey argued strongly for the primacy of the social dimension in learning, decrying the *absurdity* of spontaneous development from within; for Dewey, learning could only be understood as a socially situated process (Dewey, 1998 [1916], pp. 258, 263). Language development in children flowed on from adult responses to the *instinctive babblings* of infants (Dewey, 1998 [1897], p. 229): in this view Dewey was strongly aligned with Vygotsky (Kozulin, 1986).

The critical feature of this theory of language acquisition in children is that it is achieved through experience and interaction with the external world, through interaction with *external agents* (Dewey, 1998 [1916], p. 258). In rejecting the notion of development as an inwardly orientated process, Dewey stated:

> *What is called inner is simply that which does not connect with others – which is not capable of free and full communication* (Dewey, 1998 [1916], p. 263).

For Dewey, these external agents were typically adults with superior experience and judgement. Their experience was seen as the guiding force in selecting and rejecting learning experiences on the basis of their utility and propensity to provide continuity for learners (Dewey, 1997 [1938], p. 39).

The role of the teacher in experiential learning is typically based on expertise in a set of skills relevant to the activity. Teachers facilitate learning, providing a scaffold based on competence and experience to support and guide the learning process. Teachers are co-leaders and co-learners in experiential learning. They manage the physical setting of learning to achieve learning outcomes (Dewey, 1997 [1938], pp. 40, 59). In contrast to the conventional transmission model of learning, in which the teacher provides students with a grounding in the relevant abstract principles of a topic prior to application in the real world, the order is generally reversed in experiential learning, with learning often occurring through reflection after participation in an experience-based activity (Laubscher, 1994, p.6).

During his lifetime, Dewey was an articulate and ardent critic of traditional schooling and what he saw as its isolation from reality. He felt that the lack of experientiality in mainstream schooling was one of the reasons for the many criticisms of American education in the early 20th century, the most persistent of which was its perceived failure to address the needs of American society (1997 [1938], p. 48). Citing Rousseau's *education of things*, Dewey acknowledged the importance of connecting learning to the real world, and, in particular, the surrounding setting or context in which learning takes place (1998 [1916]). Learning, to be effective, must have relevance and application in the setting in which it occurs (Dewey, 1997 [1938], pp. 48-49). Dewey's educational legacy is highly pragmatic. He advocated authentic learning experiences to promote independent thinking, to solve social problems, and to build a better, more democratic society (P. Freeman, Nelson, & Taniguchi, 2003, p. 25).

Dewey and Vygotsky: Common Ground

As we might expect, there is considerable common ground between Dewey and Vygotsky (Glassman, 2001, p. 3). In considering Dewey's ideas regarding experiential learning, drawing some comparisons with Vygotsky's thinking allows us to connect the two in a loosely defined theoretical structure. There are strong parallels between Dewey's connecting experience with education and the role played by *culture* in Vygotsky's thinking (1978). The concept of experience and its role in education was a central feature in much of Dewey's writing, but was not emphasised in Vygotsky's work.

Dewey described *actual experience,* including the experiences of both students and mature persons responsible for guiding the learning of the young, as having an *intimate and necessary* bond with education (1997 [1938], p. 20). Going further, Dewey cited the *organic* relationship between personal experience and education as the one permanent frame of reference on which to base any theorising about education (1997 [1938], p. 25).

A fierce critic of formal education in his time, Dewey essentially rejected the notion of an education in which the teacher acts as the sole arbiter of worthy content, where only carefully selected experiences from the past are valued. For Dewey, there was a world of difference between understanding the past experiences of selected others as the sole end of education, and using past experience as a means for learners to achieve a more broadly focused set of learning outcomes for the benefit of society in the future (1997 [1938], p. 23). The centrality of the learner in this notion of using experience to achieve future outcomes is further evidence of Dewey's socio-constructivist leanings. The educational power of experience as a social force was clear to Dewey: *Every experience is a moving force...all human experience is ultimately social* (1997 [1938], p. 38).

Vygotsky, by contrast, established a distinction between formal, school-based, *scientific* learning (semantic, factual knowledge learning) and informal, experiential learning, which Vygotsky referred to as *spontaneous* learning. Vygotsky considered scientific learning to be systematic, factually, and conceptually rich, reflecting knowledge constructed through direct adult instruction (1986 [1934], p. 158). Spontaneous, 'everyday' learning – experiential learning for the purposes of this discussion – on the other hand, resulted in knowledge being constructed from subjective, personal experience (1986 [1934], p. 158).

Using Vygotsky's scientific and spontaneous categories of learning, we have established a discrete theoretical basis for experiential learning that is connected to scientific learning, but which offers different strengths, particularly learning motivation in the affective domain (1986 [1934], p. 158). Vygotsky cited clinical evidence of scientific learning capacity developing ahead of spontaneous learning in younger children, but this only happened *as long as the curriculum supplied the necessary material* (1986 [1934], p. 147). He believed this was due to the *systematicity of instruction* and cooperation between the child and teacher, noting that children found it difficult to draw abstract knowledge from their personal experience (1986 [1934], pp. 148-149). Vygotsky believed that spontaneous or experiential nature was connected to a qualitatively different aspect of cognitive development (1978, pp. 84-85). There is no evidence that Vygotsky examined the reverse flow of learning, where children might have attempted to connect their previous spontaneous learning with subsequent scientific learning; this is a connection that Dewey made very clear in his views on continuity of experience connecting to later learning. Interestingly, present day student-centred or student-led *discovery* learning is far more closely aligned with Vygotsky's spontaneous learning than scientific learning (Karpov, 2003, p. 66; Panofsky, John-Steiner, & Blackwell, 1990, pp. 251-252).

Traditional education of the type Vygotsky might have identified as *scientific*, organised in a much more systematic manner without any realistic prospect of immediate application, was strongly criticised by Dewey as having insufficient social utility in both the short and longer-term (1997 [1938], p. 19). In his criticism of the traditional model of education, Dewey questioned the imposition of a passive, *transmission* model of education in which teachers used *devices of art to cover up the imposition so as to relieve it of obviously brutal features* (1997 [1938], p. 19). These are strong words indeed.

The gap between adult-like competence and student performance noted by Dewey was seen as being so great, and the structure of learning experiences so rigid, that students were effectively *forbidden* from active participation in their own learning (1997 [1938], p. 19). Dewey noted that one of the underlying assumptions in this approach to education, apparently imposed by those in previous generations, was that future generations would be little different from previous ones and that knowledge was to be transmitted unchanged and unchallenged from previous times (1997 [1938], p. 19). Dewey was clearly not a supporter of this conservative view of education (1997 [1938], p. 19).

Unlike many other theorists and true to his experiential leanings, Dewey was highly focused on the ways in which his ideas of an experience-based education might be implemented (1997 [1938], p. 21; Wells, 1994). At both a classroom and institutional level, Dewey recognised the necessity of conducting a thorough redesign of the conduct and management of learning programs in institutions once the underlying theory of learning was changed. Dewey was keenly aware of the failure of earlier reforms as clear evidence supporting this concern (1997 [1938], p. 21). Vygotsky, on the other hand, was chiefly concerned with observable phenomena, rather educational reform.

A final point of congruence between Dewey and Vygotsky concerns the bi-directionality of interaction between the subject and the mediating semiotic tool (Vygotsky, 1987, p. 106; Wells, 1999). The old transmission model was always seen as a one-way process, with information passing from the originator to the recipient, from transmitter to receiver. Constructivists, on the other hand, acknowledged that the learner might influence others, including competent and experienced adults, during the learning process. Dewey believed that experience similarly could not be treated as a unilateral, isolated phenomenon affecting just the individual learner. Experience will always exert its own mediating force on the ultimate source of the experience:

> *Experience does not go on simply inside a person...every genuine experience has an active side which changes in some degree the objective conditions under which experiences are had* (1997 [1938], p. 39).

As learners, we are therefore not passive recipients of an experience. We have the capacity to change the circumstances of the experience and shape future experiences. In a manner similar to the treatment of culture and cultural artefacts in Vygotsky's work, for Dewey, experience had a cumulative property in which each experience was held to live on in some way in future experiences (1997 [1938], p. 27).

Experiential Learning and Constructivism

While experiential learning theory shares much with constructivist ideas, beyond Dewey, there is little direct commentary in the constructivist literature dealing with the notion of experience as a form of learning. While some, such as Moon (2004, p. 2), have asserted that *all learning is experiential,* Miller and Boud see experience as only one of the means through which learners actively construct their own knowledge of the world (1996, pp. 9-10). For Bruner, citing historical examples, *praxis* always precedes *nomos:* the experience comes first, leading to skill, and then construction of meaning from the experience itself (Bruner, 1996, p. 152).

The way in which we construct understanding of our experiences is shaped by the thoughts and words we use to describe them (Halliday, 1993). Halliday draws our attention to the fact that it is through language that the connection is made between our experiences and the corresponding knowledge that is constructed:

> *Language is the essential condition of knowing, the process by which experience becomes knowledge* (1993, p. 94).

Language provides the means by which we construct a more durable account of an experience for later re-use, reinterpretation, and recall. This view aligns strongly with the Vygotskian notion of language as the key mediating tool in the social interactions, through which knowledge is built (Vygotsky, 1986 [1934], p. 7).

Experiences occur in a social and cultural context that shapes the way in which learners construct knowledge from novel encounters. In fact, according to Miller and Boud, the experiential context cannot be excised from the experience itself (1996). Experiential learning has what might be described as a socio-emotional context, or a micro context. This is perhaps another way of describing learner affective factors, which serve to shape the way in which an experience is constructed in the minds of the participants (Miller & Boud, 1996). An important part of the social dimension of experiential learning is the extent to which individuals and groups are aware of themselves as members of a collective entity when engaged in an experiential learning task (Cates & Ohl, 2006). The setting in which the learning occurs and the nature of the problem encountered by the group will also have an impact on the relative cohesion of the group, influencing social dynamics significantly (Cates & Ohl, 2006, pp. 72-73).

There is a view that childhood development occurs as a result of participation in activities leading to transformational changes in the individual, rather than through the acquisition of knowledge and skills (Rogoff, 2003, p. 254). Echoing Dewey, Rogoff asserted that through the experience of participation in one activity, the individual might develop the ability to apply that experience to new situations, or to construct a better working model of the applications of the experience; new problems are handled in ways that correspond directly to the prior experience (Rogoff, 2003, p. 254).

Perhaps a final comment on the constructivist perspective on experiential learning should come from one of its pioneers: Piaget, who, in an observation about the nature of learning written in the latter years of his life, noted the tension between more conventional semantic learning and what he described, perhaps in Vygotskian terms, as *spontaneous* (experiential) learning (1962). While this relationship is seen by some educators as adversarial, Piaget (1962) insisted that there was much that formal education could learn from other more spontaneous forms of learning. In fact, Piaget argued in a reflection written towards the end of his life that learning conducted in a more active mode might be more *productive* through tapping into the experiences and interests of the child (1962).

Experiential Learning and Problem Solving

Ideally, learning should be connected with the learner's experience of reality. Experiential learning ideally takes place in the context of solving a problem that is encountered or experienced by a learner who is motivated in some way, either through need or interest, to seek a solution to the problem (Dewey, 1997 [1938]; Wells, 1999). As previously established in the discussion on the ZPD, the ideal experiential learning problem lies beyond the immediate ability of the individual to solve on the basis of current knowledge or skills. Through the problem, the learner becomes aware of a gap in knowledge or skill needed to resolve the problem and assistance, often in the form of physical or semiotic tools provided by a more competent individual, is required to solve the problem (Bassok, 1997, p. 1). Learner generated mistakes arise inevitably as a result of this experiential process.

As established in the second chapter discussion on the learning process, the genesis of learning as a cognitive process arises from the learner's attempts to resolve a cognitive conflict, to close a cognitive gap. Through this process, the learner becomes aware of mistakes, which in turn give rise to questions that play a central role in initiating and guiding learning through cognitive conflict (Scardamalia & Bereiter, 1992). The learner, in ignorance, or through committing an error, potentially encounters *disequilibration* (Piaget & Garcia, 1991). Learning is said to have occurred when the disequilibration has been resolved, although according to Daniels, the exact mechanism by which this is achieved is still subject to debate (Daniels, 2001, pp. 32-35).

Challenging experiential learning problems should be multidimensional, include affective domain factors such as planned disorientation, either physical or emotional, for learners, which are seen as being a necessary part of enduring learning (Owen-Smith, 2004). One way of engaging the affective domain in learning is to design learning experiences that offer a sharp discontinuity with the previous life experiences of the learner, a practice that generates *discontinuous experiences* (Williams, 2005). This discontinuity may not involve risk or particularly confronting problems, but may take place in a *place-based* setting as a core program element within a specific social setting (Theobald & Tolbert, 2006, pp. 271-274). Similarly, experiential problems should be open-ended, encouraging learner curiosity and openness, seeking to avoid the imposition on learners of pre-conceived notions (Freire & Giroux, 1992; Roberts, 2000, p. 2).

When facing a problem, learner motivation, one of the most fundamental psychological drivers, plays an important role in the process of learning (Covington, 2000; Tappan, 1998). Awareness of a cognitive gap, or conflict in the form of an error or knowledge gap, is one of the primary preconditions for learning, acting as a trigger providing causal motivation for the commencement of the learning process. In a metacognitive sense, a learner's awareness of a semantic knowledge gap, characterised by Dewey as *genuine ignorance* (1997 [1910], p. 177) or error, creates the conditions and motivation to allow the learning process to commence. Errors encountered during the process of learning to solve a specific problem actually motivate further learning and in fact where the number of errors is reduced, the latitude for learning is also reduced (Seiffert & Hutchins, 1992, p. 183).

The importance of learner awareness of knowledge gaps and errors has contributed to the growing trend in pedagogy towards a greater application of metacognitive concepts for both practitioners and learners to enhance the effectiveness of learning (Bruner, 1996, p. 64). Through detailed examination of student errors and knowledge gaps, and how they are encountered, recognised, and managed, the potential exists to develop a greater understanding of the process of learning and what motivates learning at an intrapsychological level. In developing a better understanding of error as a trigger factor in motivating learning, both pedagogically and metacognitively, the potential exists to design learning experiences that enhance the development of autonomous learning. Learners need to be able to think about their own gaps and mistakes as well.

Mistakes and errors are an important part of the experiential learning dynamic. If we consider mistakes as a form of Darwinian 'trial and error' developmental mechanism, learning occurs through encountering and recovering from mistakes – trial, error, and survival – as we seek a form of Piagetian equilibrium through the creation of new knowledge and skills (Perkinson, 1984, p. 169). Taking Perkinson's idea a step further, through the experience of less effective paradigms of learning, it could be contended that more powerful paradigms will emerge as a result of this trial and error, offering even greater explanatory power to advance our understanding of the process of learning.

Post-Dewey: Kolb's Experiential Learning Theory Model

After Dewey, there have been very few fully articulated theories of experiential learning. One exception is the model developed by David A. Kolb known as *Experiential Learning Theory* (ELT). Kolb's model is one of the most frequently cited theoretical references associated with experiential learning (Greenaway, 2005). ELT espouses a strongly Deweyan/Vygotskian foundation and incorporates a four-stage model of learning moving from *concrete experience* through *observation and reflection* to *abstract conceptualisation* back to *active experimentation* (Grabowski & Jonassen, 1993, p.253; D. A. Kolb, 1984).

While the ELT model is frequently cited in writings about experiential learning, it is a model that is essentially aimed at adult learners (Oxendine, Robinson, & Willson, 2004). ELT has been widely adopted in many different forms as a model for the design of vocational or professional training programs (Oxendine et al., 2004). It remains questionable whether the degree of learning autonomy, maturity, and perception implicit in Kolb's model is present or available to be operationalized in school-aged experiential learners.

Other criticisms of Kolb's model focus on several key areas: reflection as a learning mechanism; its fixed, invariant cycle; and the social dimension of experiential learning. A fundamental concern is that, while based on Dewey's ideas, Kolb's model makes no clear distinction between *non-reflective* experiential learning, which arises directly from disequilibration, where a real-world contradiction is encountered and resolved directly, and *reflective* experiential learning, in which the experience is followed at some later point by deliberate, purposeful reflection (Oxendine et al., 2004). Some critics observe the Kolb's experiential learning model is largely indistinguishable from more generic models of learning and as such fails to identify the unique elements of experiential learning (Henry, 1989, p. 26). Kolb also overturns Dewey's notion of knowledge being created out of the learner's contact with, and subjective, reflective interpretation of, reality through observation, asserting instead that knowledge is created through the experience itself (Oxendine et al., 2004).

A further criticism of Kolb's model is that it imposes a fixed cycle of processes in the learning cycle on individual learners; both the learners and the stages in the cycle do not appear to interrelate in the ELT model (Oxendine et al., 2004). This approach is not supported by our knowledge of cognitive processes associated with learning, in which there is rarely a set pattern of steps; instead there is wide variation according to context, need, and individual affective factors, all of which are not well accommodated by Kolb's model (Greenaway, 2005). In particular, Webb (1980) found Kolb's model to be fundamentally flawed in asserting an invariant four-stage model that is not borne out in practice. Learning, according to Webb, can occur at any point in the experiential process (1980, p. 2).

Kolb's model has been extremely influential in shaping corporate, adult-oriented experiential learning. However, significantly for schools, experiential learning for younger learners is not specifically addressed in Kolb's model, leaving an open question as to the applicability of this model to the school setting, particularly in view of the metacognitive demands placed on learners working within the ELT model of learning.

The Problem with School-based Learning

Experience is a powerful motivating force in human learning, but the theoretical connections between experiential and semantic learning are tenuous; the practical links between the two in formal education are almost non-existent. In fact, our failure to connect everyday experiential learning and spontaneous concepts with semantic, *scientific* school-based learning poses a risk that the latter will be rendered *inert and developmentally ineffective* (Daniels, 2001, p. 98); others have offered a similar contention:

> *Conceptual and problem-solving knowledge acquired in school remains largely unintegrated or inert for many students* (Collins, Brown, & Newman, 1989, p. 455).

Learning that is too abstract and isolated from the experience of the learner will have limited future effectiveness (Steffe, 1995, pp. 507-509). This is particularly the case where that semantic knowledge is abstract or not directly connected in some way with the learner's experience of the world acquired by way of the physical senses (1995, pp. 507-509). Knowledge that has a direct connection to personal experience, perceived or experienced directly by the senses is more readily incorporated into the learner's memories, and is available for recall and reflection without considerable effort in most cases (Duit, 1995, p. 275).

Experiential, *everyday* learning is typically learned unsystematically and from a very early age, but with direct relevance and applicability to everyday tasks and settings. This contrasts strongly with *scientific* learning, which is often taught in schools in a highly systematic way, with very little direct relevance to the daily experiences of learners (Vygotsky, 1978, pp. 74-75; Wells, 1999, p. 29):

> *Perhaps as a by-product of the relegation of learning to schools, skills and knowledge have become abstracted from their uses in the world* (Collins et al., 1989).

With this in mind, schools and teachers are seen by some as an impediment to learning in general, and integrating experiential and semantic learning in particular (Tobias & Duffy, 2009, p. 5). Should schools act merely as conduits for the construction or even the transmission of knowledge? For others, there is an important role for schools to play beyond student mastery of factual content for benchmark testing:

> *Although schools have been relatively successful in organizing and conveying large bodies of conceptual and factual knowledge, standard pedagogical practices render key aspects of expertise invisible to students. Too little attention is paid to...carrying out complex or realistic tasks* (Collins et al., 1989).

This *invisibility* of expertise is particularly problematic when the learner seeks to leave the formal educational environment and assume a productive role in the community. The time-honoured and examination driven focus on *conveying large bodies of conceptual and factual knowledge* that for many characterises contemporary schooling, is interpreted by some critics, such as Collins, et al., as passive transmission, but without practical application. Transmitted content that is scrutinised and privileged in high-stakes testing is largely disconnected and isolated from the direct experiential base of the learner and, we might suggest, the pragmatic concerns and needs of the wider community. Implicit in this virtual transmission model of learning is the notion that schools act in a unidirectional and unilateral fashion; learners act as passive receptacles into which knowledge is poured and have little reverse impact on the focus, conduct, or outcomes of their studies (Wells, 1999, pp. 52-53).

Schools that have not found a way of connecting semantic learning with authentic experience are in danger of become precincts of an *exotic kind of practice contextually bound to the educational setting* (Lave, 1997, p. 33). In order to avoid becoming exhibits of curious and fossilised social phenomena, schools need to adopt a practice that permits a gradually maturing approximation of adult practice through the practical application of learning – a form of *cognitive apprenticeship* (Lave, 1997, p. 33). Learning that does not have an experiential dimension is therefore in danger of remaining limited to an institutional context and having limited personal application. Developing strong curricular and pedagogical links between experiential and semantic learning offers some hope that the two modes of learning will be operationalised in the experienced world of the individual (Daniels, 2001, p. 98).

Criticisms of Experiential Learning: Theory into Practice

There are a number of significant problems associated with the implementation of different forms and expressions of experiential learning theory. These problems range from our underdeveloped understanding of the role of setting in experiential learning, through appropriate teaching methodologies, to the identification and measurement of learning outcomes associated with experiential learning (Kirschner et al., 2006; Miettinen, 2006). It is seen as too impractical, too expensive, too risky, or lacking academic rigour, and as such fails to produce new knowledge of any value (Hirsch, 2001; Karpov, 2003).

One of the more significant problems is the issue of setting and the extent to which experiential learning settings should be controlled in some way, or allowed to reflect the real world. Classrooms and other mainstream learning settings are typically *synthetic*, with many of the variables controlled or restricted in some way and in which participants are insulated from consequences; natural or realistic settings, on the other hand, introduce a greater degree of reality and uncertainty to the learning activities (Hoberman & Mailick, 1994). Synthetic experiences are supplied by moot courts or other simulated environments in which the learning can be subject to much greater control. For the purposes of experiential learning, realistic settings are by definition essentially *uncontrolled*, and as such pose genuine risks to learners; these risks require careful management (Fenwick, 2000).

Perhaps the middle road between an overly controlled synthetic setting and an open-ended, risky real-world setting is the need to establish a form of safe, scaffolded apprenticeship or mentorship, overseen by more skilled and experienced individual undertaking a mentoring role, but within an authentic setting (Schön, 1987, p. 37). An experiential practicum might approximate the real world in its presentation of actual problems in all their complexity, while removing many of the risks, pressures and consequences that attach to real world tasks (Schön, 1987, p. 37). In this form of learning by doing, Schön argued that interactions with peers and teachers are equally important, and that exposure and immersion lead to what he termed *background learning* (Schön,

1987, p. 38). This idea also closely parallels Vygotsky's notion of ZPD, in which the learning ecosystem is managed and scaffolded by a more experienced individual, but where learners are always being drawn out into the zone between their demonstrated competence and the extreme outer limits of what might be accomplished with mentorship.

Guided discovery learning is a compromise between a tightly controlled pedagogy on the one hand and an unfettered *discovery* learning approach on the other; by virtue of its empirical nature it can be considered to be a form of experiential learning (Karpov, 2003, pp. 74-76). In guided discovery learning, students discover underlying principles in a learning activity through sensory interaction under the guidance of an experienced mentor. This type of learning has regained popularity in the last decade, but for some it is flawed in its underlying theory in a number of ways. Most importantly, critics such as Karpov, have objected to the trial and error nature of any form of discovery, dismissing it as *reinvention* (2003, p. 75). Karpov also criticised the acceptance of mistakes in learning, particularly scientific learning, as inhibiting the potential contribution to knowledge implied in a less than rigorous approach to accuracy and truth (2003, p. 75).

These criticisms may underestimate the importance of discovery in developing learner autonomy and confidence. A culture of risk-taking can have a very positive impact on learning outcomes. Karpov's conclusion that independent learning should be an outcome, not an instructional premise, does not address the manner in which independence is acquired as a formal part of the learning process (2003, p. 79).

A criticism levelled at activity-based and student-centred experiential learning is that too much attention is focused on the process of learning, the learning journey, with insufficient emphasis placed on mastery of the discipline-based knowledge (Wells, 1999, p. 90). There may also be learner misconceptions that arise through 'discovery learning' where the guiding principles and concepts are imperfectly understood or lacking entirely (Karpov, 2003, p. 70). Mastery of knowledge in its true sense is a process of sequential construction: mastery is achieved painstakingly, progressively, and methodically. Activities of an experiential nature, when connected to semantic content, must be based on steady theoretical foundations, where there are clearly articulated links to the mainstream curriculum (Wells, 1999, p. 90). As noted earlier, there is no transmission of knowledge from textbook to brain; research that creates new knowledge ideally is framed using learners' own questions.

The steady accumulation of prescribed knowledge by learners for retrieval and display is already an outmoded model of education; participatory knowledge building through joint action is the only way to give students a sense of proprietary ownership in both the process and the product, as both the questions and their relevant answers will belong to each student in a very real and personal way (Wells, 1999, p. 92).

Experiential learning is incomplete as a process if it lacks some form of analysis and reflection to guide future experiences and learning (Dewey, 1997 [1938]; Lutterman-Aguilar & Gingerich, 2002; Wells, 1999). Yet the practice of reflection, which is accepted widely as an essential part of experiential learning, is often at odds with the student-centred philosophy on which many experiential learning programs are based (Estes, 2004). The common practice of post-experience reflection is teacher-centric and teacher-initiated. The power to shape the way in which an experience is processed, analysed, and remembered rests largely with the teacher, rather than the student (Estes, 2004). There is an incongruity at the heart of student-centred learning in which the teacher *speaks on behalf of the experience* (Estes, 2004).

There is a noted absence of sustained research into experiential learning and consistent program evaluation (Neill, 2004). Instead, there is a trend towards more affectively powerful, informal approaches to experiential education that avoids entirely the challenges of more rigorous, exacting research. Client focused corporate experiential learning, typically aimed at middle level management and largely based on Kolb's ELT model or a variant of the Kolb model, has driven the establishment of a healthy industry for adults with an associated body of research to support these programs (Neill, 2004). However, the same is not apparent for school-based programs where there is potentially a significant gap in our knowledge. The duration and structure of outdoor education programs are similarly not based on a theoretical model aimed at maximising the benefits to participants, but on the availability of program venues and content (Neill, 2004).

Over the past five decades, the value of experiential learning has been affirmed in general terms by various scholarly and professional journals, yet the availability of reliable and quantifiable verification of specific outcomes remains problematic. There is little consensus on what constitutes a rigorous program evaluation methodology (Hendricks, 1994; Scrutton & Beames, 2015). In order to adapt and transfer those elements of experiential learning that have applicability in other forms of learning, the main research task is to discover the more broadly applicable reasons for success underlying those experiential programs that are found to be effective (Hendricks, 1994). Prior research in this field has also focused on the merits of individual programs in isolation, rather than the broader educational benefits conferred by utilisation of the experiential mode of learning within a mainstream educational setting (Hendricks, 1994). Smith (2003), for example, reported that in one limited experiential program in the United Kingdom specifically aimed at linking experiential learning and literacy, significant results were achieved in building a connection between the experience and the academic skill, in this case, writing. Participants reported enhanced self-esteem, but it was also noted that they achieved observable improvements in their writing skills (M. Smith, 2003). Smith noted that the impact of the program relied to a large extent on embedding the experiential component within a mainstream literary curriculum (2003, p.3).

Finally, where conducted within traditional mainstream institutions, experiential learning programs may in practice merely reflect a different form of teacher-centred learning, in which the student is still compelled to follow a teacher directed course of study (Itin, 1999). There are still many implementations of experiential learning in which the student is bound to a tightly structured curriculum, and in which the main difference to mainstream didactic learning is essentially a shift in pedagogy and perhaps, setting, with the teacher-centred structure left largely intact (Itin, 1999). Rickinson et al., in summarising a review of outdoor learning, noted the use of fieldwork settings to enhance mainstream learning in the United Kingdom and in other countries is severely limited, particularly in the sciences (2004). They also noted that the setting of *outdoor* education may have a positive effect on long-term memory, but without further discussion or analysis (Rickinson et al., 2004). Furthermore, echoing Hendricks, Rickenson et al., also asserted that our understanding of the relationship between experiential and mainstream (semantic) learning is not well understood (2004). As such, the practice of experiential learning in schools remains challenging and imperfectly realised.

Chapter 4: Learning in Context: Setting

Returning briefly to the broader ideas about learning examined in the second chapter, it is perhaps curious to note that there is little meaningful attention in academic writing placed on *where* we learn. All learning takes place *somewhere*, but is this *somewhere* important to our understanding of learning as a theory or practice? There is an assumption, largely implicit, that learning is a school-based undertaking and it therefore takes place in schools or other formal educational settings. And what of experiential learning? Is the setting of an experience a significant factor in learning experientially?

Given that some common forms of experiential learning are referred to as 'outdoor education' it seems sensible to assume that provided the activity is happening 'outdoors' and is broadly educational, then the program would appear to conform to its defining characteristics. There is much more to experiential learning than selecting a setting for an activity that is solely defined by the absence of a classroom.

The role of the setting in which learning takes place, particularly in student-centred or even experiential learning, is an area of surprising neglect in the writings reviewed in the earlier chapters. Seen as theoretically unproblematic by many in mainstream conventional education, there are hints and suggestions that learning settings warrant further attention at this point in our journey. This is particularly true in the field of experiential education. This chapter seeks to assert the importance of setting in experiential learning and challenge some of the underlying theoretical assumptions used for the selection, design and pedagogical utilisation of learning settings (Land & Hannafin, 2000).

The sparse evidence pointing to the influence of setting on learning in constructivist learning theory is largely implicit: the role of setting is just not a prominent feature (Piaget, 2002 [1923], p. 269; Vygotsky, 1986 [1934], p. 56; Wells, 1999, p. 38). There are, however, some pockets of enlightened resistance. The highly experientially focused *Reggio Emilia* approach to learning, for example, found most frequently in early years education, identifies the setting as the 'third teacher', but this is something of an anomaly (Gandini, 1998).

We learned in the previous chapter that our capacity to remember experiences in finely recorded detail is influenced by the relative unfamiliarity of settings that are emotionally and subjectively significant. This is supported by research into experiential learning that suggests it is ideally undertaken by students away from their normal, everyday environment (Hattie et al., 1997, pp. 44-48). However, being 'away' from the everyday learning and living environment of the learner is a rather amorphous concept that does little to inform an intelligent selection of exactly where 'somewhere' else might be educationally meaningful and conducive to learning.

The role of setting has been discussed in a more explicit way in the recent relevant literature on experiential learning, but it is still typically viewed in an unproblematic or narrow way and remains relatively *unexplored* (Beard & Wilson, 2006, pp. 79-85). In some descriptions of experiential learning, the term *outdoors* is used to make explicit the contrast with the *indoors* associated with mainstream, classroom-based education (Beard & Wilson, 2002, p. 93; 2006, p. 87). Again, *outdoors* is not defined in an educationally meaningful way and seems to imply that for the purposes of learning, one 'outdoor' location is much the same as another. This idea will be challenged in the following pages.

The settings in which programs of experiential learning are conducted are described as *unfamiliar*, or by some as *distinctive* and *challenging*, although these qualities are not typically explored in detail (Neill, 2006). Unfamiliarity is a somewhat difficult characteristic to narrow, if we were seeking to design an ideal experiential learning setting – unfamiliar to whom? In what way might one setting for a learning activity be distinct from another? Why might it be seen as challenging?

An early and highly influential model of the experiential learning process characterised the physical setting as *neutral* and *impartial* (B. Martin, Cashel, Wagstaff, & Breunig, 2006, p. 64; Walsh & Golins, 1976, pp. 4-6), but with a social dimension that influenced the learning dynamic in the physical setting. Some researchers have now moved away from setting as a passive or neutral 'given', asserting the affective influence of setting on the learner's experience through generating feelings of unfamiliarity, isolation, dissonance, and anxiety (McKenzie, 2000, pp. 20-21; 2003, p. 14). These offer a slightly higher degree of specificity, but still hardly constitute a clearly defined set of parameters for the selection of the ideal setting for experiential learning.

There is growing acknowledgement, however, that much of the research into experiential learning has been focused on activities rather than settings and that more work is needed on the theorisation of setting in experiential learning (Beard & Wilson, 2002, pp. 90-92). For example, in one extensive survey of the parameters of experiential learning, the only explicit reference to setting was *environmental awareness* (Hattie et al., 1997, p. 48). In Itin's Diamond Model of experiential learning the social, economic, political dimensions of setting are acknowledged, and existence of interaction between learner and setting is illustrated diagrammatically, but without describing the nature of this interaction and without ascribing any particular role to setting in this interaction (Itin, 1999, pp. 93-95).

Overall, the role played by setting remains under-explored, ill-defined, or uncertain in the research literature on experiential learning. The foregoing citations share a common attribute: they point to an affective response from the learner that is induced by the setting, but without specifying what induced that response. There is an unspoken assumption that an unfamiliar and challenging setting may be memorable and may therefore lead to learning. The extent to which setting is discussed by experiential educators tends to focus on whether the mountains can indeed *speak for themselves,* and if so, what they would say (Beard & Wilson, 2006)?

This chapter seeks to shed some light on this question of the role of setting in experiential learning and the particular characteristics that appear to be likely to lead to certain kinds of learning experiences. It explores the theoretical role played by setting in experiential learning and seeks to explain why it is important. This discussion also considers the special role played by objects and artefacts, important elements of setting, exploring the interplay between the learner and the setting, including objects and artefacts. The varied roles of objects in creating learning *affordances,* and even the nature of prosthetic intelligence, are also discussed briefly.

What is Meant by 'Setting'?

For our purposes, the term *setting* is intended to mean the immediate physical and temporal location in which learning takes place, including the tools, artefacts and objects present; each setting has an embedded chronological, emotional, social, and cultural dimension (Marsh, 2004, p. 125). The term learning *environment* is used by many writers interchangeably with setting; it can, however, act as a broader term, including the location of learning, but also embracing emotions, spirituality, institutional policy settings (e.g., behavioural), local and systemic pedagogical practices, institutional and community demography, and the prevailing political milieu. For consistency, the term *setting* is adopted in this book to denote the precise location and context of learning.

While setting is seen by some as theoretically unproblematic (Van Note Chism & Bickford, 2002), acting as a *container* of human behaviour (Engeström, 1993, p. 66), others see it as *changeable* and *dynamic*, not a *static entity* to be taken for granted (Marsh, 2004, p. 125; Vygotsky, 1994 [1934], p. 346). Another perspective sees complexity in setting arising from the frame of reference through which it is viewed, for example, historical, cultural, institutional, or psychological; each perspective yields different interpretations of the impact of setting on human activity (J. Wertsch, 1991, p. 121).

The overall impact of setting on learning theory, however, has been modest, attracting little attention from researchers and is therefore perhaps not well understood. There are no unifying or general theories to guide the design or exploitation of setting in student-centred programs of learning (Land & Hannafin, 2000, p. 2; Loyens & Gijbels, 2008). For some researchers, it is assumed that psychological processes are essentially independent of setting and that learner cognitive processes are spatially neutral or ambiguous (Marsh, 2004, p. 129; Poag, Goodnight, & Cohen, 1985, p. 71). This neutrality or ambiguity with respect to setting and cognition arises in part because its impact on the learner is seen as being largely *indirect* (Poag et al., 1985, p. 104).

Even as an implicit element in many educational theories, setting does not feature as a *core* consideration in learning. An example of this is found in Vygotsky's critique of Piaget's evidence, for example, which pointed out the unacknowledged influence of *surrounding conditions* on the nature of speech in young learners (Piaget, 2002 [1923], pp. 269-271; Vygotsky, 1986 [1934], p. 55). In contrasting the social interaction between children in culturally different kindergartens in two countries, Vygotsky asserted that Piaget's error lay in assuming that the findings in one setting would be applicable to others (1986 [1934], p. 56). Indeed, Piaget noted the differences in the data, but focused instead on the developmental trend within the data stream, rather than the potentially differential impact of the two settings – Geneva and Hamburg – on the ego-centric speech of his subjects (Piaget, 2002 [1923], p. 269). Vygotsky suggested that the higher level of group activity and the consequent reduction in the ego-centric speech co-efficient in German kindergartens pointed to the potential for a different set of conclusions on the matter of egocentric speech

(1986 [1934], p. 56). Implicit in this criticism is the fact that the generalised theory on egocentric speech was actually based on a conflation of observations taken in two different cultural and social settings.

Vygotsky's own perspective on the impact of the setting on learning reflected his awareness of the complex *interactive* relationship between the learner and the setting (1994 [1934], pp. 338-339). The setting acts as far more than an undifferentiated 'container' of activity for the learners occupying the space. The same learner and space will generate a changing dynamic as the learner develops and different learners within the same space will have an individualised, even unique interaction with the setting (Vygotsky, 1994 [1934], p. 339). Learners also utilise and adapt semiotic tools found within a specific setting to reflect their own experience of the setting. This may result in some discrepancies in communication acts as individuals at different stages of development use common words, but with differently nuanced meaning to describe their experience of the setting (Vygotsky, 1994 [1934], p. 345).

Each learning setting is unique, when socio-cultural, ontogenetic (experience across the lifetime of the individual learner) and microgenetic (the moment of a specific action) factors are taken into consideration (Brown, 1988, pp. 3-4). Through the interaction between the learner (subject) and the setting, a unique, semiotically mediated relationship is established that leaves a unique imprint on the learner. The learning experience impacts on the learner, but the learner in turn exerts influence on the learning setting and associated artefacts (Wells, 1999, p. 38). Any mediated interaction between the learner and setting may result in a net change in the learning environment beyond the learner. Agency in this case is bi-directional. The learner will be both acted upon and in turn act upon the mediating agent (Wells, 1999, p. 38). Learners leave a mark on both the environments in which they learn and on the adults through whom their learning is mediated (Wells, 1999, p. 38). When we interact somewhere, with something or someone, we are changed, as are our surroundings.

Taking this notion of the relationship between learner and setting a step further, proponents of what is known as *activity theory* see setting as an activity *system* that is constructed by participants, possessing a physical, psychological, social, and cultural dimension (Engeström, 1993, pp. 66-67; Engeström & Miettinen, 1999, pp. 1-13). In *setting as a system*, subject, object, tools and artefacts, and community are integrated into an interactive whole (Engeström, 1993, pp. 66-67), each component of which is constantly undergoing construction and revision and reconstruction.

More recently, some cognitive theorists have begun to acknowledge the role played by the learning setting through its interaction with the learner

(Hickey, 1997, p. 175). *Authenticity* is an essential attribute of the ideal learning environment from a constructivist perspective: in authentic settings, learning problems can be *complex and ill-structured* to pose a challenge to learners (Loyens & Gijbels, 2008). Some have sought to focus on perhaps overlooked aspects of traditional learning spaces that might be modified to suit constructivist pedagogical approaches (Readdick & Bartlett, 1995). These voices, however, seem to represent a diffuse minority rather than offering an aligned mainstream critique of learning settings.

There are practical difficulties in creating theoretically ideal environments that offer a degree of authenticity and present learners with realistic, complex problems. Conventional classrooms are settings constructed within an institutional context, which entail economic, policy, building, and safety standards, and as such are not necessarily aligned with the theory-driven demands of student-centred learning (Land & Hannafin, 2000, pp. 2-16).

The inertia of existing setting design theory and actual institutional practice results in compromise as new approaches are heavily modified to fit into the existing infrastructure, resulting in *domesticated* implementation models that bear little resemblance to the original theoretical models that spawned them (Land & Hannafin, 2000, p. 16). This suggests that there may be a fundamental conflict between the type of setting that is needed for effective learning that is focused on the needs of the learner, and the conventional notion of an appropriate learning environment within an institutional context. We seem to construct the settings for learning that we are permitted to build, within the funding and compliance constraints imposed from without.

This seems to point to an insoluble dilemma. If theory demands authentic settings, but practical realities require artificial settings, there seems to be no room for negotiation or compromise – at least from an institutional perspective. Settings are only as real as we allow them to be, within the constraints of the legal, ethical, regulatory, educational, and institutional boundaries applicable in a given context.

There have been attempts to evolve learning settings in ways that are more conducive to learning. Virtual learning environments (VLE) in classroom settings heavily modified by technology offer a way forward, albeit within the existing institutional educational paradigm. One such approach that seeks to resolve this dilemma is the creation of 'Open-Ended Learning Environments' (Oliver & Hannafin, 2001), in which learners frame and tackle realistic problems using specialised on-line or computer network tools in modified classroom settings.

The extent to which this approach confers a discernible learning advantage over a more traditional pedagogical approach, however, is questionable. This is in part due in part to the tensions between institutional content-related constraints and the less structured objectives of open-ended learning (Oliver & Hannafin, 2001, pp. 28-29). A further theoretical concern is the centrality of Vygotskian interpersonal interaction as the key mechanism through which learning takes place; artificial or virtual learning environments essentially violate the social locus of learning.

The *Reggio Emilia* approach, originating from the experience of learners constructing their own classrooms from debris found in the ruins of conflict in post-war Italy, is based on a learning theory that emphasises the benefits of learner interaction with different materials and microenvironments. Aimed at early childhood education programs, the Reggio Emilia approach construes setting as the *third teacher* (Cook, 2006; Gandini, 1998). Based on the work of Dewey, Vygotsky, and Bruner, Reggio Emilia is strongly constructivist, bringing the setting and learner into a direct, interactive relationship in which specific properties of the setting stimulate learner exploration through all of the senses (Swann, 2008). The Reggio Emilia learning space is a *container* for social interaction, but also acts as learning content in its own right (Gandini, 1998, p. 164). While the employment of the Reggio Emilia approach is typically limited to early childhood educational programs, it does point to the possibilities of modifying learning by changing how we perceive the learning setting.

This idea of the learner's perception of the learning setting offers another way of thinking about this question. Theories of learning exploring the nature of the *relationship* between the learner and the setting, and particularly the role of setting itself in learning, are not commonplace, but one such theory, the notion of *affordances* (J. J. Gibson, 1986), seeks to establish a theoretical framework to explore the boundaries and relationship between the learner (subject) and object.

Emerging from research into human information processing capabilities in complex environments, the theory of affordances suggests that any action or experience is a phenomenon shared between the learner and the setting (object). According to Gibson, an affordance is an invariant property of the object itself, not of the subject; an affordance or *invitation* is perceived visually by the subject (J. J. Gibson, 1986, p. 139). Hence a chair *affords* the possibility of sitting, regardless of the perceptions of the observer, and may therefore be used for that purpose if the observer is capable of decoding or perceiving that which is afforded by the object. The object or setting offers something and the observer must have the skills or knowledge to take advantage of what is afforded (Zhang & Patel, 2006, p. 335). The property of a setting or object, itself, may therefore play a role in the deployment of human intelligence, drawing out latent capabilities and making possible certain types of developmental activity that might remain dormant in a different setting with a different set of affordances (Pea, 1993, pp. 51-53).

Table 1 shows how the properties of a chair might be categorised.

Object Category: Chair			
Physical Properties	**Cultural Properties**	**Affordances**	**Learner Experience**
• Dimensions	• Design	• Visual	• Sitting
• Weight	• Purpose	• Audio	
• Proportions	• Significance	• Tactile	
• Material state	• Social function	• Manipulable	
• Material type	• Semiotic value	• Portable	
• Texture	• Spiritual function	• Consumable	
• Color	• Symbolic value	• Operable	
• Odor	• Conferred status	• Facilitative	
• Mobility		• Ceremonial	
• Location			
• Shape			
• Design			
• Spatial orientation			

Table 1: Potential object properties, affordances, and learner experiences

In the table above, the object category of 'chair' is examined briefly in terms of its potential affordances. The potential affordances are determined or influenced by the physical and cultural properties of the many different kinds of objects that we might call chairs. For example, a seat in a waiting room, a pilot's seat, and a throne could all be considered to be different kinds of 'chair', but each possesses different properties and thus offers different potential actions and afforded experiences. A performer, however, might also perceive the potential affordance of a chair to act as a prop in a juggling or balancing act.

In considering the affordance offered by an object, we might also consider the extent to which the perception of an affordance is culturally constructed. This was not explored in the original thinking about affordances, but has been given some consideration in more recent accounts (Pea, 1993, pp. 51-52; Zhang & Patel, 2006, p. 335). The affordance of eating using implements such as chopsticks, for example, might be culturally constructed (E. J. Gibson & Pick, 2003, p. 16). In one culture they are just two sticks with no particular affordance associated with eating, in another, they suggest the consumption of food. This suggestion is of course a potential that is constructed in the mind of the observer. The notion that a setting or object might possess properties that are independent of the cognitive meaning imputed by the observer also presents a theoretical difficulty for some constructivists (Greeno, 1994), who believe that this contradicts a fundamental tenet of constructivism regarding the universal subjectivity of meaning.

A further development of this concept is the notion that an artefact may possess qualities that become linked to the way in which an individual perceives and experiences the world. The employment of tools or other artefacts to extend human perception in some way does present a difficulty in identifying the boundary between subject and object and what is actually afforded to the subject by the object. The boundary between the perceiver and the setting in the case of the blind using a sticks to aid in extending their range of perception is a case in point (J. J. Gibson, 1986, p. 41). Vygotsky and Luria referred to the *psychology of the prosthesis* to describe the artificial extension of perceptual boundaries by means of a prosthetic object (1993 [1930], p. 218). In this case, the prosthetic object possesses a property that affords the subject the opportunity to perceive and interpret aspects of the physical world to change behaviour. As a part of the physical setting in which an activity takes place, this type of prosthetic affordance points to the need for a better understanding of the way in which humans interact with settings, particularly in the course of learning through discovery.

If human perceptions are extended artificially through a device or prosthesis, where does the boundary lie between learner and an object that is perceptually out of reach without the aid of some form of prosthesis? And what of human knowledge that is constructed through the support or intervention of a device, such as a computer? If intelligence is the property of an individual, but is only observable or measurable in some way through its external or physical manifestation afforded by an object, then any intelligence demonstrated through some form of interaction with an artefact is potentially a property *shared* between the human mind and the artefact. Tools do not have minds of their own, but they allow human minds to extend beyond what is possible in a tool-less world. For example, would Mozart have been able to demonstrate his genius for music without the existence of a piano? The object itself is not intelligent, but it affords the possibility of intelligence being deployed or displayed.

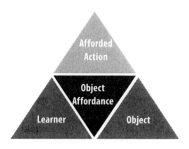

Figure 8: *Learner-Object-Affordance Relationship*

Any considered, complete, and intelligent theory of learning must then also explain how we interact with our surrounding environment and its objects and how the setting and its objects in turn influence our learning is shaped and then displayed or revealed.

Experiential Learning and Setting

Having considered briefly the idea that where learning takes place may exert some influence over learning itself, we need to return to the original notion of a learning transaction reduced to its simplest form. The basic conditions for learning to occur as set out by Piaget (1952, pp. 4-5) require just two essential components: the *learner*, bringing a set of pre-existing cognitive structures based on previous experience; and the learning *problem*, reflecting a novel situation, which creates cognitive dissonance in the learner. Learning occurs through learner resolution of this state of cognitive dissonance, either through *assimilation* or *accommodation* (Piaget, 1952, pp. 4-5). In resolving the cognitive dissonance, knowledge is constructed by the learner.

In this simple model of learning, termed *semantic learning* here, the spatiotemporal setting of the learning transaction is not – or, at least, is not necessarily – theoretically significant in the construction of new knowledge. In essence, the Piagetian model of learning transaction has just two parts (see Figure 9.): *learner* and *problem*.

Problem **Learner**

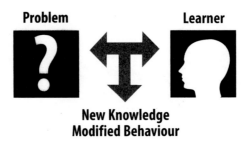

New Knowledge
Modified Behaviour

Figure 9: *Piagetian model of learning*

Of course this semantic learning transaction must take place in a spatiotemporal setting, but the 'where' is theoretically insignificant in the learning transaction. In this model of semantic learning, the *where* and *when*, are not essential components of the learning transaction itself. We can learn in this way anywhere and at any time. The setting therefore acts as a little more than a container or a boundary for the model. For the learner and learning, the experience of the setting and any objects present is immaterial. This semantic learning model can therefore be said to have a *weak* experiential dimension. This idea is explored further below.

In contrast, in some forms of learning, the setting and its objects play a much stronger role. This type of learning might be said to be fundamentally dependent on the setting in which the learning takes place. Strongly experiential learning is inextricably linked to its setting.

Taking the activity of swimming as an example to illustrate this idea, if we consider the *weakly* experiential semantic learning model above, a learner sitting in a classroom may learn something about the activity of swimming for the first time. The learner may be curious about the novel idea of immersion in water, but the classroom setting itself is not strongly or experientially connected to the notion of swimming.

In a *strongly* experiential model of learning, the same learner jumps into a swimming pool and experiences swimming for the first time. The setting, the swimming pool, creates cognitive dissonance through the novel experience of immersion in water for the learner. The pool *affords* the possibility of swimming for the learner. The resultant action, swimming, is remembered by the learner in its context and setting – the swimming pool. A learner cannot have the experience of swimming without the setting which of necessity involves immersion in water.

In experiential learning, therefore, we can see that in resolving the cognitive dissonance, the learner and problem interact within and through the setting itself: the setting becomes a *co-participant* in the learning transaction model. Thus, the basic model of the *experiential* learning transaction must comprise three basic components – *learner, problem,* and *setting.* The physical, political, economic, social, and chronological parameters of setting are all relevant and significant in this model of the *experiential* learning transaction. There is a strong interactive relationship between learner, setting, and problem, where each element has an influence on the two other elements (Wells, 1999). One way of depicting this tri-partite model is shown below (Figure 10).

Problem **Learner**

**New Experiences
New Knowledge
Modified Behaviour**

Figure 10: *Three Components of Experiential Learning Transactions*

In experiential learning, the setting exerts a strongly pervasive influence over the learner and the problem. Setting includes the available artefacts which afford possibilities for activity in the Gibsonian sense (J. J. Gibson, 1986); setting as system includes the community constructed by the learners (Engeström, 1993; Engeström & Miettinen, 1999, p. 9) as well as the available artefacts. The setting is of critical importance to the existence and nature of the learning problem and to the learner. When learning experientially, learners are immersed in settings that present problems that cannot be ignored or deferred. The setting acts as both a *facilitator,* determining the specific conditions and parameters of the problem and influencing the state of the learner, and a *filter,* shaping what is memorable and subjectively significant about the learning transaction for the learner (Miller & Boud, 1996; Tulving, 2004; Wells, 1999). This relationship is illustrated below.

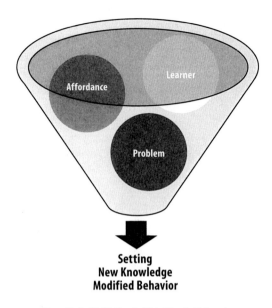

**Setting
New Knowledge
Modified Behavior**

Figure 11: *Model of Setting-Facilitated Experiential Learning*

In this model of experiential learning, each learner experiences setting in a unique way and as a result makes meaning through, and within, the setting (Bruner, 1997). The presence of setting in a learning transaction separates experiential learning from semantic knowledge: it distinguishes knowing semantically – *noetic* awareness – from knowing *autonoetically* about one's own experience (Tulving, 2004). Unlike semantic knowledge *about* a setting, which reflects subjective learner constructions of the understandings and experiences of others, experiential learning within a setting is shaped by the physical, cultural, and social dimensions of the setting directly; these qualities of setting are thus incorporated into the learner's own episodic memory and the knowledge constructed (Hickey, 1997; Tulving, 2002; Wells, 1999). A learner cannot vicariously experience another learner's experience of the world; autonoetic awareness comes only from personal experience, the setting of which is an essential component. Thus, the experientiality of learning is also reflected in the *autonoeticity* of the learning transaction: this is measured through the extent to which an experience generates autonoetic awareness in the learner, which is then encoded and made available for re-enactment in episodic memory (Tulving, 2002, 2004).

For example, the *semantic* knowledge acquired through the study of the design and operation of wood-fired combustion stoves becomes *experiential* when the learner has need to operate a wood-fired combustion stove to provide their own heating and hot water. Likewise, a theoretical knowledge of the principles of navigation becomes highly autonoetic when employed by a learner who needs to return home through difficult terrain and challenging weather conditions. When faced with hunger in a wilderness setting, the learner must deal with the problem of how to apply their semantic knowledge about foraging to meet a personal need created by the program setting. In all three examples, the setting of the problem encountered provided the conditions, and hence the potential, for personal experiential learning to take place. The role of setting thereby determines the degree of experientiality possible in the learning examined in this study.

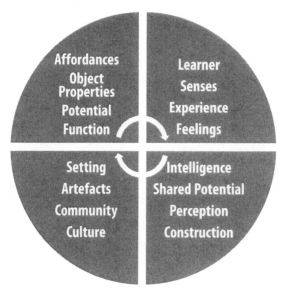

Figure 12: *Affordances and Intelligence: Shared Properties of Setting and Learner*

This has implications for the factors informing setting selection in experiential learning, as the specific properties of each setting will constrain the type of learning problems afforded. Setting selection as such is therefore actually about *problem finding* (Pea, 1993, p. 68). Settings are selected to afford a range of problems based on the previous experiences of learners.

The setting in which learning takes place emerges as a fundamental part of the experiential learning transaction model. This stands in contrast to the semantic learning transaction; experiential learning is transacted through a three-way interaction of a learner encountering a novel experience within a specific setting. The nature of the interaction between the setting and the learner in experiential learning may be described as a property of the setting or a unique property afforded by interaction between the learner and setting. Thus the experientiality of any learning transaction may be measured by the extent to which its setting facilitates the learning transaction. Experiential learning is characterised by its generation of strong autonoetic awareness in the learner.

Chapter Summary

All semantic learning transactions occur within a spatiotemporal boundary and have an experiential dimension that is not essential to the transaction itself; these transactions can be described as *weakly* experiential, due to the ontological impossibility of removing setting entirely from a learning transaction. Learning transactions in which setting plays an essential role in facilitating the learning are *strongly* experiential. The significance of the role played by setting in learning transactions is a measure of the *experientiality* of the learning.

The cognitive dissonance arises out of the relationship between the learner and the setting, which informs the creation of the learning problem and thus creates the conditions under which certain types of human intelligence, such as problem solving, are deployed and manifested (Greeno, 1994). Applying the notion of *affordances* (J. J. Gibson, 1986), settings and all associated artefacts are a special class of objects that *afford* or invite certain actions, facilitating certain kinds of learning possibilities by virtue of their own fundamental properties. These affordances are more than just innate characteristics of the setting. They are activated through the interaction between the learner and the setting and as such are a shared property existing between the learner or learners and the setting (Greeno, 1994). The setting creates the potential for a range of allowable or potential actions, which reflect what is *afforded* by the setting. If the setting is changed, therefore, the allowable, potential or needed actions afforded by the setting are similarly altered (Zhang & Patel, 2006). The intelligence deployed by a learner in solving a problem within a particular setting is therefore a *shared* property of the two components, learner and setting, working together. A further implication of this finding is that exposure to a range of settings commensurate with the full range of intellectual properties of each learner may be needed to ensure full deployment and development of problem solving skills.

Chapter 5: Enduring Learning: Memory, Reflection, and Experience

At this point in our exploration of learning, experience, and knowledge, we need to pause for a closer look at the nature of memory, how it functions in the long-term, and the role it plays in learning. For some, memory is the key indicator of knowledge-based learning. We might claim that we have learned something when we can remember, reproduce, employ, or communicate it. If it is a skill, we can say that we have achieved a measure of learning if we can replicate the skill in some way. Acquired skills, such as striking a golf ball or playing a musical instrument, which can be effortlessly replicated at will, are also another manifestation of memory function, whereby a response conditioned by practice demonstrates long-term retention of something we might say has been 'learned'.

In much of the educational literature, the role of memory in learning has become unfortunately conflated with the notion of 'rote' learning – a time-honoured pedagogical approach that seems to demand little more than supervised repetition to achieve practiced mastery of a certain canon of knowledge. This is also known dismissively as 'drill and kill', because of its renowned practical effect of eliminating any passion or positivity towards learning. It is also mastery without understanding. The slightly disturbing consequence of the move in recent decades away from rote learning towards more constructivist, student-centred, inquiry based, meaning making is that we may have become forgetful of how important memory is in the learning process. The absence of mnemonic devices to assist in the memorisation of lists, tables, dates, names, and sundry facts, does not mean that our memories are no longer welcome at the table of constructivist learning. An inquiry without a remembered contextual framework and retained factual elements to guide it is just a question blindly searching for an answer. In learning, memory matters.

Contemporary psychology tells us that the relationship between learning, knowledge, and memory through history is complex: Socrates is said to have claimed that *all learning (knowledge) is recollection* (Plato, 2002, p. 111, Trans. G. Grube). The creation of knowledge relies entirely on learning and memory: the two are tightly interconnected, mutually reinforcing, but have separate identities (Howard, 1995, p. 3). New knowledge is in fact evidence of learning and the memory function associated with the creation, and particularly, the recall, of knowledge plays an important role in learning (Anderson & Krathwohl, 2001).

Whether it is the reproduction of knowledge or the demonstration of skill, both rely on long-term memory that is stable and durable for the purposes of recall. A detailed exploration of the taxonomy of memory functions lies beyond the scope of this book, but one particular memory function, episodic memory, is critically important in experiential learning. For the sake of brevity at this point, however, we might say that there are two widely acknowledged forms of long-term memory: procedural (for skills and conditioned responses), and declarative (for knowledge and autobiographical recall).

Procedural memory is an implicit manifestation of long-term memory that operates in a manner that is largely unbidden, without prior thought or volition. Facial recognition, for example, a highly important survival skill for infants, is deeply ingrained in our procedural memory. We undertake highly specialized and complex analyses of subtle differences in facial features, bone structures, expressions, skin colour, and make important decisions about relationships and responses, all within the blink of an eye (Schön, 1987, p. 23).

Reading is another procedural cognitive function that depends heavily on largely automatic functions of long-term memory. The routine act of reading is habituated for the literate, so it is difficult to perceive these memory processes at work in a subjective sense. This function's automaticity is neatly illustrated, however, by the following oft-forwarded text with jumbled letters:

Aoccdrnig to a rscheearch...it deosn't mttaer in waht oredr the ltteers in a wrod are, the olny iprmoetnt tihng is taht the frist and lsat ltteer be at the rghit pclae.

The rset can be a toatl mses and you can sitll raed it wouthit porbelm. Tihs is bcuseae the huamn mnid deos not raed ervey lteter by istlef, but the wrod as a wlohe (M. Davis, 2012).

The fact that most readers can decipher the text with little loss of comprehension or reading speed demonstrates the brain's ability to make meaning automatically and unconsciously out of impaired textual input. Provided the first and last letters of the jumbled word are correct, our brain scans the words in the passage and predicts meaning on the basis of intuitive interpretations, largely informed by extensive experience that is stored in long-term memory. There are quite strict limits to this memory repair function that relate to the structure of the language used and text itself. Where the brain cannot disambiguate between multiple possibilities, for example, meaning is lost.

Generally, procedural memory helps us manage many routine, daily tasks with little appreciable conscious effort.

The explicit form of long-term memory, declarative memory, employs different memory encoding, storage and retrieval processes that might be differentiated as *knowing* and *remembering*. The former is associated with factual information, concepts, and ideas that are processed by our *semantic* memory; the latter, *episodic* memory, is more closely related to autobiographical events and *experiential* learning (Tulving, 2004). Long-term memory relating to personal experience is highly context-dependent and relies heavily on the subjective sensory perceptions of the learner captured at the time of the experience (Styles, 2005, p.257).

The role of long-term memory is a significant part of experiential learning because it is only those elements of an experience that are stored in memory that will be available at a later time for retrieval, reflection, and perhaps cognitive construction and personal growth (Howard, 1995; Willingham & Preuss, 1995). This is particularly important in the case of memory encoding and recall, as varying depths of memory encoding, and the presence or absence of external stimuli to trigger recall, may have a significant impact on the outcomes of any given learning experience (Willingham & Preuss, 1995).

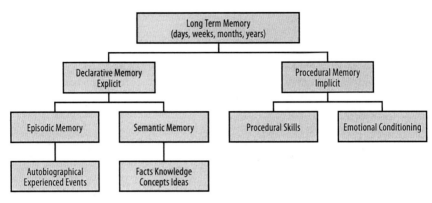

Figure 13: *Taxonomy of Long Term Memory*

Episodic Memory

In 1972, the Canadian neuroscientist, Endel Tulving, produced an influential paper, *Episodic and Semantic Memory*, hypothesising the existence of a type of memory that stored information relating to personally experienced actual past events, which he described as *episodic memory* (Tulving, 1972, 2002). Episodic memory is one of the two forms of long-term memory; it has close connections to the other form – semantic memory. Episodic memory is the stronger of the two types and is related to our experience of setting and circumstance, supported by a rich set of sensory cues and stored contextual impressions to aid recall (Sutton, 2004). Unique to humans, episodic memory has a close and as yet unresolved interactive relationship with semantic memory (Tulving, 2004, p.13). Episodic memory allows the subject to re-live a personally experienced past event (Tulving, 2002, p.xvi) or even to project forward in time to anticipate an event, based on previous experiences (Tulving, 2004, p.10-12). Episodic memory has a special relationship to time and place that semantic memory does not: an individual might know of an event that occurred at a particular time and place through semantic memory, but they can only remember it as a part of their own lived experience through episodic memory (Tulving, 2004, p.18).

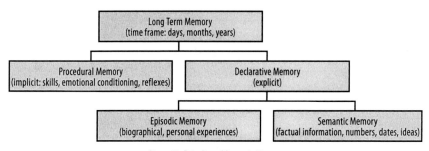

Figure 14: *Episodic and Semantic Memory*

The creation of subjective time in our memories of the past is a unique human phenomenon that is made possible through the interaction of episodic memory and physical time, which in turn creates the capacity for subjective time to be re-lived *autonoetically* in the future (Tulving, 2004, p.17). Citing the example of a tree falling in the forest creating vibrations that only become sound if there is an ear present to capture the phenomenon, Tulving notes that the slice of past subjective time – a sense of *pastness* – that is carried forward into the future is only recalled through the interaction between the physical time of the event and the episodic memory systems of the rememberer (Tulving, 2004, p.17).

Semantic memory relates most strongly to the storage and retrieval of factual and abstract information that largely lacks the strong contextual cues associated with episodic memory. Semantic memory allows the subject to recall knowledge about a particular subject, but in a *noetic* sense, that is without self-awareness of the memory as an actual lived experience, and without any temporal and spatial context (Tulving, 2002). Episodic memory, however, functions through semantic memory; encoding into episodic memory is dependent upon semantic memory processing (Tulving, 2004, p.13).

The close association of these memory functions with particular types of recall events is emphasized in Tulving's writings, but this does not amount to an absolute identity of function for the two; e.g., in re-experiencing a past event through *autonoesis*, an awareness of self participating in the remembered event, the subject may also employ semantic memory to a lesser extent (Tulving, 2002). We therefore must keep in mind that all memory functions are interdependent to a degree and they do not function as discrete cognitive processes (2002). Episodic memory creates autonoetic awareness – self-awareness – of subjective time and is strongly associated through recollection with a specific time and place (Tulving, 2002, 2004). According to Tulving, strongly recalled learning experiences are most frequently associated with episodic memory (Tulving, 2002).

In replicating Tulving's experiments attempting to establish a clear distinction between semantic memory (knowing that) and episodic memory (remembering that), Snodgrass found that the *context of encoding* appears to have a significant positive correlation with the extent to which retrieval can be associated with semantic or episodic memory (1989, pp. 170-1). This suggests potential significance for the place of setting in experiential education.

Episodic Memory and Experiential Learning

So why is memory a significant element of experiential learning? Due to the particular encoding, storage and recall functions associated with episodic memory, learning experiences that are *episodic,* activate a distinct process of capturing and storing memories in the form of a complete *episode*, containing an interconnected set of sensory data, which are more likely to leave a deep and enduring impact on the learner (Herbert, 1999). *Episodic learning* is, in every sense, *experiential learning.* We retain a personal narrative that puts our experiences into a context that helps us to make sense of the world and what has happened to us.

There has been very little research into the intentional use of episodic memory in an educational setting. In a very limited study in an Australian tertiary educational setting, consistent improvement in student mastery of semantic content resulted from the employment of *episodic-rich* materials to support or scaffold the learning (Herbert, 1999).

We love stories and particularly memorable ones. When we can put facts into a personal story, as a whole they make sense to us and we retain the story, along with the semantic content, for much longer than disembodied or context-less facts. The experiential framework or scaffolding of a learning activity thus provides learners with additional mechanisms to assist in the process of schematisation, where experientially derived stimulation forms a cognitive scaffold by which semantic memory is operationalised to organise and categorise retained knowledge (Herbert & Burt, 2004).

Semantic memory, lacking the contextual scaffolding of episodic memory, has been the subject of much educational research focusing on the enhancement of learning efficiency and efficacy. Foos and Sarno (1998, pp. 310-311) found that all memory encoding can be adversely affected by familiarity, with distinctive encoding and strong recall associated with unfamiliar subject matter and settings. The relationship between the affective domain and experiential learning is a further consideration, as some assert that memory best retains what is emotionally and subjectively significant (De Sousa, 2004, p. 67). If we make an experience novel, we are more likely to remember it; if we engage our feelings, it will similarly resonate for longer.

There appears to be little interest in the employment of episodic memory as a discrete scaffold or supporting component of semantic learning in the current literature associated with theories of learning, or indeed experiential learning. There is virtually no literature discussing the question of episodic memory and experientially-based science field trips (Knapp, 2000, p. 65). Educational psychology places great emphasis on understanding the functioning of semantic memory in learning, but the role of episodic memory has been largely neglected in past research (J. Martin, 1993, pp. 169-170). Martin adds that this neglect may stem from a belief that episodic memory is less significant educationally, a belief that he claims stems from inadequate clinical experimentation on learning activities that activate episodic memories (J. Martin, 1993, p. 171).

Some limited investigations into the role of episodic memory in learning have been conducted. For example, Casareno, in examining the work of teachers managing teenage students experiencing learning disabilities, reported that learning with an intentional episodic memory connection, properly established and reinforced, has a positive impact on the learning and recall functions (2002). On the basis of limited observations involving a comparison of memory performance in verbal and action events, Knopf found that memory performance based on experiential action events is more effective than verbal events that have a more specifically semantic knowledge focus (1995, p.131). While some recognise the importance of the relationship between episodic memory and learning, this has not been examined in any depth, resulting in the absence of ideas for the active utilisation of episodic memory in a pedagogic sense (Uljens, 1997, p. 231).

One of the reasons for this apparent lack of depth in research into memory and learning is that the taxonomy and function of memory is still the subject of vigorous debate. Indeed, the status of some forms of memory in the literature is at best unclear (Willingham & Preuss, 1995). While there is support from some quarters for further research into the ways in which memory functions in the learning process (Caine & Caine, 1994), this support is not universal.

Some question the extent to which research in the field of neuroscience, such as Tulving's work, can be directly applied to education (Backtalk, 1999; Bruer, 1999). For example, Bruer criticises the application of what he terms *brain-based research* to mainstream education, questioning its theoretical validity and the absence of research verifying some of the claims made in this field of research. Tulving himself notes that even with considerable clinical evidence to support the notion of multiple systems of memory, particularly through research performed on subjects with physiologically induced impairment of memory function, there is as yet little understanding of its practical applications, particularly among educators (Tulving, 2002).

In summary, episodic memory, as a function of long-term memory is highly durable and strongly autonoetic. The educational applications of this memory system, however, are not well understood. There is evidence of a connection between personal experience and episodic memory, and thus by extension, between experiential learning and episodic memory, which suggests the potential for the enrichment of learning through the intentional incorporation of experiential *scaffolding* utilising episodic memory. As yet, there is little evidence in the literature that this has been attempted, nor is there any substantial analysis of the pedagogical implications of this approach.

Reflection as the Mechanism for Enduring Experiential Learning

We can sense from the foregoing discussion that certain types of memory function are closely associated with experiential learning and in particular recalling and thinking about experience. Memory provides the direct cognitive 'transport system' that captures the noticed (intentional) and unnoticed (unintentional) sensory elements of our experiences in the external world, storing them away for later use, and allows recall of those same sensory impressions that are brought to 'mind' for further thinking and ultimately learning.

One of the first references to this process of thinking about experiences came from John Locke (Locke, 1952 [1689], p. 121), who asserted that our ideas were much more than the sum of our senses; he believed that we add something of ourselves to the process of thinking about our experiences that he named as 'reflection'. John Dewey also connected the act of reflection with thinking about experience: he characterised reflection as:

> ...the explicit rendering of the intelligent element in our experience. It makes it possible to act with an end in view: reflection consists of both thinking and action (Dewey, 1921, p. 171).

Reflection provides the primary cognitive mechanism by which sensory stimuli captured through experience become learning, and hence the nature of reflection itself and its contribution to the learning process need reconsideration. Another area of contention is the extent to which reflection must be explicit in the Deweyan sense. Indeed, some forms of reflection are implicit, taking place when the mind is actively engaged in thinking about something else. In another form, reflection is a type retrospective rumination about matters past, where one memory might trigger thought processes unbidden about matters long forgotten.

There are differing practices applied to processing experience for the purposes of learning, however. The role and function of episodic memory in processing novel personal experiences in reflection is a key to understanding the enduring and highly personal nature of experiential learning.

In experiential learning, the experience itself is the immediate objective of the activity, with the making of meaning taking place through reflection on stored memories to produce knowledge to follow. The learning associated with the practice of reorganising or reconstructing an experience through reflection is manifested in its ability to *direct* future experience, even tacitly and within the same program (Dewey, 1997 [1938]; Schön, 1983).

The experience must be sufficiently memorable that it challenges the habitual assumptions that arise from routine experience. Without a reflective, analytical stage, however, the sensory input from novel experience is essentially *inert*; it contains no experientially derived knowledge in and of itself for the participant and does not lead to any direct action (Daniels, 2001; Wells, 1999). Understanding an experience and learning from it can only occur through active interpretation and meaning making (Wells, 1999).

The thinking associated with any reflective act relies on the language employed, either as inner speech or as a communication act. The language employed to reflect and interpret experience to make meaning is critically important. Language shapes the inner speech associated with processing memories and ultimately shapes the way we think (Wells, 1999). The personal meaning and knowledge that is produced through reflection on experience depends on language as the essential condition of that knowing, as language informs the process by which experience becomes knowledge (Halliday, 1993). The intramental processes and inner speech employed in reflection on episodic memories of an experience affect the way in which the images and other residual sensory impressions are processed and emerge post-experience as knowledge. These processes are critically important to the experiential learning process and rest themselves on the manipulation of semiotic tools that reflect prior experience (M. Cole & Wertsch, 1996).

The structure of the reflective process and the way in which language is employed to interpret experience is therefore of interest in the context of this book. In programs of experiential learning examined in schools, the common presence of reflection as a post-experience practice contrasts sharply with the apparent absence of a unified approach in its practice. For some, like Dewey, reflection is a deliberate, even planned phase in the learning process. For others, reflection, while present, is largely implicit or invisible. This contrast in some ways mirrors the divergent theoretical perspectives on reflection in experiential learning encountered in the relevant writings (Dewey, 1997 [1938]; D. A. Kolb, 1984; Miettinen, 2006; Quay, 2003).

Operating in concert with episodic memory, reflection, as either an explicit or implicit process, can act as the instant 'replay' of an experience to make sense of it; reflection can also function as the long-term editing and restructuring of a personal narrative based on experience.

A final point is needed on a relatively new trend in learning that invokes a form of reflective practice that stands in somewhat stark contrast to the forms of reflection discussed in the preceding paragraphs. Recent educational literature has been replete with exhortations for schools and teachers to adopt various forms of meditative or reflective *mindfulness* to enhance the sense of immersion in the moment, calm the mind and spirit, and reflect on present experiences (Baer, 2003). This is a practice that has penetrated mainstream classrooms in different parts of the world. It quite intentionally avoids the need for inner speech and typically rejects the need for mindfulness in practice to direct future action. While loosely based on Buddhist traditions, the notion of paying attention to the present in a focused and balanced manner is one that appears to resonate with contemporary literature on reflection. For some, as it is a form of experience, it is therefore of relevance to experiential learning (Jordan, Messner, & Becker, 2009; Yeganeh & Kolb, 2009).

How does mindfulness differ from the more traditional forms of reflection discussed in the foregoing paragraphs? Perhaps one approach would be to consider mindfulness within the overall taxonomy of reflection as a form of *passive* reflection to contrast it to the more active and directed process advocated by Dewey and others. For its advocates, the purpose of mindfulness is found in its apparent capacity to enhance the quality of dwelling in the moment and as such it has its focus in *being*, rather than *doing*.

The different modes of reflective practice found in school-based experiential learning are explored in greater depth in the Chapter 11, which discusses the place of reflection in program implementation.

Chapter 6: Defining Experiential Learning

The final step in our journey through the theoretical aspects of experiential learning is to bring the elements of the previous chapters together in summary form to refine the working definition of experiential learning offered in the first chapter.

One necessary step in this process is to undertake a minor terminological clarification. Much of the terminology associated with experiential learning points to some implied underlying commonalities. For example, terms such as *outdoor education, outdoor learning, adventure learning, experiential education, wilderness education,* and *environment education,* tend to be used interchangeably in some of the literature on this type of learning. As they seem to be suggesting the same sort of thing, namely learning that is undertaken away from the traditional classroom setting, we might be forgiven for making the assumption that these terms reflect a similar or common philosophical approach and pedagogy. This assumption is in some cases not wholly accurate (Adkins & Simmons, 2003; Itin, 1999). For example, programs emphasising experiential learning about the environment may share settings used for adventure learning, but the activity focus and manner in which the setting is incorporated into the learning may be different.

It is implicit in some of the terms used in describing experiential learning – *outdoor, environmental,* and *wilderness* – that setting is a defining characteristic of experiential learning (Land & Hannafin, 2000, p.2). This is true to a point. Setting, particularly beyond the classroom, plays an important part in differentiating some forms of experiential learning from semantic learning.

An important clarification, however, is that not all experiential learning occurs *outdoors* (Barnes, 2005, p. 3), but the setting itself does play a key role in the learning. A comprehensive range of experiential settings may serve an educational purpose, from local and overseas urban locations, places of work, through to the family home; perhaps even the conventional classroom might be used experientially (1999).

Defining experiential learning has become problematic as it embraces a diverse range of activities and age groups, from infants to adults, from the playground to the wilderness (Fenwick, 2000). There is some agreement that experiential learning is about *ensuring that people can 'do' rather than merely 'know'* (Henry, 1989, p. 28). This simple definition is also unsatisfactory, however, as it suggests that experiential learning may not have occurred if knowledge is *constructed*, but not *applied* in some form of action, if there is only 'knowing' and no 'doing'. Both act as essential outcomes of learning, but the absence of action does not preclude the possibility of experiential construction of knowledge.

Some other commonly used definitions of experiential learning in the literature over recent decades give rise for concern, particularly when defined in a self-referential manner:

> *Experiential education is a process through which a learner constructs knowledge, skill, and value from direct experiences* (Association for Experiential Education, 2005).

In the web-based literature, a frequently cited definition, now somewhat dated, states:

> *Experiential education is the process of actively engaging students in an experience that will have real consequences. Students make discoveries and experiment with knowledge themselves instead of hearing or reading about the experiences of others. Students also reflect on their experiences, thus developing new skills, new attitudes, and new theories or ways of thinking* (Kraft & Sakofs, 1989).

This is a good start, but it also has the rather unfortunate shortcoming in seeking to define experiential learning in terms of *experience*. A comprehensive definition might also attempt to illuminate the underlying nature of *experience* in the context of this specific mode of learning.

From the foregoing discussion on the importance of where experiential learning takes place, it might also be asserted that these working definitions of experiential learning suffer from the omission of any mention of setting and context as a significant element of this type of learning. While *what is* experienced and *how* it is experienced are deemed to be significant, *where* the experience occurs is apparently theoretically unimportant. The foregoing review of key concepts, from Rousseau to Vygotsky and Dewey, suggests otherwise. Setting does indeed play a role in shaping our experiences and hence our learning. These definitions also appear to fail to acknowledge the distinctive cognitive and memory related processes associated with experiential learning.

Drawing from the review undertaken in the first chapters of this book, a comprehensive and theoretically consistent model of experiential learning should include the following elements:

1. Experiential learning is a **social enterprise** with the student placed at the centre of learning activities; learning occurs through socially and culturally mediated interaction with others (Henson, 2003; Piaget, 1952; Vygotsky, 1978, trans.);

2. Experiential learning is strongly **autonoetic**; memories are encoded and stored in episodic memory (Tulving, 2002);

3. Experiential learning relies on intentional interaction with a learning environment or **activity setting** (Miller & Boud, 1996), including its:

   a. Physical environment

   b. Socio-political milieu

   c. Economic context

   d. Chronological frame (M. Cole & Wertsch, 1996) and

   e. Cultural setting (Lutterman-Aguilar & Gingerich, 2002)

4. Experiential learning requires active participation in scaffolded, realistic **problem-solving activities** (Bruner, 1996, p.65; Gordin, Hoadley, Means, Pea, & Roschelle, 2000);

5. **Risk-taking** is an integral part of learning process, with learners expected to make and learn from mistakes to develop self-reliance (Bruner, 1966; Dewey, 1997 [1938]);

6. **Reflection** on experience is incorporated as an integral element of learning (Dewey, 1921, 1997 [1938]; Fenwick, 2000);

7. Experiential learning is behaviourally and attitudinally **transformative**, leading to personal growth (Dewey, 1997 [1938]; Miller & Boud, 1996); and

8. **New knowledge** is constructed by participants as an outcome of participation in experiential learning (Wells, 1999).

These elements are of course taxonomically awkward as they belong to different categories. The following figure makes an attempt to represent these elements in a linked and coherent way:

1. *Enablers*: shaped by theory and philosophical choices (setting and problem);

2. *Actions:* made possible by the enablers, these are actions that arise because of the problem in the setting that require social interaction, taking risks due to the novel nature of the experience, and result in some thinking about the experience later on; and

3. *Outcomes*: these are the effects arising from the enabling conditions and the actions undertaken.

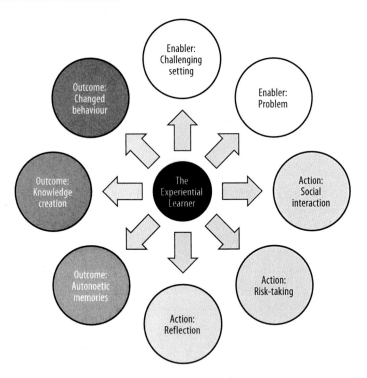

Figure 15: *The Experiential Learner: enablers, actions, and outcomes*

As illustrated in Figure 15, there are two essential enabling components for experiential learning: the setting and the problem (cognitive gap); there are three dimensions to the experiential learning transaction: social interaction, novel risk, and post-experience reflection; this leads to three outcomes:

autonoetic memories, knowledge creation, and behavioural change.

These eight elements of experiential learning may be further reduced to the following four **essential** elements of experiential learning for the purposes of program design and implementation.

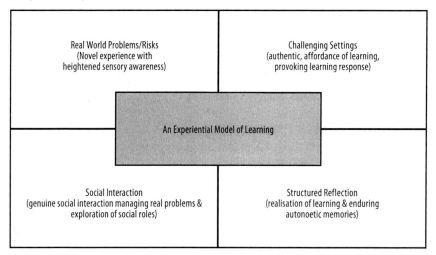

Figure 16: *Four essential elements of experiential learning*

In this idealised model of experiential learning, the learning problem is authentic and relevant, socially mediated, and located in a challenging and memorable setting; post-experience reflection, again ideally structured, provides the cognitive mechanism by which sensory input is retained and stored in an individually meaningful way.

Summary of Part I:
An Experiential Model
of Learning

Experience is the totality of ways in which humans sense the world and experiential learning is how they make sense of what they perceive (Miller & Boud, 1996). Experience of the world is a pre-condition of human learning, because in order to learn and understand, we must first experience (Daniels, 2001; Wells, 1999). Novel problems are thus handled in ways that reflect the sum total of our prior experience (Rogoff, 2003). While we experience as individuals, all human experience is a dynamic force that is ultimately social (Dewey, 1997 [1938]). Language is a social artefact that is an essential condition of knowing; our experience becomes knowledge through language (Halliday, 1993; Wells, 1999).

Experiential learning is a process of reconstruction or reorganisation of experience that adds to the meaning of experience, and which increases our ability to direct subsequent experience, or creates the potential for new learning experiences (Dewey, 1921; Miller & Boud, 1996). Experiential learning emphasises both doing (action) and knowing (understanding), where knowledge is transformative and applicable in the real world (Dewey, 1997 [1938]; Wells, 1999). Authentic settings are important in experiential learning as each transaction has a unique social and cultural micro-context which shapes the way in which we make meaning from an experience (Miller & Boud, 1996; Rickinson et al., 2004). Understanding is achieved through reflection which is the process of knowledge creation directing subsequent experience (Dewey, 1921).

Our recollections of personal experiences are encoded and stored in episodic memory, a durable form of first-person, long-term memory that is highly autonoetic (Tulving, 2002). Episodic memory is highly context dependent, fixing an experience in a setting according to subjective circumstance (Styles, 2005; Tulving, 2002). Episodic memories allow the individual to return to an experience in its setting at any point in the future, in contrast to semantic memory, which is linked to knowledge of facts without direct reference to the context in which the facts were first learned (Tulving, 2004).

Experiential learning contrasts with the other most common form of learning, semantic learning (information mastery), in that it is strongly context dependent; semantic learning is weakly context dependent. Experiential transactions require three essential elements: *learner, problem* (cognitive dissonance or gap) and *setting*. This stands in contrast to semantic learning transactions that require just two elements: *learner* and *problem*.

The evidence that experiential learning has actually taken place is found in the meaning constructed through reflection on experiences and behavioural changes arising from the learner's exposure to a range of novel sensory input captured through the interaction between the learner, the problem (learner's cognitive gap), and the setting in which the problem is encountered.

Fundamentally dependent on the temporal, physical, social, and cultural context in which it takes place, *experiential learning* is the enduring cognitive and behavioural changes produced by cognitive construction stimulated by novel sensory input from interaction with the external world.

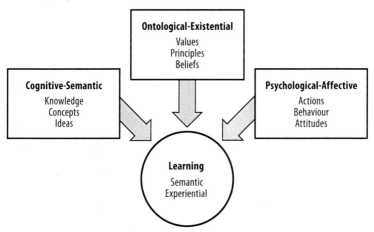

Figure 17: *A Learner's Model of Experiential Learning*

107

Finally, when combined together, the human phenomenon of learning, either semantically or experientially, stands on three pillars: the ontological-existential, cognitive-semantic, and psychological-affective. Our learning emerges from our ontological state of being to shape how and what we come to know and what we do. Perhaps another way of expressing these is the secular notion of *body, mind, and spirit.*

PART II:
Designing Learning
by Experience

Chapter 7: Introduction to Learning by Experience, Learning by Design

The second part of this book seeks to take some of the theoretical ideas explored in the first part and link them in a more concrete fashion to the design and practice of experiential learning. It draws on both learning theory and professional experience to explore how some experiential learning programs are designed and implemented.

For some readers, the first part of the book may have been largely unnecessary. The theoretical chapters do, however, provide a means of connecting learning and experience at a conceptual level. This step is necessary to move beyond the endearing but simplistic 'learning by doing' tag that is often applied to experiential learning. We can now adopt a more rigorous and theory grounded approach to create, develop, implement, and review authentic and educationally sound programs of experiential learning. We are now in a much stronger and better informed position to demonstrate to a sceptical audience that we know what we are talking about.

For those of a practical bent, this second section comprises an introduction to the principles of experiential learning program design, followed by a more detailed discussion of the essential elements of program implementation. These thematic chapters examine the selection and employment of settings to achieve learning outcomes; the place of social interaction as the framing element for experiential learning activities, and its central role as both the cause and outcome of certain kinds of experience; the role and management of risk in experiential learning; and the essential structuring and utilisation of reflection as a mechanism to build episodic memories of experiences that inform further learning.

The principles of program design discussed here have been largely developed from the study of programs aimed at learners in their secondary schooling years (ages 11 to 18). These principles are equally applicable to adult learners and, with appropriate adjustment to program expectations, activities, duration, and risk, to younger learners in the upper grades of elementary or primary school. There are also potential applications for these practices in the classrooms, laboratories, and playgrounds of schools anywhere.

The following discussion has been informed by the author's own research, conducted over two decades on two continents, on formal programs of experiential learning undertaken at secondary schools. Some of the discussion has been informed by the author's own professional practice in creating and implementing programs of experiential learning over three decades in different settings. For the sake of authenticity, direct quotes from research informants have been used where appropriate. In the interests of confidentiality, however, quotes and anecdotes from schools and educators cited in the following chapters have been anonymized to protect the sources.

When referring to 'participants' in experiential learning programs, the terms 'student', 'learner', or 'participant' might all be used somewhat interchangeably, with similar meanings intended. For the following discussions on specific programs, the term 'participant' has been used extensively to denote an individual taking part in a specific experiential learning program. The term 'student' refers to an individual enrolled in an institution and may include program participants. The term 'learner' is used when discussing broad principles of learning and refers more generally to anyone engaged in learning, either child or adult, including teachers, instructors, leaders, and even parents.

School-based experiential learning programs have become increasingly widespread phenomena in schools over the past 100 years, with a growing number of schools around the globe offering programs of varying length, content, setting, and purpose. The so-called Progressive Education Movement emerged from the Age of Enlightenment and particularly the ideas of John Locke and Jean-Jacques Rousseau, resulting in some noble experiments in the formal incorporation of direct experience in education. In the United States, the Progressive School movement of the late 19th century and early 20th century, best exemplified by those following the Deweyan model, offers a tantalising glimpse of the first attempts at putting some of the theories of experiential learning into practice in a school (Dewey, 1997 [1938]). Many other educational innovators, such as the Steiner Waldorf Schools and Montessori Schools, have since followed similar paths to reform education.

The range of learning programs and activities that embrace aspects of experiential learning is vast. Some experiential learning activities are offered as short vignettes within the flow of a mainstream classroom lesson. Others offer units of experiential learning that are more overtly structured and purposeful, still others remove school children from the classroom, and sometimes from home as well, to offer experiences of varying duration in isolation from mainstream learning and home life. The latter may be offered in dedicated facilities or discrete campuses in remote settings, often with purpose-built residential facilities. Still others have attempted to create complete educational 'ecosystems' based on experiential approaches that inform the design and construction of the physical learning environment: pre-schools founded on the Reggio Emilia philosophy offer a good example of this type of approach to setting design.

Those schools and educational systems that implement dedicated experiential programs at purpose-built, facilities, often at some distance from the usual setting for the delivery of mainstream curriculum, have taken this route because they believe that this approach confers benefits that are not typically available in the mainstream classroom. These institutions often promote the benefits derived from student participation in these experiential programs through various public communication media that typically emphasise the special learning outcomes and the unique nature of the experiential learning environment. Some emphasise a contrasting setting and the acquisition of skills that, it is claimed, will have applicability well beyond the years of formal schooling.

To give the reader some idea of the language used to promote or justify this approach, the following offers just a small sample of extracts taken from a selection of school websites that offer programs of experiential learning away from the main or home school site:

(The) outdoor activities program provides a unique and unforgettable learning and living experience. Students face challenges beyond those possible in a suburban day school, including taking responsibility for themselves, the community and the environment, while learning life skills and values including leadership, teamwork and tolerance (Secondary School 1).

(Experiential learning) provides exciting learning experiences for students: ones that leave vivid memories long after leaving...It continues (the school's) commitment to providing innovative outdoor experiences (Secondary School 2).

112

> *(The program offers) challenge and a chance to succeed in a unique environment, a place to explore and experience life, form friendships and receive positive encouragement in the development of self worth...Students are most likely to be found in the fresh air considering educational issues in a meaningful setting (Secondary School 3).*

The type of setting and the physical learning and living environments are emphasised by some schools:

> *In the stunning mountain setting students live in and learn from the natural environment. This unparalleled experience sets the year apart from any other educational opportunity (Secondary School 4).*

> *...in the beautiful National Park, students live in households of eight, gain... independence and responsibility, practice the life skills... study the environment, power and water use, and go canoeing and bushwalking...it stays with them for life (Secondary School 5).*

Another school sought to emphasize a linguistic and cultural focus for its program offered in another country:

> *(The program offers) intensive study of another language and culture. (The) program promotes personal independence...in a different setting...(where) participants learn a great deal about themselves (Secondary School 6).*

There are now many examples of such programs in different parts of the world, but their emergence as an identifiable educational phenomenon can be traced back to Dewey's progressive schools and the 'survival' programs of education that were developed during and after World War II, such as Outward Bound, founded by Kurt Hahn (Montgomery & Darling, 1967, p. 8; Outward Bound International, 2004).

One program promoting intensive physical activity in a remote mountain area invoked Hahn directly:

> *The principle behind this is a simple one and perhaps has its origins in the thinking of Kurt Hahn...Hahn believed that the skills and confidence to deal with unfamiliar territory can be developed. They are things that are learned (Secondary School 7).*

An exhaustive and detailed survey of such activities and programs in schools around the world lies beyond the scope and purpose of this book. However, while acknowledging that there is a huge range of variation in the chosen settings and range of activities offered by schools embracing this form of education, what these activities and programs are seeking to achieve in an immediate educational sense is participation in learning experiences that embrace *adventure, self-discovery,* and *life* in general beyond the classroom. They also emphasize settings that contrast strongly with the classroom: *fresh air, stunning* mountains, *unfamiliar* territory, *natural* settings, *vivid* memories; they are intended to be *unforgettable.*

There are some important implicit assumptions or beliefs about what we might loosely call 'mainstream' education in more conventional 'school' settings that might be discerned from a close analysis of even the tiny sample offered above: classroom learning is not adventurous, focuses on mastery of externally imposed knowledge that may or may not be personally relevant to learners, and to the learner may not be perceived as having a connection with life after school. We might therefore infer the following:

a. School-based, mainstream, institutional education appears to be insufficient to meet the totality of learning and/or developmental needs of school children;

b. Discovery and exploration are operationally problematic within a structured curriculum and familiar school setting; and

c. Novel memorable experiences involving risk that develop character and learning about life are difficult to achieve inside the classroom.

These basic ideas are a largely implicit, but powerful influence in encouraging schools to explore experiential modes of learning and are often present in some form in the literature justifying the establishment or existence of such programs.

The Learner Experience

So schools that offer discrete experiential learning programs in dedicated facilities believe they are serving a learning need that cannot be met in a mainstream learning environment and curriculum. What might students say about such programs?

As we might expect from their apparent popularity, these programs tend to evoke a wide range of views from participants, many of whom are fulsome in their praise of the experiences offered. For example, the following is a typical sample of responses to learning challenges from Grade 9 students undertaking a short-term residential program at an Australian independent school:

New home, routine, people, etc., and having to put up with it...learning to clean up, take care, and manage myself (Student 1).

How to make friends...Living with strangers and being away from my family (Student 2).

Learning to live with those who bug me, learning to accept everyone for who they are, (and) valuing my own opinions (Student D).

My most difficult challenge was being a leader (Student 4).

The most difficult thing was being away from my friends and family for such a long time. I think I got through it because of the busy schedule (Student 5).

I know I can be independent and that I don't need my parents to do everything for me (Student 6).

While this sample is hardly comprehensive in any statistical sense, the author's experience in studying these programs would indicate that they do reflect with some accuracy typical responses from teenagers who attend residential experiential learning programs in many different settings. For these learners, their reaction to the social dimension of the experience is often emphasised over the specifics of program location or activity.

If we dig a little deeper, however, we can see other important elements buried just below the surface of superficial student socialisation. For example, new responsibilities and self-management (1), novel setting (1), rupture of contact with family (2, 5), conflict resolution (3), self-confidence (3), tolerance (3), leadership challenges (4), and independence (6). Taking the institutional and the individual together, we might say that the elements of experiential learning are as follows: unfamiliarity (setting), challenge (risk), skills (problem-solving), and character (reflection and development).

These themes will emerge in a more concrete way in the following chapters.

Creating The Learner Experience

The chapters in this section present three different perspectives on program design and implementation: design principles, design in practice, and program outcomes. These three perspectives have been informed by research involving practicing teachers and leaders and provide an over-arching interpretive framework through which to consider how to go about designing and implementing a program with some certainty of achieving desirable learning outcomes from the programs experiences, both planned and unplanned.

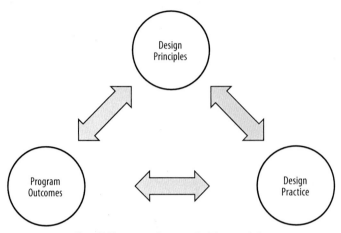

Figure 18: *Three perspectives on experiential program design*

Design principles involve philosophical factors and choices affecting key decisions and choices, including: campus location, location affordances, the relative isolation of the campus, topography, environment, climate, provision of services; the design and configuration of student living areas; the provision (or absence) of means to facilitate external communications; living and learning routines, principles responsibilities and schedules; program duration, including recesses or short breaks; participant demographics, including gender configuration, group size and structure; pre-determined behavioural boundaries, staffing qualifications, experience, role, configuration, duties, and living arrangements; and specific site utilization through planned activities and skills development. Together, they act as an expression or reflection of educational intentions in the program.

Design in practice comprises the fixed sites and activities, problems encountered, and mistakes made by students during the course of the program. This aspect focuses strongly on the experience of participants and their physical, emotional, and intellectual engagement with the students, and also considers the attitude towards risk, error, and problem solving by participating students. Together, these reveal the theory-in-action of the planned experience.

Program outcomes for students, and includes consideration of the ways in which individual students are seen to create new knowledge through their experiences, as expressed through social interaction, reflection, engagement, and memorization. They reveal the goals of the program and hence the long-term values and beliefs of the school.

Parameters of Experiential Program Design

In order to provide the reader with some sort of framework in which to understand the structural parameters that largely inform the development and implementation of all programs studied, the following lists and defines the essential parameters at the highest level.

1. Setting:
    a. distance from home school
    b. setting type and affordances
    c. contrast to home school setting
    d. isolation: permitted contact and communication

2. Social: cohort demographics:
    a. age
    b. size (overall, sub-groupings, activity group structure)
    c. gender (mixed or single sex)

3. Curriculum:
    a. theme
    b. structure
    c. focus
    d. content
    e. skills
    f. duration of program
    g. assessment
    h. integration with mainstream

4. Risk: risk tolerance and management:
    a. Autonomy: level of responsibility conferred
    b. Challenge: relative degree of difficulty

5. Reflection:
    a. mode
    b. frequency
    c. structure

Each of these parameters reflects a choice at an institutional level that must be made in designing an experiential program. For some institutions, parameters such as gender, curriculum, and cohort size are givens, determined by tradition, obligation, or market forces. Other parameters, such as program duration, distance from main school, degree of isolation, and risk reflect active choices made in the design and implementation of the experiential learning program itself. All must be addressed, however, either explicitly or implicitly in program design and actioned in some way in the program itself.

Definitions of Program Descriptors

The following are descriptions of program design parameters at the highest level. Each descriptor, includes a definition and some commentary on the expected range of possible responses and the relative impact or importance of the descriptor on the program.

Setting

There are four main parameters for a program setting: type, contrast, distance, and isolation. Each describes a specific property of the setting with respect to the 'home' or 'parent' school.

Type: The design parameter of setting describes the physical location of the program or activity with respect to the 'home' or 'parent' school. Each setting type affords a particular range of experiential learning activities that sit at the core of the program. Setting types may be categorized as follows:

a. Wilderness: describes a setting that is physically and particularly visually isolated from any form of urbanised settlement or human activity; this type emphasizes immersion in and interaction with natural environments, such as forest, desert, mountain, or coastal locations;

b. Rural: typically associated with some form of agricultural or other farming activity conducted on the campus property, rural settings are intended to contrast with the typical urban setting of many schools;

c. Urban: campus is physically located within close proximity to a 'host' community with neighbours in visible proximity, and where a degree of interaction with the host community is intentionally incorporated into the program; and

d. Cultural: campus is located in a socio-cultural setting that contrasts strongly with the host school.

Contrast: this describes the extent to which the program or activity setting differs from that in which the parent institution (and by extension the program participants) is based. The most common form of contrast is that between an urban setting for the parent institution and a remote bush setting for the experiential learning program; some programs offer a cultural contrast, where others offer a different type of urban setting. There are three levels of contrast used in the table:

a. High: the program setting differs markedly from the parent institution in a physical or cultural sense, creating the potential for a strong affective reaction from program participants;

b. Medium: Some essential elements of the setting are different (e.g., climate, geography, or size of population in urban setting); and

c. Low: program setting may be similar to the parent institution, e.g., same town or city, but may offer a contrast in terms of scale or degree (e.g., more urbanised, inner versus outer suburbs).

Distance: taking the participants' subjective perspective of 'home' as the starting point, this describes the perceived distance between the campus or activity site and a participant's home environment; distance may be measured in travel time, rather than a unit of distance, as different modes of travel may be employed to transport participants to the program site; the subjective elapsed travel time for each participant acts as a factor influencing participants' sense of journey, which in turn shapes their emotional state of mind and affective response to the experience. The duration of the program or activity will, in practice, have an immediate impact on the distance parameter: there must be a reasonable balance between travelling time and activity duration.

Isolation: this describes the perceived degree of isolation of the campus setting from the home environment and incorporates the various levels at which participants may experience isolation, including:

a. Visual isolation: participants are unable to see neighbouring properties or dwellings;

b. Geographic isolation: participants are aware of the physical distance to the nearest town, road, neighbouring dwelling, etc;

c. Cultural isolation: participants are conscious of the setting being isolated from their parent culture;

d. Media isolation: informational isolation is imposed; participants are not given regular access to any form of print or electronic media; and

e. Communication isolation: participants are denied regular immediate forms of communication with family and friends, typically telephone or other forms of electronic communication (SMS, e-mail, social media, etc.).

There are three levels of isolation found in typical experiential programs:

a. High: participants experience a strong sense of isolation from their home environment through physical separation and endure restrictions on all forms of communication and media access; real time communication with the world beyond the campus absent; some infrequent family contact may occur through regular surface mail; direct parental contact restricted to emergencies only;

b. Medium: participants experience physical separation from family and friends, but are permitted regular electronic or telephone communication; media access is relatively unfettered; and

c. Low: participants are not separated from family and participant social networks during the program; parents may visit the campus; participants may leave the program or site for purposes unrelated to the experiential program.

Social

The social parameters of experiential learning programs include the demographic specifics of the program participants:

a. Gender: either single sex or co-educational configurations may be used to develop healthy gender role models;

b. Age: the age and emotional maturity of participants determines the ideal duration of a residential program;

c. Cohort size: the overall size of the participant cohort is usually determined by factors both organisational and financial; the capacity to organise participants into activity groups smaller than a typical class size may permit more intensive, personalized work with participants; smaller groupings also permit the sharing of leadership roles on a more equitable basis;

d. Activity groupings: sub-groupings may be formed within a full cohort for accommodation, transport, catering, and activities; and

e. Leadership: activity groups require leadership and coordination and if delegated to participants (depending on age and degree of challenge), may include responsibility for transport, catering, navigation, education and site/activity information, community liaison (for programs with a linguistic or cultural theme), finances (budgeting and reconciliation of allocated funds, planning expenditure for group activities, facilitating payments for group expenses, managing accounts, allocation of funds, preparing accounts and reports on monies expended).

Curriculum

This parameter describes the nature of the course of study undertaken during the program or activity, including the degree of immersion in the course through residency status. The curriculum categories include:

a. Full: a full conventional curriculum for year level is maintained throughout the program consisting of core learning areas (esp. Mathematics, English, Sciences, and electives); this operates in parallel to the experiential curriculum;

b. Maintenance: offered alongside a specialised program (see below), this category of program includes some maintenance of key learning areas requiring continuity of contact for the duration of the program, e.g., mathematics, music, or languages;

c. Specialised: a program of study unique to the campus and program, structured around the setting and surrounding environment; typically, a specialised program operates outside of the mainstream curriculum delivered at the parent institution;

d. Residential: students live on-site for the duration of the program; and

e. Non-residential: students return to their own home throughout the program or at the conclusion of the activity.

Theme: a component of program curriculum is the program's experiential theme, which identifies the essential guiding thematic element underpinning experiential element of the experiential program:

a. Eco-footprint & science: the specialised or unique learning elements focus on the ecological 'footprint' of each participant – the amount of energy used or the impact of the individual on the local environment – highlighting the technology and science of controlling and limiting the ecological footprint associated with human activity; outcomes measured through objective criteria, such as energy and resources consumed;

b. Urban & community: learning focuses on the political, demographic, economic, and sociological elements of human settlements, contrasting different kinds of urbanisation, governmental and societal structures and institutions, economic activity, community development, and industry; may also include elements of ethnology; outcomes measured through developing an understanding of communities reflected in self-report; and

c. Cultural & linguistic: language acquisition and acculturation form the main focus of experiential activities in which the development of oracy through interpersonal communication and social interaction is emphasized; and

d. Adventure & physical challenge: utilises elements of the program setting to develop the physical culture of participants, and typically includes a perceived or subjective element of physical risk; outcomes are measured through physical performance benchmarks, such as time taken to complete a task or journey.

Structure: the structure of an experiential learning program reflects its philosophical foundation, approach to learning and intended learning outcomes. Structural choices include:

a. Linear: this is the 'journey' structure that allows all participants to commence the program at a predetermined starting point and undertake a metaphorical or physical journey to a chosen destination or end point that is some distance from the starting point; emphasizes a shared sense of group and individual progress and change over time;

b. Bookend: the bookend structure allows for regular repetition of key activities in a 'before' and 'after' structure to promote a sense of perspective and growth in participants; emphasizes the perception of personal development and allows for several iterations or cycles within a program;

c. Circular: this structure creates the sense of a 'cycle' of growth or development, where participants undertake a sequence of activities that are structured in a subjectively logical pattern, and which return the participant to the original starting point; emphasizes the subjective perception of personal development;

d. Branching: this structure permits an element of election or choice in which participants exercise some personal volition in selecting those elements of a program to be attempted or undertaken; it creates a differentiated experience for each participant, as members of the same cohort will have a more individualized journey; emphasizes choice; and

e. Free-form: this structure allows participants to plan and implement an experiential program, usually within some limitations or parameters (such as duration, cost, scope, challenge, and actual risk); no two cohorts will have exactly the same experience; this emphasizes group and individual autonomy and leadership; learning outcomes will vary for individual participants.

Skills: experiential learning programs, both residential and non-residential, may require learners to develop or exercise specific skills in order to assume some level of responsibility for meeting the living needs of participants as a routine element of program participation. These life skills are typically designed to raise awareness of systems operating within adult society (e.g., finance or energy) or to promote individual and collective responsibility for specific areas of human need. The five categories of these life skills are:

a. Living/learning environment: participants are required to undertake regular, programmed duties within the campus setting or program to create and maintain the living and learning environment; some dedicated staff members may take on more specialised cleaning and maintenance responsibilities;

b. Commercial/financial: participants are expected to make regular financial transactions or participate in purchasing of goods to support the living or curriculum needs of program participants; commercial skills include making purchases in support of activities, making transport arrangements for groups or individuals, purchasing supplies for dormitories, participation in trading or bartering systems on or off campus to meet the living needs of participants, managing records of financial or other transactions as a part of meeting the living needs of participants.

c. Catering: participants are expected to acquire supplies and prepare meals for groups and individual participants on a regular basis; this skill may also include menu planning, negotiation with management based on a diet or other plan or set of restrictions governing catering;

d. Energy Management: participants manage and provide for the energy needs of groups and individuals through tasks, such as operating wood-fired water heaters, electricity generation through management of solar or other electricity generation systems, or management and operation of other energy generation systems;

e. Sustainability/Environmental: participants are expected to engage in a range of practices designed to create a sustainable eco-system; for example, recycling, composting, active conservation of resources, resource budgeting (i.e., intentionally constrained supply of resources and materials for participants use); and

f. Cultural: participants must interact within an unfamiliar cultural context and manage/negotiate across linguistic and cultural barriers to achieve program or personal objectives.

Duration: this describes the duration of the program. Experiential learning activities may range from minutes to months. Discrete programs offered at dedicated sites typically range between one day and one year. Program duration may be determined by the following factors:

a. Program objectives: the duration of the program must be of sufficient duration to allow the educational and social outcomes of the program to be achieved; this may include the allocation of time for activity preparation, skill development, activity execution, follow-up and feedback, reflection and review;

b. Rupture of contact: experiential programs sever connections with regular life contacts, such as parents, teachers, and friends; the duration of rupture may create separation anxiety and social tensions generated by prolonged contact with an unfamiliar peer group, both of which may be productive maturational forces for participants;

c. Maturity and age of participants: younger participants tend to have a reduced capacity for prolonged rupture of contact that leads to productive growth;

d. Financial considerations: living expenses of participants are typically met by their parents or guardians as a discrete payment to the host institution and may be subject to socio-economic constraints; and

e. Institutional capacity: larger institutions or facilities with limited capacity to accommodate groups may impose limitations on the duration of an experiential program to allow equitable shared access to programs and facilities; third-party or commercial providers often impose limitations on the duration of a program.

Risk

All novel experiences contain an element of uncertainty, unpredictability, or risk. The risk parameter is broken down into two dimensions: challenge (the nature of the risk) and autonomy (the degree of independence experienced by the learner in engaging in the challenge). For school-aged learners and their parents, separation from home life is already a risk; undertaking unfamiliar activities or experiences is another significant perceived risk. Perception of risk, includes potential exposure to physical or emotional harm with significant long-term consequences.

Challenge: this describes the essential character of the challenge posed by the program overall for participants. Implicit in this is that each of the challenges poses a certain amount of risk for the learners. The five main categories of experiential challenge are:

a. Physical: participants engage in activities that pose a physical challenge, e.g., hiking, running, or cross-country skiing; these challenges are typically scaffolded in a way to pose an emotional challenge at the same time;

b. Emotional: participants face challenges that are aimed at building resilience, courage, perseverance, patience, tolerance, understanding, and self-confidence; this category of challenge typically relies heavily on participants being separated from existing support networks, such as family and friends.

c. Intellectual: participants are required to solve problems, often related to meeting their own needs, through developing an understanding of systems, concepts, and techniques; energy generation and management is an example of an intellectual challenge;

d. Technical: participants may be required to master a particular skill associated with an activity that requires both content mastery and skill mastery; examples include building and farming; and

e. Cultural: participants are faced with problems that test their understanding and tolerance of other cultures, value systems, social systems, practices, and belief systems.

Autonomy: Participants' relative autonomy is determined by the extent to which they are permitted to participate in negotiating the shaping and planning of activities with the program leaders/managers. There are three levels of autonomy:

a. High: within the context of an overall theme and a framework of challenge categorisation, participants are required to negotiate the structure, conduct, and goals of their learning with program facilitators;

b. Medium: participants may negotiate some elective or non-essential aspects of the program, but within an overall framework that is essentially invariable; and

c. Low: participants engage in a series of highly structured activities that reflect a set program; there is little, if any, scope for participants to negotiate changes to the program.

Reflection

Some of the programs studied do not require participants to reflect or review their participation in an explicit or programmed manner and therefore any reflection undertaken by participants is implicit, whereas others allocate regular time for reflection to occur, and often provide a structured means or vehicle to facilitate formal reflection, e.g., daily journal.

a. Mode: written (hardcopy, genre-based, free-form), visual (image and video), spoken (recorded or performed), electronic;

b. Frequency: daily, post-activity, weekly, ad hoc; and

c. Structure: staff moderated, participant determined, open, confidential, private, published, assessed, etc.

Together, these parameters of program design provide a blueprint or check-list for the establishment of a new program. Some reflect immutable, institutionally imposed elements, others may be subject to financial, resource, or curricular constraints at the home school. Where there is a free choice, the influence of each parameter on learning should be considered at length.

Chapter Summary

It can be seen from the foregoing design parameters that the intelligent design of an effective and memorable experiential learning program relies on much more than the selection of a convenient place and the hope that something educationally interesting might take place in that space if we leave learners there for long enough. The choices made in designing all aspects of the program, from risk appetite, through programmatic theme, through to the forms and frequency of participant reflection all take on educational significance.

The following four chapters explore setting, social interaction, risk management, and reflection as the essential elements of experiential learning programs and activities.

Key Questions

In the initial conceptual and planning stages, the following are key questions that need careful thought (and decision):

1. Why does the school want to offer an experiential learning program?

2. What are the institutional values and learning philosophies that will inform the learning offered?

3. What is the ideal setting for the program, given the overarching philosophy and values?

4. Who is the intended target of the program?

5. What is the intended duration of the program?

6. What is the intended theme of the program?

7. What level of isolation will the program impose?

8. What is the level and nature of the challenges to be offered?

9. What is the expected outcomes for the target student group?

10. What is the parent community view of experiential learning and residential settings (if offered)?

Chapter 8:
The Experientiality of Setting: Learning in the Real World

Having taken the important philosophical decision to embrace experiential learning in a formal educational program, the setting, as one of the three essential components of an experiential learning transaction, shapes everything else. Program setting is the essential force in shaping and facilitating experiential learning programs. The setting and its associated affordances will determine what is possible, feasible, or practicable in an experiential program and what is not. It provides the framework on which the other essential elements of experiential learning are based. The setting, in all of its dimensions and parameters, constrains, informs, and shapes all aspects of the experience: the frequency and type of social interaction, the risks and mistakes associated with the challenges, and finally the memories and reflections that underpin and facilitate enduring learning. Choosing the *where* for an experience to take place is therefore the most critically important decision taken in the first phase of program design.

As noted in the foregoing section dealing with the selection parameters for choosing a setting, there are distinct choices in a setting that reflect the guiding vision, mission, and values of the parent school and the experiential learning program. Settings that focus on natural wilderness, rural life, urban life, or immersion in other cultures reflect very different decisions with respect to underlying values, program design and implementation, and learning outcomes. Adding contrast, distance, and the subjective sense of isolation imposes another layer of complexity in the decision making process.

The most useful starting point in the selection process of a suitable experiential setting is to understand the nature of the existing learning environment and to determine what type of experience might best achieve the desired learning outcomes in the new setting. What sort of contrast or difference might have the greatest impact on learning? We need first to understand the essential dimensions of the daily 'routine' experience of learners in the parent institutional setting. We then need to consider how the learning environment might be different, and if so, how might that difference create the potential for learning that is not possible in a direct, experiential sense, at home. For example, we might arrange equipment exhibitions, display pictures, and screen videos about white-water kayaking, but the experience of shooting a Grade 5 rapid is only going to be possible on a river with rapids at that rating. The learning outcomes, and the risks, are in stark contrast.

Seeking contrastive pairings is a useful tool for site selection. For example, the majority of learning in a given school might take place indoors, in which case its contrasting experiential pair might be 'outdoors'. Other such contrastive pairings might include a 'city' school versus a 'country' experiential campus. There are some important qualities or characteristics of settings that have a disproportionate impact on the experience of the learner that might guide our choices when setting is considered from a learner's perspective. These choices might include pairings such as urban or highly developed human habitats versus sparsely populated rural settings or even isolated wilderness areas. Mountains may stand in stark contrast to flat plains or deep valleys, the littoral or coastal regions might contrast with inland or even desert settings. The distance between the home institution and the experiential program might create a sense of contrast or even space. There are many other contrasts possible, such as climate, terrain, culture, etc. These contrasting characteristics should be considered carefully when selecting an activity site.

This is not to suggest that the blind quest for difference is virtuous in and of itself. Difference only creates the potential for a novel experience. The choice of a setting that contrasts strongly with the existing experiential frame of reference of the intended participant is only valid if it serves an educational purpose and that purpose is understood and fully integrated into the experience itself.

Authentic Settings

One pairing of opposites that has been raised by participants and practitioners in many different settings is the idea of 'real world' authenticity versus school 'artificiality'. A setting that is perceived by learners and educators as authentic versus one that is seen as contrived or constructed creates an expectation among the learners that what will follow will be 'real'. This subjective sense of connection with a form of perceived reality may have a powerful impact on experiences, memories, emotions, and of course, learning.

An idea that emerged strongly from the research project was that classrooms are seen by learners and educators alike as inauthentic or artificial: *...the classroom is basically a fake environment* (Teacher D2). If the setting can add an element of authenticity, this creates in the minds of the learners the idea of a new world of learning possibilities:

> *The setting is what makes it; it's the biggest thing. I think the setting is massively important; it's their world, it's a new world, it's very different from the old one. The first impression of that world is going to have a deeply entrenched impact. The setting is the key in the sense that they are being dropped right in the middle of the experience, they don't have to go and get it. It's highly challenging, sometimes very frightening, (and) confronting (Teacher D2).*

Here 'real' is held to include full immersion in a place that invokes a sense of uncertainty, tension, or even fear. First contact with that new reality leaves a deep and abiding impression.

In planning an experiential program, authenticity, perceived or real, is extremely important as it is this sense of reality that connects directly with the learner, unmediated by a teacher or institution. We are taking learners out of their normal learning environment and exposing them to another environment, where we expect different learning to take place, some of which may be challenging and confronting. It is this contrast between the perceived unreality of the classroom and the authenticity of settings beyond school that creates some of the initial conditions for learning to take place.

A Distant Place: Isolation and the 'Journey'

Following on from *authenticity* comes the property of relative or absolute distance from the home setting. For some experiential programs, the distance between the setting and the home school is a defining characteristic. The purpose of this sense of subjective and objective distance from the home institution is twofold: the *isolation* creates or encourages the emergence of a discrete learning ecosystem that is sufficiently removed from the normal daily supports and interactions so as to generate a completely new set of social interactions, relationships, and peer group structures; the distance also creates a subjective experience of *journey* – this will be explored in more detail below.

In one experiential program located a half day's travel from the home institution, the setting stood in stark contrast to the parent school, which is located in a large city. It is *isolated, removed from outside influences,* and *remote* (Campus Manager A). The removal of outside influences allows for the learners and program leaders to create or restructure the pattern of social interactions, the living and studying arrangements, in fact the culture of the program. These novel social interactions between students and teachers are also supported or facilitated to an extent by other design considerations that place participants in close proximity and in circumstances that require unfamiliar forms of social interaction and cooperation:

> *The remoteness is important. The isolation is important so that we can focus entirely on the participants (Teacher A1).*

The isolation allows other design choices to be made in order to create a learning ecosystem that is largely self contained and insulated to a degree from outside interference:

> *Participants don't have access to the mass media, they don't have access to TV, internet, cable television and all the other bits and pieces that seem to influence their lives enormously (Campus Manager A).*

The environment at this school is intended to be both isolating and challenging:

> *I think the isolation is a huge key in what we do and I don't think that you could replicate this program in an urban setting. We rely on the isolation enormously (Campus Manager A).*

At another remote campus associated with a school in a large capital city, all direct communications with the outside world is eliminated:

> *We've taken away their normal environment and deliberately removed some things (Teacher B1).*

In this school, the setting is integral to the intended learning outcomes for the program:

> *(Its) location...is its greatest asset and its greatest challenge on so many levels. There are so many things that participants get out of that 'remoteness' experience that is unique (School Manager B).*

Another teacher at this school commented on the affective response of participants:

> *It's important they really feel that they're miles away from home...it's an environment that they are not familiar with (Teacher B2).*

The isolation removes the home 'time-out' phenomenon; the intervening 'circuit-breaker' that stops the impactful flow of an experience. Participants do not have the opportunity of switching off their learning by returning home to 're-set' their emotional and physical state in the comfort and familiarity of home. The isolation may also impose some limitations on the immediacy of feedback or support from family and friends. The isolation imposes a time lag on any appeal for parental support or resolution of a problem:

> *It's very easy for the students in the normal school environment to go home, either break away from a problem that had happened at school that day by having her own space, or getting on to mum and have her say I will get on to the phone and deal with it…there is going to be a week potentially between them writing home and the parent ringing up. Often problems have been solved in that time and its meant that kids have learnt some skills which they may not have otherwise learnt (Program Manager B).*

The pressure of this isolation creates learning opportunities, because there is no chance to break away from a problem by having a private space or having a parent solve it. One teacher observed that the greatest challenge for participants is *living with other participants (Teacher B2)*. With a week between writing home and the parent contacting the school to handle a problem, the participants have had to deal with the problem themselves and thus have learned some skills, which they otherwise may not have learned.

The relocation of program participants to the remote experiential program site offers an opportunity for participants to experience one of the time honoured rituals of 'leaving' home: the *journey*. Regardless of the actual distance to be travelled, or the relative isolation or novelty of the experiential setting, the typical human response to the perceived risk of leaving the familiar and going into the unknown creates a sense of anticipation, tension, heightened awareness, even anxiety for learners.

The journey to the activity site is a form of leaving ritual that offers learning opportunities that will leave vivid and durable episodic memories. For many residential programs studied, this journey takes a day to complete. Staff participating in the study frequently used the term *journey* to describe how they saw the program from the perspective of the participant:

> *It's an excellent opportunity for the (participants) to be removed completely from their normal operating environment and be immersed in a place where they are on a journey…(a) journey of self-discovery (Program Manager B).*

Different approaches to the journey are used. For some, the means of transportation (bus, car, train, boat, aircraft) is an important part of the ritual, where participants have a subjective sense of the familiar being replaced by the unfamiliar during the course of the journey, all of which is typically experienced in the company of other participants. The journey is usually the first 'shared' experience for participants. It is the first program-related common bond between participants that is progressively reinforced throughout the program through other challenges faced and activities successfully completed.

In creating the journey, the distance between the parent school and the campus offers the opportunity for an experience that performs an important function at the commencement of the program:

> *The bus trip here is symbolic. It's almost like a passageway between the two experiences (Teacher E1).*

The journey, as a 'passageway' between two worlds, acts as a form of commencement ritual that may be managed in different ways. Participants may be transported directly to the program site in a single 'phase' of travel. They may also undergo a journey of multiple phases, involving different modes of transportation. Modes of transportation not commonly experienced by participants add to the impact of the journey.

One program adopted the practice of requiring all participants to undertake their first physical challenge of the program by completing the final phase of the journey to the remote campus on foot, thus reinforcing the physical and emotional sense of a journey commenced:

> *Walking into our campus rather than being driven in or out (is) also symbolically important...to rely on your own legs (Teacher A2).*

This physical phase of the journey ensures participant engagement in the journey to an extent not possible if all aspects of the journey are experienced passively, as passengers on a conveyance.

Activities with a shorter duration typically cannot afford the luxury of a day's journey. The sense of contrast and journey can still be created, however, by adopting a novel approach to transport arrangements or the route taken to arrive at a destination. Regardless of journey duration, treating the journey itself as a part of the experience is key.

There are many aspects of a program's setting that can contribute in either an explicit or implicit sense to the learning outcomes. In the above example, there is commendable attention to detail by the program managers in incorporating opportunities afforded by the need to travel some distance to reach the setting.

This first literal 'rite of passage' in the program establishes expectations and a very specific set of values (self reliance) for what follows.

The *journey* as both a literal and metaphorical component of the experience is useful in establishing the dynamic orientation of the program. Participants are not immersed in a steady 'state' of learning; they are moving from their 'home' towards a destination that will be reached at a time and a place. This creates in minds of participants the perception of movement, change, growth, progress towards a goal, and perspective.

Arrival: Alien, Threatening Landscapes

At the end of the journey awaits an unfamiliar place for program participants. Many program settings are chosen for their natural beauty, but no matter how attractive or enticing, these environments are also perceived by participants to be different to their regular places of living and learning. Some wilderness or culturally contrastive settings are intentionally selected to create a strong emotional reaction in participants:

> We see nothing but trees here. I think that real alien feeling is where the power comes from (Campus Manager E).

In this case, the subjective sense of isolation is reinforced by the school's deliberate selection of a site from which participants can only see trees. The *alien feeling* experienced by participants reflects the intention to make the experience something that offers a strong contrast to the home living and learning environment for most participants; the Campus Manager E added:

> One of the things that we do is try to make experiences as different as we possibly can.

In removing the familiar, the commonplace, participants are compelled to confront some disturbing personal reactions to the loss of experiential certainty. This lack of familiarity may also extend to the living arrangements. In addition to the unfamiliar surroundings, participants may also find that there is a loss of privacy when in a communal living environment:

> Some of them find that this place is too alien and I guess that if they were a little older and a little wiser they would see that as a reflection of themselves...They just don't have the usual distractions: there's no TV and no parties to go to, they can't go shopping...they go into their personal space as much as they possibly can...(but) it's difficult to find their personal space (Program Manager C).

This initial feeling of alienation arising from the program setting evokes a range of reactions, such as withdrawal or anxiety. As a starting point from which participants work towards assimilation and accommodation in the Piagetian sense, such a reaction is virtually impossible to generate in the familiar lived environment of home and school. One teacher expressed this in terms of needing to sever 'links' to the socially and physically familiar at home:

> *I don't know if you could replicate this experience in (the city) because they would still have those links to the environment that they feel comfortable with and understood and they would still have the communications. Isolation: physically and socially as well, they're in an environment here that's very alien to them (Teacher E2).*

In severing these links with the familiar, the 'alien' landscapes become an initial challenge that must be faced and overcome. For programs based in wilderness settings, the surrounding terrain presents a challenging dimension that shapes the daily life, program activities, and learning outcomes in every sense possible. Teachers at one program based in a mountain setting expressed considerable pride in the implicit challenges of the program site:

> *Our mountains are pretty hard and that's a genuine challenge for everyone who has lived here. They are also really aesthetically beautiful...you get views...With our mountains you can see where you have come from and that's crucial too; that feedback, "This is what I have done" (Program Manager A1).*

The challenging terrain provides very direct and visible feedback as program participants undertake activities within the setting and negotiate the physical challenges of learning and living in beautiful, but potentially threatening settings.

The journey marks the transition. The arrival heralds the participants' immersion in an unfamiliar setting, with unknown challenges and dangers. This causes participants to experience a sense of anxiety or tension that may also be perceived as a sense of danger. This is a common reaction to a novel experience that generates the *fight, flight,* or *fright* response. 'Fight' may give rise to an aggressive, combative response; 'flight' may cause a participant to avoid contact or seek escape; 'fright' may freeze a participant into immobility through fear, unable to process the experience, but also unable to avoid or flee. Participant responses are typically one of these three and in fact a participant may move through all three in the process of assimilating to the new setting.

One campus manager emphasized that for participants, *perceived danger* is essential to the program, with *apparent* risk generating a set of responses in participants. Another teacher noted that one of the sources of this perceived danger is that the environment imposes *real consequences* for participant actions (Teacher A2). The tension and anxiety arising in participants from perceived or apparent risk associated with a hazardous environment is generated intentionally to put them on 'edge':

> *We take kids into the country with a really hazardous environment and there's a lot of risk involved…they do feel vulnerable and quite scared about it (Teacher A2).*

The alienation, fear, or anxiety induced by the setting heightens awareness of the surroundings and focuses participant attention on the first carefully curated and managed steps under the leadership and supervision of program supervisors and teachers.

Connecting Setting with Learning: Everything is Curriculum

Experiential settings are immersive and become an integral part of the learning undertaken through the phenomenon of affordances. Every aspect of living in an experiential setting is potentially an opportunity to undertake learning that is not possible in the normal home setting. In this sense, it is difficult, if not impossible, to separate the 'formal' taught or experiential curriculum, and its associated activities, from the surrounding living experiences:

> *Everything here is a curriculum. You can't look at it as lessons; it's a series of experiences, planned and unplanned…teachable moments where they just happen and you pick up on something (Program Manager B).*

Some experiences take place without planning or preparation, but arise out of the participant interacting with other participants within the setting. This may give rise to unexpected events, but which nevertheless fit into the envelope of experientially relevant activities. There is an opportunistic element to this that teachers must detect and direct, when in evidence.

The idea that 'everything' is potentially a part of the experiential curriculum also means that the participants are always 'on' as learners, never 'off':

> *They are really learning all the time. From the time they get on the bus and think about the people they leave behind to stepping off the bus and meeting the staff [here] (Campus Manager E).*

The necessity of selecting an alien setting for experiential learning lies in the fact that the setting determines or shapes the learning; schools choose a different setting with purpose:

> *So the program is about taking students out of their urban environment and exposing them to another environment knowing full well that different learning happens in different environments (School Manager B).*

The experience of the new setting is intended to create a strong connection with participants; even building design can create a direct sensory connection with the surrounding environment:

> *It doesn't matter where you are around the campus or in the house, you can't escape the outside world...When it's raining you can hear it; the roof is made of tin. All of that is not being able to escape being exposed to the setting...We have very strong values and philosophies around that (Campus Manager E).*

The appreciable differences between the home and program setting may generate anxiety, but they also engender curiosity:

> *Kids are curious and if they haven't ever been to an environment like the ones at our school, then they naturally ask questions about animals or trees or those little micro-environments and that's the platform on which you would do things to teach them about that. It's a bit ad hoc for school, where you set up an experience and hopefully those sorts of questions come out of that experience, but if not, you can be more prescriptive and point things out and take them through that journey (Teacher B3).*

If the setting does not arouse curiosity, then the teacher can construct forms of interaction that generate questions. Teachers offered some examples of experiential activities that provided opportunities for semantic learning scaffolded in an experiential framework. These examples typically consisted of outdoor activities in which participants were able to observe environmental phenomena directly, ask questions, and thereby gain a greater theoretical grasp of the underlying principles:

> *I have participants walk through the rain forest up into the sclerophyll forest and be able to identify the difference between the two...being able to hold the soil in their hand, be able to see the trees move from being quite dark green and wet to a more open forest and then go away and work with the data...and write up on why they thought those two things were where they were (Program Manager B).*

The same kind of content might be covered as factual content supported by visual scaffolds in a classroom, but the immediacy of the personal experience, the direct interaction with phenomena in situ, is missing:

> *I think in a classroom they would still learn exactly the same knowledge, but it comes back to having it right there in front of them and they can see the consequences. Especially, last year was a big one in terms of all this talking about the drought. They could actually see that there was no water in the creek...and ask, "If we don't get rain, what's going to happen?" (Teacher B1).*

Sanctuary, Routines, and Symbolism

As discussed in the first part of the book, the notion that a setting, and its associated artefacts, afford certain possibilities is a core principle of experiential learning. Those affordances, when connected with specific actions, routines, and habits, become imbedded in the experiential program and in fact come to symbolise what is taking place for the participants. Daily necessities become learning virtues indeed; what was alien at the outset becomes a sanctuary of safety and self-discovery for participants:

> *I believe to get in touch with yourself you to be put in an environment that is conducive to doing that. I am a big proponent of sanctuary and having a sense of isolation in order to be able to listen to yourself (Teacher B1).*

As the program participants overcome their sense of isolation and alienation and become more comfortable and familiar with the new setting, certain places and activities assume an importance that is disproportionate to their actual function in the course of a day. These places and activities acquire great symbolic significance for staff and participants. Certain places become special because of the activities associated with them, or because of the subjective significance ascribed to them by participants. Some daily responsibilities undertaken by participants take on an educational significance that is unrelated to risk or challenge, and which hold an important place in the philosophy of the program:

> *Chopping wood symbolises something here...It's something that they have to do that is required that they give back to their (peers) or they give to themselves. It needs doing and it's constant. They learn that in life there are certain things that you need to do...if they are not done it has a wider effect (Program Manager A2).*

The setting of the campus may impose a daily routine of responsibilities. Water usage, heating, cooking, cleaning, and other human needs provide opportunities for participants to learn about campus energy and water systems, analysing efficiency, sustainability and ultimately, practicability. Participants also undertake daily duties in the kitchen and dining areas, as well as waste management, low-level maintenance, and dormitory cleaning.

> *It's cold and it snows and the kids have to light their boilers all the time...they are such a big part of the program – lighting the boilers. They have to get the wood, cut the wood and work together...to keep the boilers alight all the time. It's a real teamwork thing. It really fits into this environment and reminds them of a simpler life (Teacher A2).*

For some long-standing programs, participants report that activity sites and commonly visited locations come to take on a highly personalised significance for a range of highly subjective reasons. Places identified as having special significance for participants in this sense include a river bed, a hilltop adjacent to the main living areas of the campus, and some of the paddocks used for livestock. They become significant due to activities undertaken there, such as reflection and program bonding rituals, or through their connection with special incidents. One teacher speculated on the reasons that certain places acquire a special significance for participants:

> *The experience of being at a place that is meaningful to them and has helped them learn what they know as the learning and educational process here has made that place special for them; whether they know it or not...I have thought about this and asked myself why is it so special to them? Is it because they run up and down that mountain during the term? Is it because it gives a bird's eye view of the campus? Is it because the Chapel is up there? Is it because a participant who came three years ago told them about it and the infamy that has come from it? There are probably quite a few reasons and for different participants, it's going to differ (Teacher B4).*

One teacher, who had been a student at the campus nine years before, reflected on what left a deep impression during her time:

> *I think my most enduring memory was actually making a contribution that was physical. I still remember putting in a gate and a post and hammering it all together with the farmer. The gate is still there now (Teacher B7).*

These special places are important for several reasons: connection with activities, connection with reflection, perspective on the immediate setting of the campus, and other unforeseeable events that are associated with the subjective experience of one or successive cohorts of participants. It is important, however, for program managers and designers not to underestimate the power of ritual and setting significance for participants where there is no obvious reason for the importance ascribed to them by participants.

Shaping the Living Environment

Residential programs offer a special opportunity for the design of the setting, and participant accommodation in particular, to create a strong contrast with the home setting. Participant accommodation offers a daily immersion experience that demands a high degree of participant engagement, and if allowed by institutional and program philosophy, in its management as well. One campus manager reflected on the deliberate choice to pursue a simpler life for participants with fewer technological conveniences:

We have been offered microwaves from parents and other small technologies and cooking gear; some have said, "let's get air conditioning in". I have said "no" on a philosophical level. When it's cold we want the kids to know they have to do something about it. Something organic, like grabbing some wood and making the effort to get it lit. When it's hot, you have to slow down. You can't run around anymore, you have to slow down and it takes a long time for the students to understand the value in that (Campus Manager E).

The rhythm and pace of the program might be adjusted to allow more time for consideration of the richness of the environment and the activities on offer:

I often have a lot of participants that can't listen to a whole song. You see what they do, they plug it in for a few moments and then switch over to another song. So it's slowing down. There's something really rich in reading an entire poem or an entire novel, actually going through the process and the hard work of admiring a work of art like that rather than little snippets...There are no phone calls and no parent contact during term and letter writing is very much part of the experience and it's almost like revisiting lost skills (Campus Manager E).

The Experiential Dimensions of Program Setting

Each of the program settings examined for this book share a common feature: they are highly distinctive, confronting, challenging, exciting, and ultimately, highly memorable. The element of *challenge* in each setting creates the physical, social, and cultural space in which students interact with each other and the setting itself, thereby creating the learning problems and associated risks that each student encounters. These challenges reflect deliberate choices in program design. However, the importance of setting as the element of the program that triggers cognitive dissonance, essential for experiential learning, which thereby initiates the learning process, remains largely tacit. In many programs, setting is still taken as a given and the central function of setting in the learning process is not strongly articulated or examined by the schools or the teachers themselves.

Program settings should be designed to offer contrast with mainstream learning environments. They should be unfamiliar, novel, and even alienating; they may make learners feel anxious, vulnerable, and isolated. The extent to which learning undertaken in these programs endures is directly connected to the range and degree of challenge posed by the setting. Settings with *high* peaks, *hard* mountains, *natural forests*, physical *isolation*, cultural *alienation*, social *separation* and *remoteness*, and personal *confrontation* all have a deep impact on program participants. Through the quality of affordance, settings should create learning problems that require learner intervention, particularly those that involve basic human needs, such as the acquisition of food, provision of shelter, habitat management, or the achievement of other specific program specific tasks.

Over time, the teachers in each of these programs have developed a high degree of reliance on the role of setting and its connection to experiential learning. Teachers learn to manage and incorporate challenges that require participants to cope, adapt, and overcome in ways that are not possible in a mainstream classroom, where the setting for learning is tightly controlled by the school, parents, and other regulatory or institutional constraints.

As well as isolation, settings may create a degree of anxiety or vulnerability for participants through perceived risk or danger, partly due to unfamiliarity, but also due in part to apparent inherent objective dangers associated with some settings, such as caves, cliffs, rivers, and seas. Settings that pose potential physical dangers may make participants feel anxious, vulnerable, and isolated. This affective dimension of experiential program settings confers a highly memorable quality that distinguishes them from the safe and well-regulated environments in which learning typically occurs in schools.

The very novelty of the experiential settings provides an important learning motivation for participants, which is largely absent from the mainstream classroom. Teachers report that the experiential settings are also seen by participants as authentic, connecting learners to social, cultural, and physical realities in a way that classrooms do not, in part because of the perceived risks. By contrast, the mainstream classroom is often characterised by teachers as a *fake* environment, insulated from the real world, especially in its aversion to risk and uncertainty.

The *authority* or *power* exercised by the experiential setting over participants, both physically and emotionally, derives in part from their perception of the setting's *authenticity*. This is a place with real problems, real risks, and real consequences, all of which entail students being much more personally engaged in the activities that take place there than in regular school.

The choice of a natural setting in some programs reflects a deliberate choice of contrast and challenge. However, tacit philosophical reasons also underpin the selection of natural settings in some schools. While care for the environment, resting on a thoughtful pattern of interaction with nature, is a hallmark of the programs located in natural settings, there is also a deeper, implicit – almost reverential – importance attached to these natural settings. In this evocation of natural setting as a mythical, revelatory space, participants are encouraged to explore their 'true selves' in communion with nature by facing and overcoming its challenges.

In summary, the three primary dimensions of program setting are *physical, social* and *cultural* (Engeström, 1993; Marsh, 2004, p. 125). There is the *physical* dimension of setting, reflected in the impact of terrain, climate, facilities design, and immediate location/ environment on the learning program. There is the *social* dimension of setting in which interaction between participants is shaped or created through the deliberate isolation, separation from family, and forced congregation with others who are often relative strangers. Finally, there is the *cultural* dimension of setting, reflecting a choice of mainstream urban culture, rural culture, natural or wilderness culture, or foreign culture. While the first two dimensions are easily discernible, the third dimension, culture, reflects a more subtle range of choices and values, particularly for those programs that choose a setting that is physically close to the parent school, but is still within a distinctly different cultural setting, for example urban versus rural settings, or urban settings that highlight the contrast in the socio-economic status of different communities.

A common aspect of challenge in each program setting is that participants are isolated in some way. Isolation is achieved at the must fundamental level through the removal of participants from their normal home and school and placement in an unfamiliar setting. Teachers working in the experiential programs studied referred specifically to *isolation, removal, remoteness* or *separation* as a key characteristic of experiential program settings. Isolation and contrast with the home environment are credited as significant factors in creating desirable conditions for learning experientially.

There are different ways in which isolation is defined and realised. In some cases, isolation means a *setting apart* or *withdrawing*, and also a *severing* of direct connection with family, friends, school and community. This may be achieved by means of distance, unfamiliarity of setting, or rupture of contact. In some of the programs studied, isolation was achieved by means of physical distance. In one program, based at a location some considerable distance from the home school, the participants became aware of the isolation and distance by virtue of the time taken to undertake the journey. In other programs, *unfamiliarity* of setting was an important isolating factor; it could be in close proximity or remote, but it was distinctly different to the parent school. While some programs achieve isolation through remoteness from human habitation, others based in highly urban settings in other countries use a combination of physical distance and cultural *unfamiliarity* to isolate participants.

Another common aspect of setting is its *authenticity*, where participants have real problems to solve in settings that are clearly in the real world. Residential programs should be designed to allow participants to participate cooperatively in the management of the participant living environment. Participant problem solving is, in part, facilitated by setting design that involves an intentional simplification of the living environment. These simplified design characteristics create the need for *self-sufficiency* and *teamwork* from participants; these choices structure participant activity on a daily basis within the setting.

For programs offered over a longer duration, it is fairly common for a version of a more traditional school curriculum to run in parallel to the experiential activities. In some cases, the curriculum is modified in some key ways, such as amending the structure of the school day or week to continue experiential programs during daylight hours. At another school, the connections are more opportunistic, with *contextual* connections being drawn between texts employed in the academic program and the learner experience of the program environment. This approach creates some time-related tensions with the demands of the experiential program, with both aspects vying for scheduling priority. At the same time, due to the isolation of the setting, both campus programs struggle to integrate the normal classroom learning fully with the academic programs being undertaken at the parent schools. One school adopted a highly innovative and largely unstructured approach to the setting itself, a central business district in a large city. Academic work was undertaken, but free of curricular constraints from the home school.

Chapter Summary

Settings *isolate* learners through distance, unfamiliarity and rupture of social contact; they *provoke* strong emotive reactions through confrontation, alienation, conflict and fear; settings are intended to be *authentic,* and designed to pose *real problems* for learners to solve; and settings are *worthy of study* in their own right, as highly specialised learning environments. Ultimately, the setting is judged by staff teaching at all programs to be the program's *core* element and hence offers an experience that cannot be replicated in the classroom.

Key Questions

In setting selection there are many potential questions of importance to be considered. The following are just 10 of the essential questions that require careful thought when choosing the setting of an experiential program.

1. What is memorable and distinctive about the setting?

2. What is the cultural, geographical, and social context in which the setting is located?

3. In what ways does the potential setting contrast with the home school?

4. What affordances of potential educational value can be identified in the candidate setting?

5. What learning activities, including self-management, are possible for participants living and learning in the setting?

6. How is separation, isolation, remoteness or distance realised in the setting?

7. What is the likely sustainable duration of an experiential program in the setting?

8. What logistical support and communication access is offered by the setting?

9. What supporting infrastructure exists in and around the setting?

10. What risks does the setting pose and how are these risks to be managed?

Chapter 9: Learning Agency and Experience in the Social Laboratory

In this chapter, we consider the *learner*, the second of the three essential elements of an experiential learning transaction (setting, learner, problem). Accordingly, our focus shifts from 'where' to 'who' and perhaps 'what'.

This chapter considers in more detail the social dimension of experiential learning, and in particular examines how the experience of learners, individually, and in groups, influences the formation of social and cultural identity. As discussed in the previous chapter, the setting of an experiential learning transaction shapes all aspects of the social interactions that take place. Having selected the ideal setting for an experiential learning program, rich with affordances for unique learning challenges, appropriately supported and supplied, the next important design question focuses on the learner and learner agency. How the setting is used and the ways in which learners are brought together to participate in activities forms the core of the following discussion.

It would be a mistake to think of experiential learning as a simple process in which we select some likely participants, deposit them in a judiciously chosen location away from school and wait for something useful or interesting to happen. As Dewey noted, not all experiences are equally educative; we need to be selective and this requires design and intention.

While the range of potential human interactions in an educational setting is alarmingly broad, there are certain categories of interactions and behaviours that are commonly observed and which offer rich opportunities for personal development. Cooperation, collaboration, competition, and conflict between participants are all common phenomena in any educational context. They are remarkably easy to impose, instigate, or influence in what we might call 'immersive' experiential settings. This is where participants are isolated from external contacts and influences and thrown together with a number of other participants to undertake a series of challenges. These forces act to reshape, or completely deconstruct and reconstruct, any pre-existing social order within a group of participants. They even exert influence over the construction and employment of individual social personas over time. The more intense the forces of isolation and challenge are, the greater the potential impact on the social dimension of the experience.

These intense social phenomena are particularly marked in the residential programs. When thrust together, both day and night, the residential setting creates novel patterns of social interaction among participants. These novel patterns of interaction reflect the different challenges, pressures, and demands generated in these programs and their associated living conditions. The social forces created by some fundamental life needs require participants to work together in a sustained and ideally harmonious manner. They exert pressures and influences that are largely absent or perhaps only fleetingly evident in the home school setting.

The following discussion focuses on the intense nature of the social interaction that typically takes place in an experiential program. It offers some insights regarding the educational benefit of these social interactions and the way they impact on the group and individual personas of participants. The heart and social soul of the remote experiential program – the 'house' – offers a useful point of departure for this discussion.

Residential Living: The 'House'

Programs are often structured around the necessity of compelling participants to spend an extended period of time together in a highly structured environment away from home. For some programs, the requirement for participants to live together in a structured residential setting is seen by schools, parents, and teachers as an essential element of the program design. As soon as we remove a learner from their normal place of residence and place them in a manufactured social setting, we change the group social dynamic profoundly; this has a highly visible flow-on effect to the individual participant.

Perhaps unsurprisingly, for many participants in experiential learning programs, the most memorable element and the key focus from a practical living perspective is the *house*. The 'house', or dormitory, unit, residence, home, tent, campsite, vehicle, vessel, even cave – the place where participants live – forms the central physical and social heart of daily life during an experiential program. The house assumes an importance well beyond its physical characteristics and functions: it is the stage on which many friendships and conflicts are played out; it is also the sanctuary in which the anxious, the homesick, the unhappy, or just exhausted seek respite from the pressures and challenges of the outside world. In the house, participants need to negotiate how they will live and with whom over the course of a program:

> *They face challenge right from the word go by being put into a house with people they know and people they don't know. So they don't organise who is going to be in the house before they come and I think that's crucial.... the fact that everyone comes with that same feeling...In other words, no one comes with an advantage as far as who is in the house (Campus Manager F).*

One of the first challenges in the implementation of the program is the alignment of participant and staff expectations in relation to life at the campus and the program itself. The commencement of the program is acknowledged to be challenging for participants as the social dynamic of the 'houses' begins to impose itself on them individually and collectively:

> *The hardest thing the (participants) do here is arrive in that house. The have got ten people with them that they probably don't know very well and they have to learn to deal with that and I think that's the most profound learning that happens here, in that they just couldn't get it anywhere else (Teacher E2).*

One of the design features in the residential and learning environment that can have an immediate impact on social interaction between participants is the extent to which resources may be deliberately, or of necessity, limited. If there are constraints, participants may need to negotiate and share amenities and facilities. For some, this poses an almost insurmountable personal challenge:

> *One thing that seems to go hand in hand with a privileged background is the need not to share: you can have your own TV in your room, you can have your own phone in your own room...You were able to live a very isolated lifestyle within the comfort of your own home, if you wanted to. Relationships with siblings were often not really valued, because they are not all in together. Families do not live as a big group and not always but often these kids had TV dinners (Teacher D2).*

This type of fragmented, somewhat isolated and self-centred lifestyle is quite typical for many of the students attending the schools examined in this study.

Abundant provision to meet all personal needs is perhaps an important, but somewhat implicit, family value. This contrasts sharply with the sharing, collaborative, and group-focused philosophy that informs all of the programs studied. Residential living is a highly social, interdependent, and shared experience:

> *Any kind of residential situation requires teamwork by necessity otherwise if there was no teamwork, forty, fifty or sixty kids in one place can't possibly work, so it forces kids to stop being selfish and to make sacrifices and to think about the group as an organic whole (Teacher D2).*

Participants are bundled together in an 'ark' of survival and shared experience. It compels them to find ways to work together, live together, argue together, and make peace together. The social chemistry can be intense, even unpredictably incendiary at times.

There are different approaches to the extent to which any participant has choice in the selection of house mates. Some schools use random selection to avoid the protracted and sometimes socially awkward negotiations that accompany participant selected peer or residential groups. Other schools allow participants to choose their companions, but acknowledged the problems that flow from such practices, some of which did not emerge until well into the program, particularly when the social pressures of communal living led to the implosion or disintegration of a friendship group.

Programs that adopt random selection as a mechanism for assignment of living spaces noted a social virtue in their practice:

> *Their conversational skills are phenomenally improved half way through the year...It's an amazing level of familiarity and acceptance (between participants) because they are randomly chosen (Teacher A3).*

This randomizing approach produces an opportunity for personal growth that is also recognised by participants:

> *They themselves acknowledge that they wouldn't have made those choices... they wouldn't have grown (Teacher D2).*

The other benefit of this approach is that it allows the dynamic of the program and the experience itself to shape the social structure that emerges in the house; it is not burdened by pre-existing relationships or structures from the home school.

Management of the social dynamic within a house, whether chosen at random or on the basis of a pre-existing peer structure, requires care and patience. The chemistry does not always work. In such cases, program managers must have firm policies governing group selection, but must also have strong support practices to manage the inevitable conflicts and crises that arise in each house unit. In some schools where the parent voice is strong, parental expectations may clash with school policies and beliefs:

> *I have had parents come up here and say my child's in a house and unless you shift them, I'll take them home. I would answer, "Sorry, that would be your decision." And they would take them home (Campus Manager F).*

The most common approach is to adopt some form of 'fairness' as a guiding principle in the establishment of the social dynamic of each house. Beyond this, many practical aspects of living together, such as cleaning, and in some cases self-catering, may also exert an influence on what happens in the house:

> *The house works. It's sort of driven by the participants, I guess. I like to think of myself as a shepherd, I'm just there to advise them and help them and not tell them necessarily what to do but as you can imagine the dynamics are different and what will work for one house may not work for another and vice versa. Pretty much what participants have to figure out is what is a fair position to them in a house in regards to cooking. Then when it comes to food they have to think not just of the physical act of cooking, because we often have dietary requirements so we have to take all of that on board and have to work a system that is a fair one (Teacher F2).*

The learning that takes place in the house, like experiential learning in other settings, is difficult to anticipate; it is all about the house as a micro-setting affording the possibility of learning. The daily routines of living, eating, sleeping, washing, resting, playing, and working create almost limitless opportunities for experiential learning. For some, this is simply because they are asked to take on responsibilities they have never handled in their home setting. In this context, the house provides a forum for a particular kind of intense social interaction that contributes strongly to the overall learning outcomes of the program:

> *It is an interaction between the internal place and the external world and that happens incidentally, simply because relationships are ongoing here and are constant and the remoteness and the natural environment and then some of the formal process that we have in place continue to put them into small crises, which then facilitate, to some degree, introspection (Program Manager E).*

Participants, both as individuals and in groups, experience the house in different ways. The unique chemistry of each house group generates its own learning eco-system in which different learnings might take place. Research informants observed what they described as 'incidental' learning taking place, but anticipating what might arise with any given group was difficult:

> *There's the incidental, informal learning that occurs through the interaction with relationships and the place itself. Incidental learning is the stuff that's never planned. I mean it is planned in a way because there are structures that create certain learning (Teacher D2).*

Some teachers hold to the idea that experiences can be planned, others see the learning emerging from the chaos of life:

> *There is a lot of incidental learning that goes on, I don't think it can be systematized because experiential learning just like life, doesn't happen in a prescribed order, it just happens and so the way that the learning is used by the participant is equally probably random, I don't think it can be planned (Teacher D3).*

The incidental and apparent *ad hoc* nature of the experiences and the consequent learning to an extent impedes rigid planning of the type associated with more tightly controlled teaching environments.

Where arrangements for fairly low level responsibilities are left in the hands of participants, interaction in the form of negotiation and cooperation is demanded of all:

> *For example, the participants live in a small cottage and are self sufficient for breakfast and snacks. They have to organize all daily functions including cleaning and laundry; and they have to interact with each other, they have to work together. It's through the interaction of the participants within those structures, that I think contributes to the most significant learning here (Program Manager E).*

In most programs, personal space in the house is at a premium. This is sometimes a deliberate choice in the design of the house or the campus. The imposition of deliberate limitations may create challenges that are powerful learning experiences:

> *Why I think it will make the unit most memorable in a tough challenging way in the end is the sheer lack of personal space. This goes more often unsaid but that's going to be an everyday grinding down thing – for almost every kid (Teacher A1).*

Pressures build within dormitory groups as a result of prolonged contact in a confined space:

> *I think what you see is dangerous fascination in boys in dormitories. Like throwing kids around, swearing their heads off as loud as they can. A few times*

this term we have had kids lose it; good kids, but just out of emotional energy, I reckon, and that takes some working through (Program Manager A1).

The close physical environment within the campus shapes attitudes and patterns of interaction between participants:

They learn about life, which you might call tolerance. They have been chucked in with a group of thirteen other boys, with two showers, two toilets, two big rooms, a dorm and a study. There are learning experiences in that that you can't replicate. You learn very quickly that you can't operate day to day without talking to others. They learn a lot more about how to cope and appreciate others (Program Manager 2).

This atmosphere of social tension creates a unique relationship between participants and the supervising teachers or instructional staff. Rapport between staff and participants is built through the intense, daily interaction that occurs in the dormitories:

There are a lot of 'one on one' chats that we have with the kids. To have fourteen girls in my dormitory, I am constantly chatting to kids about where they are at, how they are feeling, and are they achieving the things that they want to achieve. (Teacher A2).

Clearly, the relationship between teachers and participants extends well beyond the academic and pastoral connections that are a normal part of school life. The social dimension of residential experiential programs involves the constant, active and thoughtful participation of all teaching and residential staff.

Access and Interaction

With participants accommodated on-site for an extended period of time, out of reach of parents and other peers, the sustained *access* that teachers have creates the potential for enduring bonds between participants and their teachers. The sheer volume of time and contact creates possibilities that are just not possible in the home school:

We have the participants with us twenty-four hours a day and…learning can actually happen at any time. It doesn't have to be between set hours in a normal school…We may decide to call it the weekend or decide to call it an academic day. Our edge is unlimited access (Program Manager A2).

In a school setting, students return home each day, effectively escaping from the direct pressures and demands of the school setting and its social interactions. This respite is not available to participants in a residential program. While space may be limited at remote campuses, time is available in abundant quantities: time to live and learn, time to bond, and time to contend:

> *The uniqueness of this place is that participants don't go home at night. They are confronted by each other as (the participants) say because the conflict here is far more complex, because they can't run away from it.*

This sustained and open access to participants creates the impression of 'acceleration' in the pace of learning and maturation: *It's more intensified and accelerated here, because of where we are. (Teacher F2).* The intensified and accelerated learning creates a high frequency of 'teachable' moments for participants. The sustained immersion in the learning environment and contact with the program teachers results in unprecedented direct 'access' to the learner:

> *It's almost like windows popping up in the participants, you can almost see it when the penny drops, you can see this moment and for each of them it's different, where they just get it and suddenly they are interested and suddenly... as a teacher you can go right in and put in some tools and you can help them to help themselves (Program Manager C).*

There are some downsides to this constant access: teachers certainly feel the pressure of that intensity and acceleration. The typical classroom teaching routine consists of a block of time with a group of students that concludes within an hour or less:

> *I think that in some ways being a classroom teacher is quite easy for the teacher because you really get to sell your product for forty-five minutes as a staffer and you probably don't have to worry about some aspects of the kid's life before arriving. I mean, (when) a kid's had problems outside class and they didn't choose to talk to me about it, they weren't my problem (Teacher D2).*

Experiential learning programs, however, create sustained contact and thus promote more intense and personal interaction between teacher and student:

> *I think it's harder in an experiential setting where you realise: "Oh, that safety net's gone. I can't just leave at the end of a lesson. I am stuck with this kid." I'm thinking of one particular kid, who I was stuck with for more than a month; he was really difficult and I had to cope with him. As a teacher that made an enormous difference to me and I learned a lot. He said he learned a lot from me. I think that it's a very growing experience for both the teacher and the kid to have this constant contact. They see you in a very different light from they way they see other teachers (at school), but it doesn't mean that it's always easier, I think it's probably a lot harder (Teacher D1).*

The extended time frame of the program creates abundant opportunity for the development of a degree of personal connection between teacher and student that is simply impossible outside of a residential boarding program in a regular school. This contact creates the possibility for tensions as well:

> *The participant and the staff member with which they might have conflict, they have to be sitting and having meals together, and seeing them around the place; they are going to go on an outdoor program with them. There is significantly greater interaction with other people on a very regular and constant basis than you get in a day school (Program Manager E).*

The relationship that develops between participants and teachers during each course is important in shaping the tasks undertaken by the participants. This relationship is shaped by the design of the campus teaching spaces. In some programs, teachers are accommodated separately for both work and living; interaction is a little more restricted to 'on-duty' times. In other programs, teachers are not given separate office accommodation and this encourages a very different dynamic in the teacher-participant relationship:

> *Not having a separate staff area where we are locked away and not having discrete breaks away from the participants is at times very frustrating because you don't get that breathing space, but at the same time, (it's) great, because you are always accessible, whether you want to be or not, and the participants really know you...I think that's something that you wouldn't get in a regular setting (Teacher C2).*

A strong distinction must be drawn between the relationship that exists between the classroom teacher and the student in a conventional setting, often informed by procedural or pedagogical considerations, and the highly personal bonds that can develop between participants and their teachers in an experiential setting. These bonds are largely based on trust developed through extended contact. These bonds also impact the ways in which teachers perceive participant learning:

> *In a classroom setting, I am forced to give a tick or a cross or put a number, or a percent or give a ranking, or something else. So I compare one participant to another participant. In experiential learning, I can praise a participant for problem-solving, for identifying what the problem was...and I am not comparing them to the other person (Campus Manager D).*

Some programs require all teachers to take part in all program activities in order to generate a richer, more multi-dimensional relationship between participants and teachers:

We are much closer because we are out here doing the same things all the time (Program Manager A).

The sense of shared challenges and shared successes has a strong, positive impact of participant perceptions of teachers:

So we don't have the teachers along for a ride, they actually are heavily involved in running the program. Maybe that's one of the reasons that the attitudes of (participants) change and they look at you and see that you have so many strings to your bow, you're not just a one-dimensional human being (Campus Manager E).

From a staff perspective, teachers working on experiential programs generally report a depth of relationship with the participants that extends well beyond the experience of the teacher working only in a classroom environment:

You get to know the (participants) on a much deeper level because you don't only see them in a classroom. You see them in the house in the mornings, once they have woken up, you see them after school and you spend a lot of your spare time hanging out with them, taking them for rides and runs, you see them at night, you help them with homework, you eat meals with them (Teacher E3).

The sustained and intensive nature of social interaction at the campus is more likely to generate robust relationships based on a genuine understanding of the individual:

Rather than it being a job, it's more like your life, and they are a part of your life, not just a part of your work life, but a part of your whole life. They get to know what's going on in your life and it's harder to hide a bad day, or it's harder for them to put on an act, you get to see what they are really like because they can't sustain an act for the whole year. I think because they get to know us better and we let them be involved in our lives and we feel that we can have more fun with them and be more open with them. You feel respect. I mean you are a teacher in the classroom, but outside of the classroom you are not really a teacher, you are their mum, or their sister, or their outdoor leader (Teacher E3).

The interactions between participants and instructors or teachers rest on a social contract that is explicit in some settings and tacit in others:

If you are a teacher who demands power and structure…it's not going to work very well. However, if you are a teacher who wants to work with them and sit down with them and exchange with them and give your own opinion as well as listening to their opinion and converse with them as a social or teacher-participant relationship, then you are going to do far better and survive a lot longer and be more effective. (Program Manager C).

A central aspect of experiential learning programs is that teachers need to be willing to give up practices acquired in mainstream schools or teacher training programs and adopt a pattern of interaction with learners that exists almost exclusively in this type of setting. This is not an easy task.

Experiential programs may lack certainty and structure due to the emergent nature of experience itself. Novel experiences lead to novel reactions. Tolerance of ambiguity, which will be explored in more detail as an element of risk management in the following chapter, and immersive engagement at a personal level with participants, are both core elements of the professional expectations placed on supervising teachers. Teacher skill mastery and co-participation, therefore, place some unusual demands on the selection and professional development of teachers, not to mention their pre-service training. The emotional and physical demands placed on teachers in these types of programs extend well beyond the more routine and largely intellectual challenges of the classroom and the school yard.

Program Structure: Linear Narratives, Fast Time and Slow Time

We have established that participants will interact with teachers and each other in unexpected ways when away from school, especially in the intense, immersive environment of the remote campus. The sustained access to learners that experiential programs tend to offer creates another shaping dynamic that impacts on the relationship between participants and instructors. The next question to be decided is that of program duration and pacing. Essentially, this is a question of how long does the experience need to be and at what pace should it be experienced from a participant's perspective? This is not an easy question to resolve.

There are many different views on program duration. An experiential learning transaction can take but a moment or occupy the best part of a season. In a remote setting, particularly where there is some travel involved, some schools would take the view that a week is enough, for others a year seems to be too short. Culture, curriculum, and costs tend to be driving forces when determining program duration. The purpose here is not to prescribe a particular length of program, but to point out some of the factors that might determine the optimal length of a program duration in a particular school setting.

The duration of the program does seem to exert an accelerating dynamic that creates pressures for shorter programs. Time for rest, recreation, and reflection may be sacrificed to accommodate a full program of activities and experiences. The views of experiential educators varied greatly:

I have worked in lots of residential schools and one was for just a term. I felt that although we changed a lot, everything was just happening at a much faster pace. I feel here it's a more sustained. You are here for a year and you don't have to rush the learning so much; it just unfolds itself...It's a bit more of a marathon, rather than a sprint. You put in as much effort but it's just not so intense and rushed (Teacher A4).

Another sentiment expressed by some informants was that the experiential program had to be given time to develop naturally, with its own structure and rhythm. In this sense, the duration had to be sufficient to *let the experience speak for itself (Teacher A4)*.Thus, the experiential activity, ideally, had to be of sufficient duration to allow the participant to build up a sequence or series of experiences, impressions, memories, and stories to form a coherent and episodically memorable personal narrative.

The internal chronological structure of the program creates a certain pattern of expectations and pressures, challenges and responses for all participants. Experience across different programs, and over many years, has shown that there is an almost predictable pattern of behaviour across and within each cohort of participants. On longer programs, the highs and lows, the elation and the conflicts seem to follow a certain, discernible rhythm:

There is certainly a pattern to it as a general rule. They come with nerves and excitement in the first week. Early on in the second week the novelty is a little worn off about living with other people. I often see conflict arise in that second week (Program Manager F).

Programs generally experience an increase in tension and conflict after the initial settling in period. The lead up to any major event in any program also creates its own social dynamic, with anticipation and the prospect of external forces influencing internal campus structures.

In one program, the anticipation of conflict observed over many years led to a modification of the program structure:

By Week Three they fall apart and we actually plan to send them out on expeditions that week. We break them up from their house groups (Program Manager B).

Incorporating the anticipated affective response of participants into the structure of the program allowed the development of interventions to act as a form of relief valve for social tensions.

In another program, this build up of tension among participants was caused by the arrival of parents for an open day at the campus:

There's a build-up of excitement to a visiting weekend (where participants' parents are permitted to visit). After the visiting weekend, for some kids it's a down period. They pick up again, you know, there's the excitement and the nerves before exams and the anxiety right before assessments (Campus Manager F).

The intrusion of external elements, such as parents, adds a further complication to the social dynamic, one which is not always viewed positively by schools.

The conclusion of a program in which participants have been separated from home and friends casts something of a shadow over the final days:

Then there's a week to go and in some ways there is a party atmosphere in which time we keep them busy. There's a lot of rituals involved, including all the things we do in the last week. It's a tradition and lots of fun and a great social event (Campus Manager F).

Informants reported that these programmed milestones and rituals, such as the parent visit and the final performances, act to focus a great deal of participant energy at key times in the program. Knowledge of the impact of these events and the consequent patterns of behaviour they generate provides teaching staff with a form of social blueprint that allows some preparatory and remedial work to be carried out with individuals and groups at critical points in the program. For individual participants and groups, the impact can be unpredictable, however.

Any discussion about program duration tends to focus on the more visible metrics, such as the number of days. A more obscure and perhaps implied dimension of program duration is the rhythm or pace of the experience. If the experience is truly to be allowed to 'speak for itself', it must be allowed to unfold at its own pace and be experienced in a more or less linear sequence.

For programs of shorter duration, there may be pressure to cover and complete a notional checklist of items. An experience that is given the time and space to speak for itself is quite likely to unfold at a pace that cannot be rushed.

Philosophically, this brings us to an important choice when considering program structure: the structure and pace or rhythm of the program. One of the perceived benefits of a slower pace and simpler life for participants in experiential programs of longer duration is the chance to withdraw from what we might term the 'hyperlinked' life, where we jump from one strand of possibility to another, without following anything from beginning to end. Returning to a quote used in the previous chapter, one program manager commented at length on the hyperlinking or branching behaviour he had observed on a frequent basis:

I often have a lot of participants that can't listen to a song in its entirety. You see what they do: they plug it in for a few moments and then switch over to another song.

Program structure is designed to create spaces for more introspection or the patient and deliberate appreciation of an experience that proceeds at a more leisurely pace:

So, it's slowing down: there's something really rich in reading an entire poem, or an entire novel, actually going through the process and the hard work of admiring a work of art like that, rather than little snippets. (Program Manager F).

Taking the time to follow a narrative from its beginning to its end may be a challenge for younger participants accustomed to the branching nature of unfettered information access in digital form. The provision of alternative branches and choices removes the participant from the underlying reality of a narrative by another level or step. For some participants there may be a frustration associated with waiting for a story to unfold at its own pace, and the removal of alternative possibilities or convenient exit points.

Similarly, there is a 'linear' nature to an experience that goes from beginning to end. Immersion in the experience requires a certain kind of patience and time. There may be some anticipation associated with waiting for an experience to start, its commencement, a sequence of actions that may flow or stop and start, and finally, a conclusion. Recognizing that this linear structure may be somewhat foreign and challenging for younger participants is an important part of the necessary preparation for any experiential learning program.

The organisation and structure of the experience may allow some degree of participant construction. For example, all of the programs studied reported that each cohort of participants experienced a unique set of events and social chemistry. Each cohort tends to develop its own linear narrative in the form of a story that connects the experience into a single, unique narrative thread. Participant ownership of the experience is the end result.

One other factor to consider in apportioning time in any program, regardless of duration, is 'slow time' in which the intense nature of social interaction or program activities can be processed in some way by individuals. Time is managed in many programs to allow for reflection. Some of the activity time is therefore deliberately structured to leave gaps, to create space for the participants to experience time that is 'off-line' in order to achieve a specific outcome:

We actually, give them moments of 'I'm bored'; some kids can't handle that because they have always been entertained with something (Teacher B1).

Shutting down or switching off is a deliberate program choice that must be incorporated in a formal way into the program schedule. From the outside, it may appear to be an inefficiency, but it can have a powerful influence on learning.

No matter the length of the program, for some participants it will be too long, for others, too short. Finding the balance so that it offers participants the right balance to achieve its core elements and outcomes is critical to the educational success of the program.

Program Structure: Bookending

Ideally, program duration should be of sufficient length to permit a sense of journey, growth, change, development, and progress. One way in which this sense of change is experienced subjectively by the participant is through activity repetition or 'bookending'. This is a key structural element or pattern incorporated into the design of some experiential programs where the pair of 'bookended' activities provide a clear 'before' and 'after' experience for the participant.

When attempted the first time, it is expected that participants may find the task or activity excessively challenging or particularly striking in some way. For challenging activities, the first iteration is expected to result in hardship or even failure. The first round of the activity sets the bar very high with respect to challenge and expectation. When attempted later in the program, the anticipated ease with which the task is completed by most, if not all, participants, is intended to provide a sense of perspective and progress; it offers the participant a clear sense of the distance travelled to that point in the program. As such, bookending is an important feature of the 'journey' structure of programs.

As a confidence booster and an instrument to instigate reflection, the completed set of bookends acts as a highly effective educational device. In reflecting on bookended activities, many practitioners offered commentary on the way this structure contributed to the sense of accomplishment experienced by participants:

> *It gives participants such a chance to really develop and they get to do things twice and see how far they have come. They go to the same place and realize how far they have come in terms of fitness and their ability to overcome a challenge (Teacher A4).*

For those attempting a physical challenge at the beginning and the end of a program, there is the strong contrast in the emotional reaction of participants to the activity:

The participants are just blown away as to how scared they were the first time (Teacher A2).

Returning to the site of a previous emotional and physical challenge and meeting the challenge with ease is a powerful experiential tool in building a sense of confidence and capability.

Physical challenges are not the only form of bookend. In other programs, experiences or events are used to commence and complete the journey. This repetition is like an experiential motif that the participants return to like a familiar refrain in a piece of music. It offers a familiar element of completion or closure. One program used a very simple daily event – viewing a sunrise and sunset – in a metaphorical way to create the sense of a journey:

We are very much into bookends up here so on the very first morning that the participants are here they get up and watch the sunrise and the very last night they are here we go down together and look at the sunset on the last day. So all the way along we try to say, "This is you at the starting journey and look at how different you at the end of that journey" (Teacher F2).

Lost in Space: Communication and Isolation

In the previous chapter, rupture of contact through isolation was discussed as an aspect of setting selection when establishing a program. The extent to which participants remain cut-off from the world of home and school through communication constraints determines the degree of relative isolation practiced during a program. Participants may be in the next suburb, state, country, or hemisphere, but their sense of isolation or connection will still be determined to some extent by their capacity to access various forms of written and verbal communication media.

The existence of a direct channel of communication between the participant and close friends and family during the program is an important philosophical decision, as it has a direct influence on the subjective and actual isolation experienced by the participant. It also affects the extent to which the experience itself is created and owned solely by the participant or constructed in a shared way through interaction with parents and friends.

Several programs with long histories assert the need to maintain a sense of isolation through the withdrawal of all forms of immediate, electronically mediated communication with the outside world. This practice, which intentionally maintains a sense of isolation for all participants, has also created the perhaps unintended virtue of encouraging participant introspection through a largely obsolescent vehicle for personal communication: the hardcopy letter. This 'virtuous' isolation creates space for other emphases:

> *There are no phone calls and no parent contact during term and letter writing is very much part of the experience; it's almost like revisiting skills...the practice of writing. That form of communication is where the participants are far more deliberate in what they write (Program Manager F).*

Hand-written letters, as a system of home-school communication, are deliberately cumbersome. They do not permit any form of timely parental intervention in response to concerns expressed by participants during the course of the program. This has the intended purpose of building resilience and independence in each participant; they know that there is no immediate assistance or emotional support from home for any situation. For young participants, this may be challenging emotionally:

> *If, for example, participants had email and every decision they had to make they (asked) their parents, or their brothers or sisters, or their friends, then that decision is not their decision. We try and get them to build independence through them making their own decisions (Campus Manager A).*

Many school-aged participants find the very deliberate and somewhat mechanical process of writing down their thoughts and waiting for a response via surface mail frustrating. Indeed, some teachers commented that many participants lack the skills to communicate highly personal and sometimes profound thoughts effectively in writing, perhaps pointing to another mainstream educational shortcoming.

The parents of school-aged participants, likewise, find that program time passes slowly and news takes a painfully long time to arrive. Said one of the teachers:

> *I think they are aware of the isolation. They have to get used to writing letters and adjusting to the fact that it takes five days to get there, and the fact that you can't just automatically contact family and friends. Yet they have new friends around them that they can talk to instantly (Teacher B2).*

This imposed physical isolation does have an upside for many participants, however. Many find that a residential experiential learning program is their very first extended period of freedom from direct parental supervision and scrutiny. For these participants, there is the first glimpse of freedom:

> *Being independent...being away from mum and dad and being in the new environment, all of the kids develop independence...the biggest thing here is resilience...just the strength to overcome difficult situations. We develop those skills that you need for that: a strong mind (Teacher 2).*

Social Hierarchy and Social Masks

Perhaps less visible phenomenon from the outside is the long-term impact that intense and sustained contact with a participant community has on the school peer group social structures and individual personas each participant develops to 'survive' during the normal school day. In a residential program, the daily 're-set' when students leave school and return home for some 'time out' is absent. An experienced teacher observed the way in which prolonged exposure to a closed community peer group profoundly transformed perceptions of self and others:

> *Kids can have an image at school and they can keep up that image from 9 to 3 or whatever the time is in school but up here because they are living it 24 hours a day I think by the end of eight weeks everyone has cut through that façade and they tend to see people for what they are and that can be a good thing or a bad thing (Teacher F2).*

New social connections and relationships appear from almost from the start of each program, in part emerging naturally due to the new living and learning conditions in which participants spend their days:

> *Our residential program is a (social) leveller. I mean you have in the home school environment all sorts of hierarchy, all sorts of politics, and all sorts of issues that participants grapple with in their relationships with one another. You have participants that have more money than others, you have some whose Mum and Dad are working very hard just so they can send their child to this program. You have the participants who take over the school, because they are the in-group of Grade 9s. It's the whole power play stuff. However, when you go to the remote campus, very few have had that experience and it is so remote. I call it a **leveller** because everyone pretty much gets down to the same level... and we find that participants start working together, participants start problem solving together, participants start making connections that they otherwise wouldn't have made at the home school (School Manager B).*

The social experience of each participant is therefore different to that experienced elsewhere in the school. The notion of levelling suggests an active process in which social structures are forcibly or deliberately swept away for a period of time. The environment itself imposes a different set of obligations and demands on participants and this tends to impact on the social networks and relationships. As social interactions change within the new living environment, the social structure of the participant group as a whole begins to change in quite fundamental ways.

The setting, social interaction, and the challenges of living combine to form a mechanism of natural selection for peer leadership structures. Power within the social group in particular appears to undergo a form of redistribution, leading to a change in the participant *pecking order*:

> *I think the change is driven by people who are a little further down the pecking order or a little further down the hierarchy. They will associate and mix above and below. The people up the top learn very quickly that they don't have the same power here as they do at the parent school, because there are a lot of opportunities here (Teacher F3).*

Those participants finding their status eroded by the new environment are faced with difficult choices as they experience a loss of status and power within the new group social structure:

> *You have top dogs from each campus, so they can either assimilate or not. Sometimes, they are not popular because they are nice people, they are popular because they are powerful people, but here they lose some of that power (Teacher F3).*

One teacher offered an interesting insight on the extent to which a participant's status was at least in part determined by their capacity to contribute to the needs of the group in a meaningful way:

> *At the parent school, participants may have had a set of relationships, where they value a person. For example, "She's the leader, because she's cool." When they get in that house and after a few weeks they start to realise that although she's cool and beautiful, she can't plan, she can't cook, she's hopeless and they don't value her opinion as much because in this new context these other values are coming through (Program Manager B).*

Participants not high on the social pecking order may decide to engage in aspects of the program out of interest or motivation. Their participation and the resulting altered social dynamic results in greater recognition, greater responsibility and hence greater opportunity to shape events and ultimately the group structure itself; these participants effectively emerge as a new leadership cadre:

> *There were some kids who barely spoke at the home school, but they wanted to come to those group meetings every week and be able to have a chance to hear what was being said and to make a comment if they wanted to. We had some of those cool kids as well, the ones who were leaders, not necessarily with the leadership badge at school, but who were leading and they all improved as well. It was really interesting; it was a kind of individual decision as to whether you wanted to be in that group. Those lower status kids stepped up (Teacher F1).*

Participants who did not enjoy the status or recognition of formal leadership roles in the home school were able to find a forum, an outlet, to make a contribution that might otherwise have been silenced or unheard.

Another teacher described the phenomenon of participants discovering their 'voice'. This is where the experience itself unlocks something inside a participant, resulting in a change in behaviour and participation level, particularly the frequency and quality of their communication about the experience:

> *You would get participants who were quiet, suddenly discovering their 'voice', discovering abilities, and realising they were able to contribute. I remember one participant: he was in a bit of trouble and had a bit of a reputation, having this amazing experience, enjoying being able to share that with participants and having the participants enjoy the sharing of it by him (Teacher D1).*

Those who embrace and undergo change to adapt to the changing circumstances emerge across all programs as superior in their engagement and the observable or behavioural outcomes achieved. Those who may not have arrived with much status from the home school can still achieve:

> *I believe that some kids do find it difficult here while other kids actually shine. I think it's something to do with some kids who are better at adapting to change (Program Manager F).*

On the other hand, those who arrive with a strong track record of achievement within a tightly structured and carefully curated educational and social setting may find unexpected challenges:

> *Some other kids are so called good kids within a very strict structure back at the home school. Within that framework and structure of what we normally call school, they shine but when it comes to here and they have to make decisions about making choices about the way things are, they are given more freedom, they are apt to do the wrong thing (Program Manager F).*

The lack of structure, and certainty, the absence of clearly stated boundaries, and a limited set of expectations are liberating for some participants and confusing for others.

Part of the social agility that is common in remote experiential programs is manifested in the ability of some participants to see opportunity in becoming a different person. Participants find they can earn peer respect through their actions and contribution to the group, not because of pre-existing power structures or popularity, but through their ability to be flexible and offer real leadership as and when needed:

It's usually people who can cross over the 'border'. The leaders here are the ones who can lead the popular ones as well as the less popular ones. These people don't dominate because they are popular or they are strong. They become leaders because people are willing to be led by them because they are respected. They learn a lot about what it is to respect and what it is to earn respect and what it is to deserve respect, not just power (Teacher F3).

Participants step through a barrier or cross a boundary to join in a newly formed 'community' in which personal feelings might be revealed or disclosed safely. The expression of community emerges in new trust relationships, cooperation, and collective negotiated goals and behaviours. This new set of relationships enables the emergence of a new social structure.

Part of the respect equation focuses on the ability of individuals to meet the needs of the campus community at critical times in the program. These participants were not necessarily popular or charismatic in any sense, but were visible and recognised for their ability or skill and as a result, earned the respect and acknowledgement of peers. This recognition effectively translated into a new form of social power for those participants:

We had it again this term with a couple of boys who were really socially inept, but technologically brilliant. They ended up mixing sound for the dances, concerts, and performance nights. It got to the point where in the weekend if something went wrong with someone's computer, they would fix it. They gathered an enormous amount of respect...because they were able to cross boundaries. People were willing to see them as valuable members of the community, not just some geeky computer nuts (Teacher F3).

Participating staff commented at length on the changing social dynamic that emerges over the course of a program, a dynamic that commences right from the start of each program when participants arrive with an attitude that is different to that prevailing at the parent school:

When they originally arrive, they come up with quite an open mind that they want to be friends with everyone – at least that is their ideal. So they are quite open to being friendly and probably more engaging than they are with kids at the parent school because of the whole notion of 'community' (in this program) (Teacher F2).

Starting with an *open mind*, the social interaction that develops in the emerging community created at the remote campus produces some surprising attitudinal changes over the course of the program:

Two female participants sat down with me and said, "There is only one good guy here this term." I said, "What do you mean only one good guy?" They said, "There's all these guys here that we wouldn't give a second glance to." By the end, one of the girls actually reflected that they were forming very close friendships and sometimes relationships with boys that they would not have given a second glance to before they came. We allowed them to see past the structured hierarchy (from the home school) (Teacher F3).

Again from the same teacher, a reflection on the changing nature of social interaction that allows participants to see other individuals at a deeper level, stripped of outer layers or *shells*:

Again I think it's because they don't just see the exterior, they don't just see the social group, they see the person and they realise that that person is worth knowing and they realise that they are quite willing to know that person and I think that they lose their outer shell; the outer shell on some people is invisible. You know it's there but it's not something that you can see (Teacher F3).

One experienced program manager acknowledged close physical proximity through the program setting as an important mechanism for imposing or facilitating changes in the group social structure. These peer group structures, however, were not completely random creations of an alien environment. She believed that the abilities and views that emerged unexpectedly from some lower-status participants in the changed environment were actually already present in latent form in the individual. It was the influence of the setting and its associated pattern of intensive social interaction, however, that allowed these latent capacities to emerge in such a socially visible manner:

It's the interaction that everything has in this setting, everything is connected, so you need to understand the other people that you are interacting with and how that affects you and how you affect them (Program Manager B).

One of the benefits of running a remote program that is to an extent independent of the parent school is the opportunity it gives some participants with a poor academic or behavioural record to 'reinvent' themselves during the program:

We say to them: "This is a chance for you to start again. If you are a naughty kid, you don't have to be anymore". Some of them really respond to that, they just see that as a way to completely change. Often naughty kids who have been suspended, or who have constant teacher altercation, swearing, yelling, throwing things, they come in here and they are angels with us and we say, "What on earth was everyone complaining about this student for? They are great" (Program Manager C).

One program manager used the metaphor of the 'mask' to explain the phenomenon whereby participants become aware of discrepancies between their public and private personas. The intense social interaction that takes place during the months of living together with other participants in a confined space creates a heightened awareness among participants of what is presented to others:

We have many masks that we present. I'm helping the participants to understand that the one they might be wearing at the moment to manage relationship situations, or just to manage being in the world that they are in, isn't necessarily the one that they have to wear all the time (Program Manager E).

For some participants, coming to an understanding of the *mask* they present to others is a difficult experience:

(Participants) are challenged by the masks they wear and then over time they learn that there are effective ways to relate to the world…and the ability to choose that is sometimes improved by how they are supported through the different experiences that go on here (Program Manager E).

The fact that some masks may reflect a choice, even an unconscious one, comes as a surprise to many participants.

A program manager cited the example of a female participant who became aware of her regular public mask and decided to change:

One girl had been presenting this persona, this mask of being very gruff and short tempered, moody, and dark. Through a series of different sorts of interactions over time, she came to realise that this was not really how she actually wanted to respond; it did not show how she wanted the world to see her. The motivation came from within her to make some changes. All of a sudden she was a different person in the sense that she walked about the campus without the scowl, her face was more open, she was able to articulate exactly why she had been going through this moody stage, why she needed to make the changes and then she made the changes (Program Manager E).

There are two main processes by which a participant becomes aware of their social *mask*: one is through immediate reaction to the responses of others; the other is through long-term, considered individual reflection. Through the process of reflecting on their experiences and interactions, participants are often confronted by what they present to other participants, friends, and even family:

I know the participants are definitely challenged by their own masks; they are challenged by reflection here, formal and informal, and many of them are confronted by themselves and how they see themselves in relation to other people...they want to be themselves (Program Manager E).

This outcome is highly individualised and driven by a complex and highly personalized process of insight and understanding. To an extent, this does emphasize the difficulty many programs have in measuring growth in self-awareness and confidence in an objective or quantitative way:

I believe what they learn a lot more about is their own sense of confidence in the world that they are operating and it's hard to measure against any standard. It's utterly personal. It's not only related to where they are at in their own personality, their own beliefs and values, their own sense of themselves, but also their motivation (Program Manager E).

The process of examining one's social masks and choosing to modify them or drop them altogether is again highly personal and context driven. For many younger participants who lack confidence in their real 'inner' selves, the mask is a defence against a gnawing uncertainty about their self-worth. Dropping such a carefully constructed and vigorously maintained defence relies on a trust of others and a self-confidence that many teenagers do not possess. Through these programs, many participants do reach a point where they can trust others and consider dropping their mask, if only for a while and among other participants who 'understand' them.

Another mechanism for a kind of radical reassessment by individual participants is the 'crisis' – an event or moment of despair or despondency that forces a cry for help and a thorough re-evaluation of some dearly held personal beliefs. Somewhat paradoxically, participants who experience a series of crises at an emotional or personal level during a program are more likely to benefit from working through these issues with staff, whereas participants who remain largely unaffected are more difficult to reach:

A kid who has a lot of crises throughout their time has the potential of learning a lot more about themselves if they choose to take that on and work with it. So the kid who might be struggling and decides to stay here and to work through that with their peers and adults, often has expressed a greater understanding of how they can interact with the world, manage their emotions more effectively, improve relationships by how they deal with conflict that doesn't push people away and but just to help themselves defining the boundaries (Program Manager E).

As participants become more aware of their own public and private personas, they also become more aware of the nature of the social structures around them. The social order within each cohort of participants tends to undergo significant change during the course of the program. One staff member at a year-long program noted the intermingling of groups of participants that would normally remain socially distinct in the parent school:

> *The cool kids had come being cool and the dorks had come being dorks and they came back and they were friends with each other and they all mixed and this hadn't been forced on them by the school (Teacher E4).*

The status and performance of individual participants in an experiential setting sometimes confounds expectations, with participants who demonstrate dominance in a social context at the parent school sometimes failing to live up to expectations in a residential setting. A teacher remembered the difficulties and early departure experienced by one participant:

> *I remember one girl who was unquestionably the 'Queen of the Hill', a very, very powerful character. She had a whole group of maybe even as many as a dozen kids running round at her beck and call. She was the leader. She came back to school within the first term. She couldn't deal with a whole lot of things, but it was really about the fact that she was just like one of the other kids. She'd been put on a pedestal; she'd been given a sort of a role by her peers that she couldn't maintain. She never showed any of the leadership that perhaps she would have been expected to show to attain her leadership status within the group (Teacher E4).*

The intense social interaction that occurs throughout the program creates stress and conflict for individuals and the group as a whole. The intensity of social interaction often leads to an increased acceptance of individual differences and for some the willingness to engage in social interaction that might not have been possible in a mainstream setting:

> *Learning about tolerance, they see each other so often in so many different contexts. They can't ignore each other they can't get away from each other. They are exposed to people who they may not have spoken to or had anything to do with in a different world, in a different environment (Teacher E1).*

In addition to generating some conflict, the intensity of the experience also accelerates the developmental processes for many participants. Isolation also plays a role in providing a suitable setting for a concentrated focus on the development and understanding of 'self' and a heightened awareness of the social context in which the participants live. One teacher commented:

> *Participants mature a little more quickly and they go away possessing a greater knowledge of themselves. They have a clearer understanding of their own values*

because they are isolated and are away from other influences. I think they have a better understanding of the environment from where they have come from socially. Certainly they have a much better relationship with their parents (Teacher E2).

She added that the most important learning outcomes lie in the personal growth achieved by individuals:

I think they learn the values that their friends and families have at home may not be the only values that they can have. They learn about what it's like to live in a small community rather than being one person in a massive big metropolitan area. They learn about themselves and what sort of people they are, what things they can cope with and they realise that a lot of stuff that they thought they didn't like, they find that they actually do like: a lot of activities and outdoor stuff that they have never had a chance to do. They also learn about being independent and a lot of relationship skills...(both) intrapersonal and interpersonal skills (Teacher E3).

The personal growth may be found in the perspective participants develop on themselves and on others: their friends, peers, and family. This perspective may come through distance or proximity, through contact or isolation.

These outcomes are not transmitted, but are constructed by the learner, possibly over an extended period of time, and awareness of the learning emerges not only through formal reflection and debriefing, but also through informal social interaction. One teacher shared this unexpected realisation of learning articulated through the post-program responses of some participants:

I don't think it's something that is taught; I think it's something that the participants themselves realise over a long period of time. I realise this by little conversations they have with each other, like: "My friends when I went home, they couldn't believe what I was wearing" or, "They just have no idea what the house is like." The participants talk about how they learn to occupy themselves and be themselves and not to rely on multimedia bombardment all the time...I mean before they didn't realise that where they have grown up and society and culture has had an impact on them but now they can see what impact it has had (Teacher E3).

It is not just through the spoken words, but through the meaningful silences – the intentionally empty spaces in between the sensory overload – that participants learn and grow in appreciation of the experience and the stillness that follows.

Program Outcomes: Returning Home

At some point, the experience does come to an end and participants return to their homes and schools, perhaps changed and more self-aware. Experiential learning is particularly prone to the 'hidden curriculum' phenomenon in which learners may not learn what is intended by the curriculum designers. An experience is a highly subjective and personal thing and it can be difficult, bordering on impossible, to anticipate the experiences of each participants and predict their learning outcomes.

There are some frequently observed post-program phenomena that warrant brief discussion: the 'reinvented' participants who find it hard to fit in back at the home school; and the seemingly uncaring attitude of teachers, parents, and friends at the home school who seem not to understand the transformative nature of the experience. The discussion is warranted because these phenomena point to two rather important aspects of experiential learning: it is transformative and it is very different to the learning experiences of students in mainstream schools. The sharp discontinuity between the two experienced by participants serves to emphasize the contrast in learning. The lack of understanding points to the highly subjective nature of the experience and the challenge in sharing this experience and its significance with others.

Vicarious experiential learning, by definition is not possible. We can only learn *about* another's experiences; we cannot experience them directly ourselves.

In considering learning outcomes, one of the unanticipated consequences for participants at the conclusion of experiential programs is the difficulty of re-integration back into a mainstream academic curriculum at the parent school. For those who have carefully constructed new masks or reinvented themselves during an extended time away from the home school, escaping from a set of reinforced expectations on return can be problematic. As one of the campus program managers noted, the journey back to the parent school at the conclusion of the program often resulted in disappointment for both participants and their teachers:

> *What they actually want is responsibility and respect. With the history that they have built up and the name they have built up themselves, they can't escape that label while they are back in that environment. Some of them have complained when they have gone back because their teachers are still treating them the way they were before in Year 7 and Year 8 (Program Manager C).*

Teachers at one independent school in an urbanised area reported to instructors at the remote campus that participant behaviour and attitude post-program was markedly different:

> *The teachers at the parent school notice that there is definitely a change...they come back much more independent and free thinkers. They don't just accept exactly what's told to them. They ask questions and then they challenge norms and ideas and potentials (Teacher E3).*

Reintegration into mainstream schooling after the program, however, is a difficult and at times a disappointing process for many participants. The changes experienced by many participants in the program are not completely compatible with the conforming expectations of the parent school. A remote campus teacher confided:

> *Participants' values have changed. They are frustrated that they can't build the same relationship with the teachers at the parent school that they did here and they all of a sudden have to wear a school uniform and comply to rules and expectations that they see as superficial and not important anymore (Teacher E3).*

A teacher at a remote campus that imposed a fairly simple, almost Spartan lifestyle on its participants noted the impact this setting had on the behaviour of participants, particularly in relation to participant self-image and what was projected to other participating participants and staff:

> *They find they don't need TV, they don't need Internet, they don't need DVDs, they don't need to be constantly entertained. After a while of being up here they don't care what they look like, they walk around school wearing tracksuits and Ugg boots and everyone accepts each other, they are just being themselves (Teacher E3).*

One key area of potential tension for younger participants is the parent-child relationship after the conclusion of the program. Most teachers consulted offered anecdotes about the changes wrought on family relationships post-program. These changes were not necessarily viewed as universally positive or welcome by parents. One teacher observed a dynamic that changed for the better:

> *They used to fight with their mum all the time and they are really ashamed as to how they treated their parents and since being away they have realised that when they go home they are so happy to see them, that they realise how important that they actually were. They took them for granted and they also realised after having to do everything themselves, get ready for school, get their own breakfast and they don't have a mum to ask, "How was your day at school?" (Teacher E3).*

On the other hand, one family commented on the impact of a more assertive and independent child on family harmony. The school had not prepared the family for this change, which became a matter of some contention in the home. The parents questioned the erosion of compliance and obedience in their child, apparently induced by a program aimed at building self-confidence and independence.

While these anecdotes offer differing experiences, perhaps somewhat polarized, this question of accommodating in the purely Piagetian sense the changed situation created by the learning outcomes achieved by the program is one of critical importance for the home institution, both philosophically and operationally. The institution must be prepared to accommodate the changes arising from the learning program offered. It must also educate its parent community, where relevant, to embrace the growth created by the program.

Chapter Summary: The Experiential Social Laboratory

This chapter briefly reviewed the impact of the setting, and particularly the residential setting, on immersive social interaction, the ways in which these interactions in turn serve to shape the experimental personas or masks employed by learners, the nature of experiential program structures, the potential impact of program duration and finally the ways in which program outcomes may affect post-program learning. The ways in which these programs have an impact on learner social structures and peer groups is of particular interest, particularly given the time and effort exerted in managing these elements in mainstream school settings. The identification of such a powerful tool to reset and restructure a peer group is clearly something that should be looked at more closely.

Previously constructed social personas from home and school, are often developed by participants to 'survive' in social or institutional settings. These institutions are places that may value a relatively narrow set of social and academic skills, or sporting and cultural talents. When these values are effectively stripped away under the influence of powerful social forces arising from sustained and specialised contact between participants operating in a new environment with different needs, priorities, and values, dramatic changes to social structures are inevitable.

We might ask why the forces that exert such a powerful influence over the formation of individual identity and peer group formation in the home school setting are weakened or absent in immersive experiential settings. One possible explanation is that in contrast to the typically individually focused assessment methodologies adopted in mainstream school settings, where merit is ascribed to individuals displaying certain privileged behaviours or traits, task outcomes in experiential learning programs are more often measured on the basis of collective performance: communal living, group survival, collective physical chores, and shared research and reporting tasks. Another possible reason is that the group's needs in a new setting are different and this changes the dynamic forces that shape peer group formation.

Peer groups may evolve significantly over a relatively short period of time and the resulting changed social dynamic effectively amounts to a resetting of the social order, generally creating a spill of positions of power or privilege, which in turn has an initial *levelling* effect on participant social status, followed by a re-ordering of social ranking. High status participants in the home school context are subjected to a form of tacit re-evaluation within the group on the basis of relevant skills competence and capacity to contribute in the new setting and may be reduced in status. Previously low-status students may be elevated on the basis of newly revealed competence in relevant skills or the demonstrated ability to serve the practical or living needs of peer group members in the new setting.

The changed social dynamic allows, encourages, and even compels, participants to experiment with different social personas, as they seek to become what they believe is a more accurate and authentic version of themselves. This perception of greater social *honesty* among participants leads to more open public and private reflection on experiences. Participants may also interact with program facilitators and even members of the public in ways that contrast strongly with their prior typical classroom social interactions.

Modifications to peer group structures are particularly evident in the residential programs, where the setting itself creates a social environment which constructs and shapes social interaction in ways that are substantially different to that found in the parent schools and homes, where participants have considerable volition in their interactions with members of other peer groups or complete strangers. Within the residential setting, participants are typically compelled to mix with, cooperate with, and even live intimately with participants with whom no social relationship previously existed. This constructed social interaction generates strains arising from unfamiliarity, lack of personal space, the imposed need to share and cooperate, and an inability to achieve release of built up tension, until expressed as frustration, conflict, and anger. These reactions are tolerated and even expected, with teachers facilitating the development of negotiating skills to diminish tensions, share access to resources, and resolve conflicts.

The key factor influencing social status and interaction in residential programs appears to be social utility. Participants who emerge as leading figures have the demonstrated ability to offer something – knowledge, skill, or attitude – that meets a peer group social or physical need that is not available from another source within the setting. The setting itself generates the group need and the participant that can meet that need in some way is accorded an elevated group status as a result, regardless of previous social status. This element of social status due to distinction is in contrast to the similarity, which typically forms the basis of a coalescing social force in the formation of home school peer groups.

Peer to peer contact is markedly different in the non-residential experiential program observed during the study. This appears to confirm the impact of setting on participant interaction. One conclusion that can be drawn is that the non-residential programs' lack of sustained peer-to-peer contact in the confined, isolating environment of the participant dormitory results in a largely undisturbed set of pre-existing peer group relationships and hierarchies.

Participants working in settings that are embedded within a community that is not directly connected to the school are expected to have regular or even frequent interaction with members of the host community. Street pedestrians, workers, residents, vendors, street people, and even refugees, all may come into contact with the participants in ways that are not planned, but that still shape the participant experience of the setting, but not the peer group structure. These interactions tend have a much more random quality, however, as they are purely chance encounters. While the encounters are expected and are an intentional consequence of this choice of setting, they are also subject to a high degree of uncertainty. There is an essentially *opportunistic* aspect of social interaction in this kind of setting and when they do occur, their impact is often brief and only rarely enduring.

In summary, participant social interaction in the residential experiential programs studied is profoundly influenced by the nature of the challenges and the setting in which these challenges are met, at both a collective and individual level. This results in changes to peer group structures and status, and also leads to experimentation with the social personas adopted or projected by individuals. This change occurs invisibly, implicitly, and yet inexorably. And what of the mechanism that produces such profound social changes? A program manager offered a remarkably simple insight into the reason for this:

> As teachers, we haven't done anything but put them into the same box (Program Manager B).

While it is difficult to anticipate who might be the beneficiaries (or indeed the victims) of this peer group reordering, it is a phenomenon that we might reliably anticipate. In residential programs, it can be a potentially disruptive social force. Accordingly, it warrants more attention.

Key Questions

In this chapter, we have reviewed the social dimensions of experiential learning. The following are some key questions concerning the status and role of the learner as a social being:

1. What are the philosophical and ontological perspectives of the institution with respect to the learner?

2. What is the culture of the school and its attitude to experiential learning?

3. What are the educational objectives of the program?

4. How long will it take for the average participant to meet or approach those educational objectives?

5. Are there any other educational objectives that must be met concurrently?

6. How long can the participants be away from their mainstream program at the home school?

7. Is it feasible or necessary to run a full academic program in the remote location?

8. What is the attitude(s) of the parent community to participants being away from home and isolated in remote settings?

9. What are the participant costs of living and studying in the remote location and who meets these costs?

10. What are the logistical considerations for maintaining a program staff in the remote location for the duration of the program?

Chapter 10: Learning is Risky Business

If *setting* is the essential stage on which experiential learning takes place and the *learner* acts as the principal agent in the experience, *risk* shapes what we intend or allow to take place and what we might limit or forbid; it is the 'how' of experiential learning.

It is of course a clichéd truism to state that learning is a process of trial and error. Most learning activities in any setting act as the 'trial' component and teachers work with learners to eliminate the 'error'. The extent to which error is absent is probably the most commonly employed benchmark of academic achievement. A 'wrong answer' is seen as a sub-optimal outcome. In one sense, learning is about the elimination of errors, a process that takes the learner from 'wrong' to 'right'. In its ideal state, we might think that perfect learning is error-free. A perfect lesson plan, executed perfectly, should therefore produce an utterly predictable and perfect outcome.

Of course, the real world is not perfect and not entirely predictable. As soon as we inject human agency into the learning process, we seem to introduce the possibility of error and the unexpected. Given our apparent need to find the right answer to any question, our natural inclination is to limit factors that lead to error or to avoid error completely. Similarly, if risk is a measure of our exposure to loss, harm, error, or negative outcomes – the probability that something negative may occur – we may seek to mitigate risk by taking pre-emptive steps to eliminate this exposure.

This approach reflects the deficit view of risk and error, which in the broad domain of human experience may not be entirely helpful from the perspective of life-long learning. To explore this further, we might consider the following questions:

1. What is the role of risk in learning?
2. What is the role of error in learning?
3. What do we lose by eliminating either?

In order to limit exposure to the uncertainties of human agency, we might let the experience 'speak for itself' as was advocated in an earlier chapter. To eliminate risk, we might tighten our control over experiences, removing all uncertainties and unnecessarily complex elements. To eliminate error, we might simplify challenges to the point where they pose no threat, where participants cannot fail. These solutions are, of course, patently absurd. We have no way of predicting what the experience might 'say' that is of educational interest, which introduces another layer of uncertainty. Our capacity to control the life experiences of a learner is finite and logically self-defeating if our ultimate goal is to prepare the learner for life beyond the years of formal education when control is no longer possible or desirable. Through simplification, we lock learners into an artificial world of infantile simplicity, bereft of intrinsic interest for the developing learner and completely disconnected from the expected complexities and real risks of adult human experience. We find ourselves in something of a bind: by reducing risk and error in the short-term, we actually increase their probability in the long-term.

In fact, learning, and particularly experiential learning, as a process of developmental change, cannot be separated from risk. The more interesting the experience, the greater the range of potential outcomes; and the greater the uncertainty, the greater the risk.

Ideally, we should consider controlled risk in learning to be a form of inoculation, preparing learners for life in a much more challenging and dangerous world beyond school. By introducing challenges that contain a carefully calibrated measure of risk, we help the learner to develop defences against the potentially infinite risks that await in adult life.

This chapter explores the essential presence of risk as a precondition for experiential learning to take place. It also discusses the philosophical and practical aspects of risk in the context of experiential learning. This discussion considers the nature of risk associated with learning in novel settings and circumstances; it also explores the ways in which risk contributes to learning outcomes. An essential element of this is what we might call the 'margin of error' or the tolerance of error, which is considered in the context of risk mitigation and management in highly challenging experiential programs.

Novelty and Uncertainty

The majority of our daily experiences are largely unremarkable, often because they are repetitions of events that have taken place many times before in our personal experience. For an experience to be educative in the Deweyan sense, it must not only have the possibility of connection with future experiences, the property of *continuity*, it must also be *novel* in some sense: it must be something we have not experienced previously. The extent or degree of novelty is a point for discussion later in this chapter, but for the sake of this introduction, *novelty* is an essential quality of any experience that has an educational purpose. Experiential learning depends on the experience itself providing some form of unfamiliar sensory input that causes a cognitive dissonance for the learner. As a novel experience by definition lies beyond the learner's existing experiential frame of reference, the precise nature of the consequent interaction between the learner and the novel experience within the setting is inherently unpredictable and hence entails risk.

As educators, when we facilitate or instigate some form of activity or social interaction within a potentially challenging setting, we create the potential for multidimensional uncertainty. This environmental and social uncertainty creates a margin for *error* that entails an element of risk in experiential learning that schools and teachers seek to manage, but cannot eliminate entirely. As each experience is unique to the individuals experiencing it, so too are their reactions to the experience, making the experience itself inherently unpredictable; its outcomes are similarly uncertain. Any uncertainty creates risk.

There can be no novel experience without introducing uncertainty and risk and it is the *tolerance of risk* within each program that informs and constrains the challenges emerging from the setting and the social interaction that occurs within the setting. The tolerance of risk creates a 'learning space' between what is known, controlled, or understood, and therefore deemed to be safe, and what lies at the dangerous outer edge of social, institutional, or legal tolerance of uncertainty in an educational setting.

In a mainstream school setting, the vast majority of potential mistakes or errors are relatively benign. On occasion, mistakes may give rise to unexpected affective responses in the learner, which at the extreme end of the spectrum are potentially hazardous or even life-threatening, but these are statistically rare indeed. In experiential programs, on the other hand, the range of potential outcomes in a given, 'real world' situation, including life-threatening ones, is broad and the likelihood of severe consequences arising from a mistake, sometimes even simple errors, is perhaps much higher: the margin for error is therefore much narrower.

There is therefore a tension in experiential learning between control and risk and this is explored in some detail in this chapter.

One of the hidden impediments to learning experientially is the tendency for competent adults to intervene in problem solving situations. There are several plausible reasons for this: for the sake of efficiency (it is quicker for the adult to intervene and get things moving along); for the sake of safety (a lot of unfocused and uncoordinated activity might be dangerous); or for the sake of visible success (the intervention allows a challenge to come to a successful conclusion). These responses are all well intentioned, but potentially work against learning.

One of the reasons for this is that the world has become more risk-aware and institutions are being held to much higher standards of accountability for any and all risks. Liability has become part of the daily vocabulary of school administrators and we might contend that educators have become risk-averse as a result. This phenomenon, whether reflecting awareness or aversion, has imposed some constraints or accountabilities on experiential educators and programs. According to one program manager:

> *The world has changed in terms of everything being a little bit safer and people are less inclined to push things and go against their comfort zone (Program Manager A).*

In making the world of learning safer, the degree of challenge has been reduced. The experience of the learner must be moderated to conform to societal expectations based on legal precedent and regulation. Intervention and control by competent adults is mandated to ensure the safety of children.

The practical difficulty this imposes on all learners is the apparent sharp discontinuity of expectation that occurs at the point of transition from childhood to adulthood. In order to prepare learners for this transition, adults in caretaking roles (parents, teachers, etc.) must incrementally step away from intervention, allowing children to bear ever greater levels of responsibility and risk. In fact, creating a 'zone' of managed transition between child protection and adult accountability is one of the key justifications for schools to embrace the risks associated with experiential learning. At some point, we have to pass over to our children control of their own destiny.

Learner Centricity, Mistakes and Control

Passing the locus of control in an experiential setting from competent adult educators to neophyte learners poses some practical challenges. In fact, it goes against every professional instinct to put the learners in the driving seat in a learning activity. Formal classroom education, even 'student-centred' learning, is usually predicated on the assumption of adult control, with teachers setting tasks, guiding the learning, setting the pace, and concluding the activity with some form of assessment or summary to close. When outside of the safety zone of the school, the apparent need for adult control is even more pressing.

The espoused philosophical position in most programs of experiential learning is to adopt a participant-centred approach. This is where participants plan, direct, organise, and lead each activity. A teacher at an urban experiential program gave an example of a copybook series of learning transactions observed during a program:

> *Participants directed the learning: they took control of the learning... initially under guidance, but the participants knew what they had to do without being told. Without being shy, they were able to organize themselves, manage themselves, direct themselves and learn together, either in groups or separately and then share that knowledge (Teacher E1).*

This is the learner-centric ideal, with both collaborative and individually focused learning that is then shared between learners. The role of the educator is almost invisible, offering some preliminary guidance, which then fades into the background as the learners take control. There appears to be little explicit risk in this approach, but in practice experiential learning demands a high degree of vigilance and flexibility.

With participants 'directing' learning, individually and collectively to the maximum extent possible, the specific role of the teacher shifts from that of a leading problem-solver at the participant activity level, to a role in which the level of difficulty in any problem-solving situation is constantly monitored and adjusted according to the ability of the participants. A teacher described herself in the following terms:

> *As a teacher, my role was very different to what it normally would have been in a school...the input came from the participants themselves in response to the environment...it was them organizing and managing themselves (Teacher E1).*

Risk is thus managed dynamically by teachers who understand the learners and who have a finely calibrated sense of the potential threats at any given moment and how those threats might be managed or mitigated. Part of this risk management and mitigation lies in the boundaries or limits that are set, either implicitly or explicitly.

If boundaries are to be set, however, for some experiential educators the ideal experiential learning environment is one in which control is minimized to the extent possible and may be largely invisible to the participant. According to a program manager:

We want the kids to interact, we want conversation and we want them to have fun, we want them to feel relaxed and we don't want them to feel that they are in an environment where they are constantly controlled and manipulated (Program Manager E).

This manager added that this approach was about participant perception of freedom, rather than the objective reality of freedom. While participants are given room to move and interact socially, there is also the strongly embedded practice of close monitoring that may lead to intervention, or diminution in the degree of freedom exercised, if necessary. He emphasized:

We want them on the edge of feeling a bit of freedom, of feeling a degree of power, but not too much (Program Manager E).

At one campus with a more aggressive approach to learner freedom, teachers expressed the belief that learning unfolds naturally from real-life encounters that occur through structured activities. As one informant explained, there is an accepted randomness attached to these learning transactions:

There is a lot of incidental learning that goes on. I don't think it can be systematised because experiential learning, just like life, doesn't happen in a prescribed order. It is probably random; I don't think it can be planned (Teacher A2).

At a different program with a strong focus on learner immersion in authentic urban life, a teacher highlighted the fact that outcomes, and even the course of a learning activity itself, may be uncertain or unknowable:

I think (we have) real responsibility and real problems. A lot of learning that happens in a classroom, it's not designed to have real problems; we know what the aim is and the result. In an experiential program, it is to do with things that are not step-by-step where we already know the outcome (Teacher D3).

The apparent *ad hoc* nature of experiences and the consequent 'emergent' learning effectively impedes rigid planning of the type associated with more tightly controlled and structured conventional teaching environments. This places the emphasis back on teaching staff to have the skills to exploit incidents in the pursuit of learning objectives. Experiential educators have to learn to adapt, adjust, and extemporize when circumstances change or the learners themselves take the activity in an unexpected, but promising direction. The almost instinctual adjustment that must then be made by the teacher while observing the risk parameters of the setting and the activity is a heavy demand indeed.

When working with participants who are perhaps unwilling to take risks, or who remain inside their level of comfort and competence, teachers may find it difficult when setting a higher degree of challenge. One teacher expressed frustration over participants who were frequently risk averse:

I actually find it more difficult working with a kid who never gets lost compared to someone who has frequent navigational issues, because you can only challenge yourself when you are making those mistakes. So if they are not making mistakes, they are not challenging themselves to the full degree. They have to draw on more than themselves (Teacher D3).

However, in drawing on their own resources, participants, particularly younger ones, encounter another challenge:

A lot of participants that are 15 don't have a lot problem solving strengths... because people solve their problems for them (Campus Manager D).

How then do learners without practical, real-world problem solving experience acquire problem solving skills, we might ask? If we consider the educational, ethical, and perhaps legal dimensions of the answer, it is both simple and complex:

Participants have to learn about problem solving from making mistakes. They usually have to communicate with a competent adult or they have to access resources, but they have to rely on more than their own knowledge base (Program Manager D).

In fact, participants are ideally immersed in experiences that demand problem-solving; the manager added:

I think the beauty of an experiential learning program is that you don't solve their problems and you allow them to flounder and allow them to realise that if they don't work on their problems they are not going to be solved (Program Manager D).

An integral part of the problem solving participants undertake throughout experiential learning programs expect and anticipate mistakes within certain limits. There must be an understanding by educators and practitioners, however, that this not the most efficient way of getting something done:

I like to give them parameters and sit back and let them make mistakes within reason and that often takes time to allow them to make mistakes and going through that whole process of dealing with the consequences and recognizing that they are mistakes and the working through that and the problem solving and then reflecting at the end of it. (Program Manager B1)

Experiential educators are thus risk managers in real time and at times must be inhumanly patient in allowing learners to make mistakes that impede progress and activity efficiency in the name of effective learning. Of course, the confidence of a teacher to allow a group of inexperienced participants take on challenges is itself dependent on experience. Letting a situation 'run', while maintaining a form of watchful situational awareness takes skill. Said one program leader:

> *Once I got more comfortable in my role, I got better at doing this. My role wasn't to find out when they made a mistake, but to let them discover the mistake for themselves as well. For me that's true responsibility. I am not looking over their shoulder as a safety net, although in the worst-case scenario I am there (Teacher D1).*

She added:

> *The more confident you are, the happier you are to allow them to run with problems and not to solve them. In the early stages when you first start...you want to fix the problems (Teacher D1).*

With experience and judgement comes the ability to manage the fine balance between control and benign neglect:

> *I will know when to intervene and when not to intervene and when to probe with a question and when not to probe. It would be easier for me to solve the problem for them, because I know we would get to the destination faster. I know that I can control it and therefore it won't get beyond what I know I can do (Campus Manager D).*

The teacher monitors the flow of the experience and employs probing questions to elicit responses from participants about the nature of the activity, the challenges faced, and how these might be tackled. The determining factor for intervention is not efficiency or speed, but facilitation of learning.

Intervention: Safety or Larceny?

When matching risk to learning outcomes, the point of intervention in an experiential learning activity certainly emerges as a contentious topic among educators. For some, intervention to solve a problem is seen as a necessity; for others, however, it serves as a means of last resort. There are conflicting views, but one highly experienced manager made the provocative claim that in taking charge, teachers took away from participants a chance to learn:

> *I **rob** them of an opportunity to let them solve it themselves. And as I become more confident as a teacher, I can sit back for longer and observe for longer and predict what's going to happen, to a degree, and I can see the progress with the participant by asking a question, by facilitating it towards a resolution without then giving an answer (Campus Manager D).*

One teacher reflected at length on an incident in which she withheld intervention to allow the participants to solve a problem that arose from their own mistakes:

There were two girls responsible for getting us back to campus. They took us in a completely different direction, and realised that they were unable to find where they were on the map and they both decided that it was too hard for them; they were not going to do it anymore. I had never been in that situation before. I said: "We will stay here until tomorrow morning, but you girls are going to get us home." We sat for probably twenty minutes while they complained and then they actually realised that this was their responsibility and they asked for other participants' assistance, who up until that point hadn't stepped in. They said, "Let's do this." They managed to get redirected. All five of those participants together made the right calls to get us back. That was a bit of an experiment for me, because I would often feel the need to guide the process, but that particular day these two girls were quite able and so they interacted and reflected afterwards. They wrote at the evaluation at the end that that was a highlight for them in being able to get through when they really realised that they were responsible for their decisions (Teacher D3).

Intervention would certainly have been justifiable at the point of learner 'surrender' at the lowest ebb. Post-program recognition of this low point as a 'highlight' would seem to suggest that intervention in this particular case may have taken something very precious away from the participants. There is a fine line, however, between persevering to achieve an outcome, and becoming mired in abject failure to the detriment of the learner's self-esteem.

This notion of teacher intervention 'robbing' participants of learning opportunities was raised by teachers and managers at several schools in different settings and with different program philosophies. There appears to be a clear recognition among practitioners that independent learning by mistake with minimal intervention is desirable. Even the discovery of the mistake is often left to the participant:

(The participants) had what I think was true responsibility and accountability because if they made a mistake they then had to discover that for themselves, then had to find a solution to that for themselves (Teacher D1).

Some offered a form of scaffolding to assist participants working out that a mistake had been made:

The first thing is to ask them to identify what the issue is and then if they can't make the next step to identify a set of steps to solving it (Campus Manager D).

Guided discussion is frequently used as a powerful tool to allow participants to discover their own mistakes and find solutions:

I like to let the situation evolve to the point where participants realize that they had a problem and they needed to fix it. Then I discuss that with them and I am able to move them on (Program Manager B1).

Participants, however, must be given room to make those mistakes, but at the same time, consequences may follow:

I would try my utmost to warn them first thing, but ultimately, if they choose to wander off in the wrong direction and (metaphorically) fall off a cliff, it is part of the mistakes that they have to make. Although it's very dangerous making mistakes, giving them the freedom to make mistakes is part of growing up (Teacher F3).

Much of the foregoing discussion has been focused on the implicit assumption that the type of mistake made is not potentially harmful or life-threatening. What are the consequences, however, that might flow from a participant's mistake? It has already been suggested that in some outdoor environments, mistakes can be lethal or highly hazardous. These are the areas in which there is little or no room for error and some of the 'safety nets' observed during the research, both physical and metaphorical, were well hidden, but 'high-tech', highlighting the readiness of teachers to take charge when needed.

In the most extreme conditions under which an experiential program might operate, communications – immediate, direct, and reliable – tend to be the area on which most attention is focused. Preparation is also seen as an important part of eliminating errors or reducing their impact:

Kids have to lead the trip. Each kid has an allocated time in which to lead the group and they have to organise meals in that time, cleaning up, packing, walking, arranging breaks and snacks and things like that. That's tough on them, especially when it's cold, wet, windy and snowing. Lots of kids struggle with that. That's the chance for people to make mistakes and learn to do better next time...I think any prompting of mistakes or creation of mistakes in this territory has to be carefully managed to avoid a fail situation, which is not productive either (Program Manager A1).

In a physically challenging setting, where the consequences of failure may be well beyond the educational value of a high-risk success, teachers work on finding supports or scaffolds that create the right result, but within a learning zone in which participants become aware of the challenges and perhaps their shortcomings:

I think you need to...nudge them across the line if you have to, so they learn a little bit perhaps, but learn it clearly. I would be more prepared to let a kid make mistakes on a group discussion. I would be prepared to let that go for a while, providing I was there the whole time. Other kids fight, that's fine; that's not going to worry me, because I can control that and arrest it if it gets nasty (Program Manager A1).

Asked if they would allow an error during a relatively risky outdoor activity to continue, with consequences compounding for the participants, the majority of teachers working in the most hazardous environments were in favour of some sort of intervention following an interval of tolerance:

I have followed participants where a couple have gone in the wrong direction... It's all of a sudden dawned on them that they have travelled for a long time since they knew where they were and have started to argue with each other...That is where we usually step in and say, "We are not getting anywhere by arguing about it...do we know where we are? What do we see around us and how can we backtrack and go to our last point where we knew where we were?" And then put it back on them... then catch up with them later on and say, "Well, you have been lost. Did you learn something from that and how would you deal with it next time?" (Teacher A3).

In reflecting on the tension between intervention and freedom, teachers may also reflect on their own learning during the course of a program. One staff member, for example, noted that the capacity to endure hardship during the program was often underestimated by teachers:

I have learnt that I can be much tougher on kids without losing them. Kids are much more capable that what I thought before. What kids do when they haven't got a choice is actually pretty extraordinary (Program Manager A1).

Participant error is also seen as opportunity to learn, and the handling of participant errors seeks to strike a balance between participant learning autonomy and excessive intervention. Provided safety is not an issue, participants are expected to take a leadership role in resolving problems:

If it's not detrimental to them, I let them do something a certain way and they become so frustrated with each other, or they just give up, or there's a tantrum. You have to judge that and might have to step in and help them out. I would be reluctant to tell the whole group to stop. I would approach a participant and say, "What do you reckon?" I would try to do it that way so that it's coming from them (Program Manager A2).

This suggests that there is an ideal approach to error discovery in which the teacher or leader finds a more indirect way of encouraging participants to re-evaluate:

I like to give them parameters and sit back and let them make mistakes within reason and that often takes time to allow them to make mistakes...dealing with the consequences and recognizing that they are mistakes...problem solving and then reflecting at the end of it (Program Manager A1).

This is, of course, time consuming. Teaching staff work with participants, scaffolding their problem-solving with leading questions that suggest certain lines of inquiry without providing a direct way out. It is up to the participants to discover where they went wrong and then seek a solution. This is frustrating for participants in one sense. It is, however, intended to avoid generating dependency on the teacher:

I was quite glad when the participants got to the point when they were frustrated with me...they couldn't find out what my opinion was, but they were able to go and formulate their own and deliver that to me (Program Manager).

It is the teacher, however, who ultimately determines the degree of challenge that each participant can handle:

There are lots of things we do here really to test and challenge them and we push, coerce, and encourage to really bring out the best in participants...it's part of our tradition...it's not something that's hidden or new (Campus Manager A).

Another teacher at this campus found a virtue in the setting of high 'fixed' expectations. He believed that this motivated participants to try even harder than they might have otherwise, if the target had been more negotiable:

There is less flexibility at our campus, but sometimes that less flexibility brings the participants up...and encourages them to go to that next level (Teacher A1).

By pushing, participants may step up and try the *next level.* The purpose behind this approach is to strengthen the resolve of participants, embolden them to give them an experience of hardship that ends in success:

The biggest thing that's different from the other programs is resilience...just the strength to overcome difficult situations. We develop those skills that you need for that; a strong mind. I think they just have to experience things that are tough. They develop that resilience because they know that's the way it is (Teacher A1).

The implicit understanding expressed in this view is that students in mainstream schools do not have enough 'tough' experience and the remoteness and physical demands of this particular program offer something not available at home.

Error and Consequences

In the same way that a novel experience cannot be separated from risk, an error cannot be truly isolated from some form of consequence. The range of consequences arising from an error may of course cover an enormous spectrum from mild disappointment to severe injury, or even death, with many points of ascending severity in between. One of the risks undertaken at an institutional level is that while consequences from a range of potential outcomes may be anticipated and evaluated, the truly novel experience may give rise to the truly novel mistake and lead to unanticipated and inherently unforeseeable outcomes. This possibility must be considered carefully and with all due gravity. Various 'escape' routes, both actual and metaphorical, should be anticipated and mapped for practicability, speed, and effectiveness.

For most mistakes made by participants in remote experiential settings, however, the consequences imposed on a participant feature a loss of one or all of the following: time, energy, and convenience. All are precious commodities to participants; all offer a fitting consequence to an error resulting from poor planning or execution.

Beyond providing a form of feedback to participants on performance against a standard or expected outcome, some programs working with younger learners limit access to 'precious' commodities as a means of encouraging or enforcing certain behavioural expectations. For example, at one remote campus, when a participant's behaviour falls short of expectations, there are consequences imposed by campus staff that are typically shaped around some major elements of student life at the campus:

> I reckon the three big things that are powerful incentives for kids are about food, sleep and social times. If we give them those, or take them away, they can be very effective control mechanisms, for want of a better word (Campus Manager F).

Consequences that are tied to some basic participant needs are seen as a practical means of influencing or facilitating desirable behaviours. Consequences in some campus programs are negotiated within the campus community and with learner participation. This provides participants with an opportunity to set their own expectations and standards and then determine to what extent access to free time might be limited as a result of an error of judgment. Warnings for shortcomings, along with commendations for strong performances, are communicated to participants, with the possibility for some negotiation at various points in the follow-up process:

If this house has done a fantastic job you get an extra half hour's sleep in. If you are mucking around at 10:30 at night and you have been warned a few times, you are up at 7:00 instead of 7:30. If you have got to the point where things aren't working you are going to have detention between 4:00 and 6:00 while everyone else is socialising (Campus Manager F).

Errors and mistakes are not just the product of an incorrect choice during a formal learning activity. They also arise from routine social interactions and events that are part of the daily lived experience of participants. An approach to participant expectation and behaviour management common across each of the programs studied is the notion of risk and reward, rights, responsibility and consequence. The word 'punishment' in the sense of an unpleasant, but perhaps unconnected or arbitrary, response to undesirable behaviour is almost completely absent. Instead, teachers refer to the rights and responsibilities that are enjoyed and respected by all participants. Breaches of responsibility by participants result in consequences that typically entail a loss or curtailment of relevant rights and privileges. Individual and group responsibilities are a core part of the values practiced in these programs. Connecting consequence to a breached responsibility does take careful thought.

Perception of Risk

While risk can be evaluated and managed by experienced program experts with a deep knowledge of the local environment, by virtue of the novel nature of the experience, participants do not share the same capacity to assess risk. One teacher commented that participants, using their urban experience as a guide, struggled to determine with any accuracy the actual level of risk in a new setting:

So while participants here are quite able to walk down the street to the train station as it gets dark, if you said to them in the first week or two, "I want you to walk to the farmhouse in the dark", they would have the perception that that wasn't something that was safe (Program Manager B)."

This phenomenon tends to create in participants a risk perception 'gap' between perceived and actual risk. One staff member at a remote program stressed that despite the participants' perception of working without a 'safety net', there is, in fact, an extensive network of support and supervision, albeit well hidden, both on campus and off. Great care is taken, however, to ensure that participants are not made aware of these safety systems and mechanisms so as to preserve the perception of risk and freedom:

We take kids into the country with a really hazardous environment and there's a lot of risk involved, but we have a lot of staff and I feel comfortable in taking participants out into that environment because I know that they have been well prepared for it...they do feel vulnerable and quite scared about it (Teacher A3).

Some of the mechanisms in place to assist participants with coping with risks may be invisible, or may rely on 'hidden' skills that are accumulated slowly, deliberately, almost imperceptibly throughout a program, but which are available when needed most. This may include times when activities are often conducted in circumstances that are physically and psychologically challenging:

I think they have just had to experience things that are tough. They develop that resilience. Last year we had participants on a three-day hike and we just had snow which covered the whole low and high country and that was the first time that they had ever had to deal with snow. They had to put up with being wet for three days; they just had to cope. We knew that these kids would be fine with whatever happened because they had had that experience early (Teacher A2).

As participants develop resilience and coping skills, teachers report that their capacity to manage risk in hazardous environments improves. Participants are able to make important decisions that carry enormous levels of potential risk, without hesitation or anxiety:

Participants spend something like sixty days in a tent a year here. So they become quite familiar with weather and it is a very important part of what they are doing here. For example, if it is forecast to be snowing on campus in a couple of days, that will affect what they do and what they pack and greatly influences what we expect them to do (Campus Manager A).

As a part of this growing capacity to make key decisions without direct adult or expert intervention, participants are encouraged to observe conditions, analyse risk, and take appropriate precautions when preparing to enter a hazardous environment, or undertake a challenging activity.

Where participants are allowed to make mistakes, the extent to which they can deal with the consequences must be considered carefully, particularly where these consequences may have a 'real life' impact on the participants. Consequences that have 'real life' impact, include unmet physical needs, such as food or water shortages, or delays imposed by navigational errors:

If they can't read a map initially, I don't want them to get lost, but when they have more experience, I think it's healthy for the participants to get lost because it's also very rewarding when they get themselves out of a situation. If they run out of food, they realise that by using their own initiative, they get by (Teacher E2).

The point of intervention in a situation might be determined by the perceived consequences of failure to intervene; it might reflect the relative skill level of the group, and the prevailing, or anticipated, conditions at the time of the point of intervention. Participant mistakes are treated with a great deal of care: some mistakes or judgement errors are allowed to stand or unfold to create learning opportunities that are entirely within the control of the participant:

Getting lost would be the big one and you might just make some suggestions as to how they could fix it...This doesn't happen often. I mean if they decide that they are going to have a lazy day, have a long lunch and sit around, that's their decision. I am not going to tell them to get up and start walking because I don't think that's the nature of the experience (Teacher E2).

Across many programs in different contexts, the expectation should be that if there is a policy of non-intervention, or the intervention protocol has not yet been triggered, the teacher is comfortable and able to withhold any interference. Teachers expect that participants will encounter difficulties during the experiential activities, some of which typically arise from participant inaction or poor decision making:

Like getting tired, getting sore feet, getting lost, getting wet, running out of food, getting angry with each other; all those things that happen when not making basic decisions on a hike (Teacher E2).

These problems, largely arising out of participant mistakes, are widely accepted as a part of the learning challenge associated with experiential program. The resolution of mistakes by the participant tends to build resilience and a sense of accomplishment:

At the end of a hike when there has been something challenging, for instance, if it's been raining the whole time or they have run out of food. I think they find the experience much more rewarding rather than when they come back from a hike when everything has gone to plan. They don't have the same sense of achievement (Teacher E2).

In allowing mistakes in order to build problem-solving skills and a perception of achievement, there is an acknowledged element of risk for both staff and participants:

The (participants) have a lot of responsibility attached to their experience here. We trust them a lot and expect a lot from them. For example, once they have got used to the place, they are able to run on running tracks in groups of four on their own, right out on the mountaintops (Campus Manager E).

The allowable 'margin for error' and risk appetite among teaching staff varies according to program familiarity and experience; it may also be influenced by subjective factors such as the prevailing dynamic within a specific group of participants during a particular program:

> *Because I am new to this area I would probably be a bit more wary about getting too far from where I know I am. I am still learning what the weather conditions do so I need to feel confident in my own ability to get the (participants) out of a situation that they might get themselves into. You might also take into account how the group is going (Teacher E1).*

Risk appetite is always on the minds of experiential educators: how much potential trouble can be tolerated before shutting participants down? The expectation that mistakes will occur as a natural and fully anticipated outcome of any experiential learning activity is perhaps a fundamental underlying assumption in all of the programs studied:

> *If participants weren't going to make mistakes it wouldn't be worth bringing them here (Teacher A1).*

If this is the expectation, it follows logically that teachers must make room for mistakes to take place and for the participants to find solutions:

> *To make the space to allow participants to make mistakes and then have the time to work that out and also have the time to deal with those problems because in terms of my managing of the program for me, it was important to make space for them to do all of those things (Teacher D4).*

How then does the teacher form a reliable judgement regarding the tolerance of error and the potential benefits accruing from withheld teacher intervention? This is determined in part by the school's own explicit or tacit views on risk.

School Culture, Protective Parents, and Risk Appetite

The extent to which risk is embedded in the philosophy and practice of experiential learning in a given setting is largely a reflection of school culture and parental expectations. Legislative and statutory factors may serve to shape the operating environment. Not all schools can accommodate the idea that an activity might, of necessity, generate situations in which participants make mistakes for which intervention is not forthcoming.

During the research, a high degree of variability across programs was observed. One teacher with extensive personal experience working two programs was able to illuminate how this variability was reflected in practice and the learner experience. One program had a very strict approach to risk mitigation; in another program, risk was not just tolerated, but considered to be an indispensable part of the learning. The conservative risk management approach in the first school created a culture in which participants are expected to be 'rescued' from their mistakes:

> *It's not quite the done thing to let the participants make a mistake without coming to their rescue. But I know personally that in my current school, I have been less inclined, particularly in outdoor programs, to let things get too out of hand (Teacher E1).*

In another institution, one with a greater tolerance of error that allowed activities to unfold in a more laissez-faire manner, the same teacher commented:

> *I would just let them go for it and if they were still walking at 1:00 a.m. that would be fine and that did happen. Often that happened because I planned it that way. I was quite comfortable to let the kids run the trip and sleep in till ten in the morning and take five hours to pack up and consequently get back to campus about four in the morning (Teacher E1).*

The prevailing ethos of the school and the program exerts a distinct and quite pervasive influence on the way in which decisions are made in the field by teachers when faced with difficult or ambiguous situations in experiential activities. In some cases, however, informants expressed an aspiration to change the school culture and encourage greater participant risk taking:

> *I would like to see the participants hone their risk taking abilities. Forget about the assessments, not just catering to the criteria, actually take a risk, do something new and test the theory out properly, don't just spew out what you know in order to get good marks (Campus Manager E).*

This hunger among teachers for authenticity and originality from participants was evident in many of the programs examined. One acknowledged impediment to this aspiration to encourage risk-taking, however, is the negative impact of parental expectations:

> *They are just used to rescuing their child from every situation. I would say the participants have to accept the consequences, because a lot of them don't have consequences at home. There are a lot of consequences in life and you need to learn to accept the consequences for what happens (Teacher E3).*

For some participants, personal acceptance of consequences was seen as a much needed and frequently absent element of their home and school education.

Paradoxically, parent attitudes can send mixed messages to schools about risk. One program manager at a conservative school noted that parents who were prone to intervening to protect their children from challenges were also appreciative of what they saw as the positive changes in their children arising from risk taking and acceptance of consequences:

> *The reason that the parents thank us is they get home participants who are not so protected (Campus Manager E).*

Parents were happy with the end result, but found the process difficult to endure.

Teachers are often willing to remove some protective measures, but may need parental consent or forbearance to do so. Suffering and danger can be managed, but not eliminated:

> *Participants really should be learning things on their own and suffering the consequences if they don't. Obviously you don't want the participants in danger, but, I think you can protect them while letting them experience themselves without being overprotective (Teacher E2).*

The balance sought in all of this is between *suffering* and *protection*. Risk may result in hardship, but may also lead to learning, development, independence and resilience. Protection removes or reduces the potential for pain and suffering, but it also robs the participant of the opportunity to become more resourceful and self-reliant.

Chapter Summary: Responsibility, Risk, and Reward

Risk is an essential precondition for experiential learning to occur. Experiential learning depends on the experience itself providing some form of novel sensory input that causes a cognitive dissonance for the learner. As a novel experience by definition lies beyond the learner's existing experiential frame of reference, the precise nature of the consequent interaction between the learner and the novel experience within the setting is inherently unpredictable and hence entails risk.

Social interaction between learners taking place within a challenging, confronting an unfamiliar setting creates multidimensional uncertainty. This environmental and social uncertainty creates a margin for error that entails an element of risk in experiential learning that schools and teachers seek to manage, but cannot eliminate entirely. As each experience is unique to the individuals experiencing it, so too are their reactions to the experience, making the experiential learning transaction itself inherently unpredictable.

There can be no novel experience without introducing uncertainty and risk and it is the *tolerance of risk* within each program that informs and constrains the challenges emerging from the setting and the social interaction that occurs within the setting. The tolerance of risk creates a space between what is known or understood and therefore deemed to be safe, and what lies at the outer edge of social, institutional, or legal tolerance of uncertainty in an educational setting.

Risk is moderated in different ways in each program, according to participant ability, but more frequently in accordance with institutional *risk appetite*: this is a largely invisible parameter of programs reflecting school culture, parental acceptance and demand, legal precedent, and professional practices and standards. Institutional risk appetite shapes and constrains the experiential latitude accorded to teachers in the implementation of any program or activity.

The type of risk present in the programs studied varies according to setting, social dynamic, degree of challenge, the nature of the activity, and the tolerance of risk in the parent institution. Participants face *physical* risks that pose a range of potential dangers from mild discomfort through to serious injury, or even death. Participants face *social* risks that range from exposure to mild forms of social embarrassment, isolation or ostracism, through to extremely harmful forms of bullying, self-harm, and obsessive behaviour. Participants may also face *cultural* risks depending on the program setting. These range from mild disorientation caused by superficial cultural differences through to fully developed culture shock that causes serious psychological symptoms requiring medical intervention.

Each of these types of risk – physical, social, and cultural – can be moderated or managed in some way. Risk can be minimised or exaggerated in practice, through intervention points, thresholds delimiting scaffolding support, and the degree of difficulty inherent in the program settings and tasks set. These adjustable parameters of risk can also be interpreted by individual teachers according to personal conviction, professional judgement, and relative level of experience, both in their working with participants and with the setting itself.

In the higher risk programs, participants are granted freedom to make decisions and make mistakes. Teachers provide scaffolding to a varying extent, but may also wilfully withhold their opinions to ensure participants are making their own decisions and make their own mistakes. The greater the range of mistakes tolerated, the higher the level of risk implicit in the activity or program. In high risk programs, the range of possible outcomes may be very broad. There is a tacit responsibility for risk that is shared between the institution at a policy and culture level, the teacher at the level of dynamic situational risk, and the individual participant based on this grant of freedom and acceptance of responsibility for consequences. Participants focus on the freedoms given and teaching staff monitor the outcomes of free decision making that will inevitably result in mistakes, some of which may be hazardous in some way.

The point at which teachers intervene once an error has occurred varies greatly, reflecting legal precedent, institutional values and culture, parental expectations, and the anticipated or estimated capacity of participants to succeed in a given activity. Participants might shine in the absence of adult intervention, they might be *nudged* to success by teachers, or they might suffer consequences for abrogation of responsibility. These approaches reflect the institutional value of the role of the teacher lying beneath the surface promotion of participant leadership. The degree and timing of teacher intervention varies enormously. For some, it is judged so as to avert catastrophe, while allowing a level of success. For others, it is the pre-emptive intervention to avoid discomfort and adverse parental reaction. Ideally, the balance between responsibility, risk, error, and intervention rests in a zone of optimised learning that equates to the notion of the Zone of Proximal Development applied to experiential learning, albeit with the additional dimension of risk.

One of the implications of this aspect of experiential learning for younger participants is the importance of the collaborative role of the parent in setting the standards for both risk and success. It is the parental tolerance of risk that is pivotal to maintaining program challenge. At the same time, it is the parent who determines the degree to which participants face risk in the programs. Some parents find this dichotomy particularly challenging, given the role to which many are accustomed as 'saviours' of their children at the first sight of trouble. Unable to rescue their child from challenge and risk due to isolation, parents observe the learning process from a literal distance. Some express gratitude for the removal of protection, but the parent-derived tension for teachers in all programs, between risk and protection, exposure and shelter, is ever present.

In summary, for experiential learning to occur, participants are exposed to novel situations in which there is uncertainty and, therefore, risk. There is a constant tension between risk and protection, exposure and shelter; safety and challenge, and the balance between the two, exert a constant pressure on teachers in all programs. Schools set policies and determine practices within legal and ethical stipulations and constraints; parents exercise the right to determine risk appetite, albeit at a distance; teachers manage risk on the ground, setting the degree of challenge, immediate level of risk, and the margin for error; it is the learner, however, who ultimately exercises the greatest power through the decision to engage, or not, in the experience.

197

Key Questions

In this chapter, we have reviewed the nature of risk, its essential presence as an integral component of experiential learning, and how it is evaluated and managed in some of the programs studied. The following are some key questions concerning risk and its management in experiential learning:

1. What is the institution's stated position on risk in education from a legal, ethical, and policy perspective (legislative and regulatory context)?

2. What is the 'risk' culture of the wider parent community?

3. Does the institution have any existing policies and practices relating to risk mitigation and management: what is the risk appetite and culture of the school?

4. How have negative outcomes arising from educational programs been managed by the institution in the past (precedents)?

5. How 'protective' and proactive in intervention is the parent community?

6. Has the institution undertaken a thorough risk analysis of each program and activity?

7. Are activities with a heightened risk profile the most effective way of achieving the desired or intended learning outcome?

8. Has the institution offered and maintained currency of training for staff in areas of perceived heightened risk?

9. Does the institution engage third-party expertise to mitigate risk through the provision of specialist consultancy services or the direct provision of expertise in the field?

10. Are all programs reviewed regularly with particular attention paid to incident reports, management, and development of program execution?

Chapter 11: Enduring Learning: Reflection in Practice

As *homo sapiens*, it is our capacity to think about things in an abstract sense that marks us as unique. We think about what has gone before, what is happening in the present, and what is likely to happen in the future. We think about our past experiences and project them into the future; we imagine things that have not yet come to pass as if they were real; we think in the abstract about things that do not, and cannot, exist. One way of describing this kind of conscious deliberation about the past, present, and future, is the term *reflection*. As noted in Chapter 5, reflection is:

> *...the explicit rendering of the intelligent element in our experience. It makes it possible to act with an end in view: reflection consists of both thinking and action* (Dewey, 1921, p. 171).

It is an explicit form of cognitive activity focused on making meaning from past experience. It is closely associated with memory function and the extent to which an experience is retained in detail in the memory of the participant, it informs action.

For the purposes of this exploration of reflection in experiential learning, the Deweyan conceptualisation of reflection as a conscious, intentional process linked to future experience and action is adopted. There are other forms of mental ruminative activity that may be associated with the term 'reflection'. For example, immersion in passive mindfulness is considered by some to be another form of reflection. This type of meditative practice is not included in the working definition of reflection in this book and as such is not discussed here.

In practice, reflection in the experiential programs examined is manifested in different and apparently contradictory ways. While reflection appears to be an important feature in all forms of formal experiential learning, there is a sharp distinction between two modes of practice or implementation observed. The first mode is immediate *guided-explicit* reflection; the second mode is deferred *emergent-implicit*.

Some see reflection, like Dewey, as an explicit, deliberate, often highly-structured and guided process that takes place immediately after an experience. The other mode of reflection is a form of implicit and indirect thinking that emerges naturally in the mind of the participant over time. In the former, learner agency is present, but is exercised to varying degrees within an externally imposed structure or schedule influenced by teacher agency. In the emergent-implicit model, learner agency is strong and may approach being absolute. Each mode has its advocates and critics; it is largely a matter of philosophical choice.

In this chapter, the practices and purpose of reflection are examined in some detail. The explicit modes of reflection observed in use and the media employed in some schools are also discussed. The arguments in favour of the delayed emergent-implicit reflection approach are also considered. The chapter concludes with an examination of reflection as an essential educational practice.

Let the Experience Speak: Emergent-Implicit Reflection

The questions of planned or implicit reflection and the optimal time for reflection to be undertaken are polarizing issues among practitioners and program leaders. Two of the programs studied and a number of practitioners at other programs shared the view that any form of structured reflection immediately following an activity or during the program is not desirable. This approach is one in which the experience itself is allowed to unfold without teacher-led scrutiny or structured evaluation, both of which are viewed as forms of unwelcome or unnecessary interference. Reflection is not formally accommodated within the program and only anticipated in a formal sense at its conclusion.

Philosophically, this approach values overt action in learning rather than thinking about it. Learner agency in the emergent-implicit process of reflection is held to be close to absolute; teachers and managers believe that reflection will take place at some point after the experience, but that process is entirely in the hands of the learner. It is up to the learner to reflect, but when and how is not stipulated. This approach is summed up in a memorable quote from one campus manager, who believed that the experience was sufficient for its own purposes: *the experience speaks for itself.*

If we look beyond the idea of the self-sufficiency of experience, other reasons were offered to justify this approach to reflection. For some, there is no time for reflection; some believe that participants are not ready or able to reflect at the time of the experience, but with time and further maturation, it is held that this will take place when the learner is ready; for others, reflection must follow action at a distance, allowing time for the reflective process to unfold at the natural pace of the learner. The essence of these positions is that the experience will provide all that the learner needs at the time and that with further time, and growth, the learner will reflect on the experience when the time is right. The experience is a seed that germinates in the mind of the learner and in the right season, it will ripen and bear fruit.

Some educators see this separation of experience and reflection as a form of active-passive time division:

> *Reflection time for us is at the end of the year when we sit back and reflect on the year. We don't build in a lot of reflection time during the year. So this place is really about doing rather than reflecting (Campus Manager A).*

For some teachers, the intensity of the experience precludes the possibility of embedding meaningful reflection in experience, and may also interfere with its memorability:

> *It's more difficult to reflect during the program than it is for them to reflect once they have left. Reflection is more lasting, I think, when they have left (Teacher A2).*

The idea that learners are not yet ready to reflect during a program was summed up neatly by a teacher who had previously attended a year-long experiential program at a remote campus as a participant. He offered a personal perspective on the idea of deferred reflection and realisation of learning:

> *I think the campus is a place that you don't really appreciate until much later. I don't think that you can have any understanding of what value an experience like that offers until you are much older and have had experiences outside. It's not really until you get out into the world that you realize how unique that experience was. I probably didn't appreciate it while I was there, not that I didn't enjoy it, I loved it (Teacher A4).*

For this teacher, the experience, while enjoyable at the time, was not ripe for reflection at its conclusion. It was only after further experience of life that the earlier experiences made sense.

This observation suggests that for some experiences there is a form of experiential 'qualification' required for effective reflection. One may not be able to reflect without the requisite post-program experience in other contexts to render reflection useful in some way. This sentiment was echoed by another teacher at the same campus:

> *The majority of participants mature as the year goes along and have changed a lot over the year and really at the end of the year they understand the importance of most things (Teacher A5).*

Further experience provides perspective that facilitates a form of ranking or prioritisation, whereby experience is reinterpreted in the light of later experiences and reordered into a form of considered, dynamic hierarchy of personal importance and utility. This view suggests that participants may not be able to determine the significance of an experience until much later.

Some of the evidence offered in support of the deferred reflection mode centres on the assumed limited capacity of younger participants to engage in reflection. One of the reasons offered for this approach is that certain younger age groups of participants do not find the process of reflection easy or educationally useful:

> *Kids at this age, especially boys, in my experience, don't reflect well. I mean they can, but generally they don't. I don't think their mental or emotional capacity is up to their physical one just yet (Program Manager A1).*

This manager added the intriguing caveat that structured or 'forced' reflection might actually interfere with the way in which an experience is remembered by the participant:

> *It comes across as shallow and boring and goes against us with most kids. I think that experience has integrity that it might not otherwise have if it's been debriefed. I never try to force that stuff on kids (Program Manager A1).*

This view holds that formal reflection compromises the value and veracity of the experience. If reflection cannot be done well, then it shouldn't be done at all.

Teachers at all schools participating in the study raised concerns about constructed, programmed, obligatory reflection. At one school where reflection was practiced through teacher-led facilitation after each activity, concerns were raised about the process tainting the outcome. This particular type of reflection is carefully and tightly framed by teachers in the form of an activity 'debriefing'. A concern raised with this approach is that in order to satisfy the demand for some kind of reflective response, younger participants might invent a reflection that they believed would satisfy the demands of the 'task'. The key question here concerns the capacity, either learned or innate, possessed by teenagers to 'reflect':

Our kids of fourteen or fifteen are not accustomed to reflecting and analysing and don't do it particularly well. They are used to the 'cop-out' comment: 'I don't know', and it obviously works in a classroom environment (Campus Manager D).

While expressing a degree of 'professional' cynicism, the suspicion that learner responses to probing or difficult questions might be inauthentic is well-founded in the experience of the author. Younger learners in particular, often operate on the assumption, reinforced by thousands of instructional hours in the classroom, that teachers are seeking the 'right' answer to any questions asked. There is therefore an understandable reluctance to offer a highly personal response to an experience, if there is a chance that it is not the desired response. At worst, "I don't know" is a safer, neutral response; from the learner perspective, it is preferable to appear ignorant than wrong.

In the school mentioned above, the structure and practice of reflection at times tended to generate the sorts of answers participants expected the teachers wanted to hear. For teachers accustomed to detecting any absence of sincerity or authenticity in participant interactions, the requirement to conduct structured reflections was seen as puzzling and perhaps pointless:

At first I was a bit confused (about debriefing), I thought it seemed all a bit of a waste of time actually (Teacher D1).

Troubled by concerns that participants might not be ready to reflect, or that their reflections might not be authentic, some teachers understandably find the approach that leaves the responsibility and timing of reflection in the hands of the learner appealing. We could summarize this view as follows: if a learner is not yet ready to reflect on an experience, don't force it.

Similarly, this school of thought does not accept the notion that reflection can be facilitated or instructed:

I don't think it's something that is taught; I think it's something that they realize over a long period of time (Teacher F2).

Reflection is thus seen as a naturally unfolding cognitive process that occurs over an extended time frame. It cannot be incubated, force ripened, or rushed in any way.

At this point, we might be forgiven for expressing some curiosity regarding the optimal interval between the experience and its corresponding reflection. *A long period of time* is not a chronologically precise term. How long? Without resorting to tiresome clichés about the length of a piece of string, it is clearly assumed by schools and programs that adopt this approach that the reflective process will take some time, but no one offered a precise estimate of the time needed to complete the reflective process. An experienced program manager offered the following, somewhat sobering, estimate:

> They might go through the whole experience and not realise it until **months** or **years** down the track and only then start to appreciate what they went through (Program Manager B).

Anecdotes supporting this observation of deferred reflection and implicit learning were rich and plentiful. A teacher commenting on the participants' realisation of learning achieved through post-program reintegration with their peer group in the home school setting, noted that concluding the program and leaving the campus triggered some reflective responses. Program participants became aware of their own growth through the reactions of non-participant friends:

> I realize this by little conversations the participants have with each other, like, "My friends, when I went home, they couldn't believe what I was wearing", or laughing at this and saying, "They just have no idea what the 'house' is like". Participants talk about how they learn to occupy themselves during the program and be themselves and not to rely on multimedia bombardment all the time. They just mention this to one another informally (Teacher F2).

The teacher added that this post-program perspective was transformative:

> I mean, before they might not have realized where they have grown up, that society and culture has had an impact on them, but now they can see the impact it has had (Teacher F2).

Without any direction from program educators, many participants also reported back to teachers on improved relationships with their parents after returning home:

> They used to fight with their mum all the time and they are really ashamed as to how they treated their parents and since being away they have realized that when they go home they are so happy to see them, that they realize how important that they actually were (Teacher F2).

Even schools that practice direct, structured reflection acknowledge the fairly common existence of this deferred learning phenomenon. A program manager overseeing a 'guided-explicit reflection' program offered in the middle years of secondary schooling, acknowledged that participants often did not really understand their achievements until well after completing the course:

> By the time they get to Year 11 and 12, they reflect back on that time and often say, "Oh, I learnt that when I was at the remote campus and didn't realise that

I was learning it." *That's part of the experiential learning concept (Program Manager C).*

In this case, it would appear that some form of learning transaction has taken place, but only at a subconscious level in the mind of the learner. Realisation of learning did not occur until much later when a cognitive trigger prompted a reflective event – the 'aha' moment – at which point, the learner has a conscious reaction to the earlier experience. In some cases, this response appears to have been triggered through reintegration with the home environment, or re-establishing relationships with parents and friends who were not part of the experience. For others, it appears to be merely a function of time.

The experience of practitioners favouring this view of reflection is that a timeframe of years between the experience and 'realisation' seems to be unremarkable, and even expected. The emergent, almost 'free-range' nature of this approach is inherently unpredictable. Remarkably, it depends in large part on the faith educators place in the learner's post-program experiences contributing to an on-going process of cognitive maturation. This faith believes implicitly in the inevitability of the outcome, but without expectation regarding the point at which this outcome is achieved. From a theory to practice perspective, the difficulty lies in demonstrating a reliable connection. This is overwhelmingly complex due to the inestimable number of other influences and experiences involved, most of which lie beyond the control of the experiential educator.

As a final observation about the emergent-implicit approach as an espoused theory of reflection, it should be noted that there is an underlying assumption that formal reflection in a program must be organised and must involve adults. If reflection time is not scheduled, or if participants are not undertaking reflection under the supervision of a teacher, this view assumes that reflection is not taking place.

In fact, as we shall see in a following section regarding modes of reflection, any form of communication, both spoken or written, such as a letter or e-mail to a friend or parent, even an idle conversation with a co-participant, can, and in fact does, act as a vehicle for reflection, albeit informal. While they may not receive official recognition as reflections, these private communication acts are highly personal and authentic expressions of post-activity thinking. They help the learner to make sense of the experience and shape future behaviour. As such, they are a form of enacted theory of reflection that is highly learner-centred and gives significant agency to the participant to frame reflection in a uniquely personal way.

In summary, of the emergent-implicit approach we might say that if the experience does indeed speak for itself, its voice might be personally authentic, but might not be heard by the participant for some time.

Shaping What the Experience Says

We now shift focus to consider the more structured and intentional approach to reflection. There are many different practices and mechanisms used to construct or prompt reflection-induced learning in a more predictable and perhaps timely fashion. This is entirely rational, relying on the natural inclination of thinking, reflective practitioners to prompt or provoke a learning response from an experience in a more direct and deliberate manner.

The key question in reducing this seemingly random process to something more predictable and controllable is the nature of the cognitive trigger that precedes the realisation of learning. If this learning process can be triggered in a more predictable and programmed way, then the learning outcome may be achieved within a timeframe that permits the attribution of some degree of causality. Some teachers see this trigger not as a single, transitory event, but as stepped, developmental process contained within some form of structure or scaffold, in which the participants' memories are stored and ordered in some way for later retrieval. This view is certainly supported by the manner in which episodic memory is understood to function.

Most teachers interviewed had an understanding of the need to offer participants some form of interpersonal exchange after an experience, through which they could explore its educational meaning at a personal level. This is based on the view that participant memories require *something that gives a frame of reference...something that physically ties a participant to a concept (Teacher D3)*. Thus, the memories of an experience act as one key part of the framework, the other is the structure provided by the teacher or facilitator.

One experienced classroom teacher, who had worked at two very different experiential programs, offered a personal definition of the significance of debriefing and reflection within the context of experiential learning from the perspective of these two programs:

Experiential learning means to me rather the opposite of what the classroom is. The classroom teaches you theories, which you are then supposed to, at some undefined point of time in a real world, apply. You know, you learn partial fractions in Senior School in the hope that maybe someday in your mid-thirties you'll be on a building site and be able to use them. I don't know, I never use maths for anything. The part of learning that we used at the remote site was the opposite. We actually saw the stuff, sometimes quite confronting stuff, and you then had to do the learning afterwards, preferably on scene, as it was happening in front of you. The teacher could remove the kids and say, "Do you see this, let me explain to you what is going on." (Teacher D2).

The immediate connection between experiential stimulus and the teacher's intervention through feedback to prompt understanding creates a very tight, closed loop between the experience and the making of meaning from that experience. The structure allows the teacher to immerse the learner in an experience and then provide timely context and expert commentary, if necessary.

Within the ranks of those who support some form of organised or structured thinking about an experience, there are two different camps: one group favours the more formal type of teacher-led reflection that some refer to as a 'debriefing'; the other group advocates for a more informal, conversational, participant-focused reflection:

I guess reflection is an acknowledgment of learning change and recognition. You always know that they are reflecting and you can do it in a million ways, but it's that unplanned stuff that they just do at whatever stage that is most important (Program Manager B).

The insertion of a reflective stage by the teacher is intentional here, but the manner of reflection is emergent, drawn to an extent from the dynamic relationships and narratives within the group at the time.

In encouraging and leading more playful and personalised reflection sessions with the participants, one teacher offered an anecdote on a creative way in which a shared experience of mass media entertainment played a useful role in facilitating a more informal process of reflection:

Occasionally, I will have a 'sitcom moment' – we've all seen sitcoms where the person suddenly gazes off into the distance and gets thrown back to something that has happened in a previous time – so occasionally I will say: "Let's have a 'sitcom moment'. So what are the things that you guys remember and reflect on that have happened earlier in the term?" (Program Manager B)."

This approach encourages a more imaginative form of storytelling that begins to shape a narrative of the experience in the mind and memory of the participant. The use of the 'sitcom' metaphor is appropriate, given the highly episodic nature of the autonoetic memories created through this process.

Using reflection as a form of self-regulating and highly personalised system of learning evaluation is another way in which this practice contributes to learning. Most informants in the research who practiced explicit reflection acknowledged the significance of reflection as a more reliable and participant-centred means of identifying outcomes:

> *Change definitely occurs: however, unless a participant says: "This has changed me", there is no measurement of where they were at the start, only at the end where they write self-reflections (Program Manager B).*

Where reflection is practiced as an integral part of learning experientially, it serves as a means of measuring learning progress, a form of cognitive yardstick:

> *I think that the participants would say themselves that they do heaps of reflective work as they go along and they start to see where they have progressed – where they have made more mature decisions, or where they created a piece of work that is either of a higher standard, or is a more sophisticated way of thinking (School Manager C).*

In those programs practicing explicit reflection, the focus is not just limited to program activities. Teachers also see reflection as a structured way of affirming aspects of the lives of participants beyond program activity skills and general academic pursuits:

> *I think what reflection did is that it deepened the learning, gave them an understanding of what was going on in their lives, gave them an appreciation of what they actually were doing in undertaking the various tasks and experiences they were going through and it gave them a chance to be able to see that they were growing (Teacher D4)*

Another teacher at this remote campus also drew a strong connection between the process of reflection and the integration of the experience into the overall understanding of the learner's previous life experiences:

> *Through talking about what they were doing, through talking about what they achieved, it helped them to appreciate what was happening in their lives. So through that process, I think they had a better understanding of (the experience) and with a better understanding of it, they were able to apply it to other situations in their lives more fully, and actually integrate it into who they are as people (Teacher D1).*

In fact, in contrast to the emergent-implicit school of thought on reflection, this teacher took the notion of evaluative reflection in experiential learning a step further:

> *To not have reflection I think would have taken away some of the impact of the experiences that they went through. They needed to be able to reflect on what they were doing and what they had achieved at different times (Teacher D4).*

This leaves us with an alarming dilemma: to reflect may compromise the *integrity* of the experience, yet to not reflect may diminish the *impact* of the experience. We seem to be faced with a tough choice: integrity or impact.

Guided Reflection: The Risks and Pitfalls

On balance, from the research undertaken for this book, there would seem to be strong evidence supporting the adoption of some form of structured reflection. However, it is well understood by some teachers that the way in which reflection is handled by the facilitator has a disproportionate influence on the judgements that are made by the participants in the reflection process. In the wrong hands, reflection might not be quite so positive. This highlights the importance of selecting appropriately trained and experienced staff to manage the reflection process. A program manager commented on the fine balance that a teacher needs to maintain in reflection:

I suppose how you actually get participants to reflect will determine whether it's either a positive or negative experience, because sometimes if participants perceive too much, or they are somehow being analysed and judged, they will give you what you want to hear, or are negative about it. That's a really fine line and that comes back to the type of teacher that is required for this sort of program (Program Manager C).

The potential impact of *audience* on what is remembered is also potentially important. A participant might remember an experience in a particular way in response to the assumed expectations of an audience, such as a parent or friend. A complex set of interrelated experiences or interactions might be reduced to a throw-away line designed to satisfy an audience or avoid an unwanted conversation. One teacher, experienced in both outdoor and classroom settings, offered an intriguing perspective on this reductive process:

Younger participants in particular tend to qualify an experience in one sentence. For example, you will have been on a camp with a child and they've had a ball, and then I have had a note from his mother saying how much he hated camp and how unhappy he was. You may say, "Well I was with the kid for a whole week and he always had a smile on his face, he never complained and every time I asked him how he was going, he only said it was good. He has come home and has turned the experience into a sentence. You know and maybe there was just something at that moment, maybe he didn't feel like talking, to you, maybe he was in a bad mood, maybe he was tired and he just said he hated it." From that, the whole experience has been coloured by his own recording of the experience (Teacher D2).

The experience is reconstructed according to the context of the post-program interaction. If this is the case, it is even more important that the key conversations that trigger reflective cognition after an experience are managed carefully, sensitively, and neutrally.

A further perceived risk from the guided-explicit reflection school is the fleeting nature of the experience itself. There is a belief that the cognitive processes surrounding and following an experience are volatile and must therefore be handled in a timely manner. One teacher made a telling observation about the transitory nature of the experience and the powerful impact of externally facilitated summary judgements:

> *In a sense, an experience only teaches for the second that the experience lasts and what stays with learners is the way that they have been **directed** to understand the experience afterwards; the way that they have turned the experience into a story or into a lesson. Without that process, the debriefing, the role of the teacher, the experience in itself can be lost (Teacher D2).*

This view emphasizes the risk that any form of debriefing or reflection may have a disproportionate influence on shaping the way a participant remembers an experience. The learner narrative that emerges from reflection will, to an extent, be a co-constructed story, involving both learner and teacher. This process of construction, however, is seen to extend the life of the experience, capturing it in a form for later retrieval, further reflection, and perhaps deferred learning.

We are therefore left with two starkly different alternatives: allow the experience to rest undisturbed in the memory of the participant, awaiting an opportunity, probably unplanned and undirected, to take root in a cognitive sense and bear fruit; or grasp the fleetingly narrow window of opportunity to generate a more structured and guided response to the experience. Each approach has its merits and potential shortcomings. In practice, the choice is largely indicative of institutional and individual philosophies regarding the purpose and practice of reflection.

There are some caveats that must be applied in making this choice. It is perhaps fair to say that the increasingly prescriptive levels of institutional and educational accountability, adopted by, or imposed on, most schools would dictate preference for an educational outcome that is more reliable, predictable, and perhaps intentional. It is much more difficult to demonstrate a causal link between the experience and the learning, if years separate the two events. On the other hand, the programs that have adopted the deferred, implicit approach tend to be offered in institutions with long histories and trusting parent communities. These learning communities have the benefit of cross-generational evidence of learning that have built faith in an approach that emphasizes patience and trust in the learner over precipitate and potentially manufactured outcomes.

Modes of Reflection: The Experiential Narrative

Whether emergent-implicit or guided-explicit, reflection takes many forms. In this section, we need to consider briefly what form that reflection might take. We can certainly discern the general principles of reflection from educational philosophers and thinkers, such as Dewey, but these very general concepts are of little practical value when we find ourselves faced with a group of wet and weary learners at the end of a three-day wilderness expedition. Reflection ultimately requires some form of concrete action.

Reflection in practice may be manifested in some form of social interaction, possibly spoken or textual, and may also comprise individual reflective thinking undertaken in silent isolation. While reflective thinking might be largely invisible to the observer, there are other modes of reflection that are manifested in tangible artefacts. Unsurprisingly perhaps, we can divide these artefacts into two broad categories: visual and spoken.

The following discussion and analysis explores reflection in action in experiential learning programs and examines the processes used to produce the tangible artefacts of reflection.

Time to Reflect

Reflection is programmed formally in many of the programs studied. Some offer a half-hour 'quiet time' at the end of each day to write entries in a personal journal. Others schedule time at the end of each day's activities as a way of concluding an activity. One school scheduled a day of isolation for each participant at the conclusion of the program during which time participants were expected to undertake a final, formal reflection alone. This activity is referred to as a 'solo' expedition:

> They have a day of solo to reflect. The night before their final presentation they
> are encouraged to think about their time at the remote campus (Teacher B6).

The 'solo' is also a well-known 'rite of passage' component scheduled at the conclusion of the extended or 'Challenge' course offered by Outward Bound. It is considered to be a testing, but ultimately worthwhile experience.

The time(s) scheduled for reflection to an extent manifests one dimension of the institution's enacted values regarding reflection.

211

Written Reflection

All programs incorporating formal reflection schedule time for reflective writing to take place. Some schools produce more formal templates to structure written reflections as responses to predetermined prompts. Other schools employ a range of written genres to act as vehicles for reflection, such as diaries, journals, personal responses, letters to parents, learning logs, etc. As noted earlier, those programs not practicing formal reflection may also facilitate a form of unofficial, personal reflection through the provision of time for participants to conduct personal written correspondence with friends and family.

The specific genres associated with written reflection take many forms, but in essence they provide a vehicle for a personal response to an experience. This response may be structured or prompted in some way, either through the genre itself, such as an 'activity report', or through the application of a particular task within a more content-neutral genre, such as a letter home explaining what occurred on a given day in the program. It may also be completely unstructured, leaving the participant completely free to decide on both the form and the content.

One program undertaken in a large capital city offered a good example of a tightly structured vehicle designed to elicit a set of broad responses from participants. The school produced a series of booklets in which participants recorded their reactions and evaluations of experiences that had occurred throughout the program. The booklets were seen as a means by which participants could demonstrate concrete understanding of their experiences:

> *There's a lot of reflection and questions and evaluation of each experience that they do: when they go to the art gallery, when they go to the cathedral, when they go and visit, or have a talk, like a multicultural representative coming in. Rather than just sitting there and experiencing it and then walking away, they evaluate it. They don't have to actually answer questions, but they have to give their own opinion and have to think about and reflect on it. We need to have evidence of that understanding (Program Manager C).*

This approach exemplifies the philosophical position discussed earlier that without the focusing realisation of experience through the production of a reflective artefact, the experience might be lost.

Personal correspondence in the form of a letter, either hand-written or electronic, is in common use at all programs undertaken at remote sites isolated in some way from participants' homes. Only one of these programs permitted any form of immediate voice communication, via telephone. Most imposed 'splendid' isolation for which the only remedy was to write to those outside of the program 'bubble'.

For some participants, the letter offers a prosaic vehicle to capture the mundane, the everyday flow of the programs routines. Mostly unremarkable in terms of personal insight, these letters are seen by both writer and recipient as important records of the experience. Participants and parents reportedly saved these letters home for years afterwards:

> *The parents have this pile of letters at the end of the year where there is a chronology of their child's experiences (Campus Manager B).*

Other participants, by far the larger proportion according to program teachers, use the personal letter in a more intimate and sometimes cathartic manner:

> *Often participants will use letter writing for escaping frustrations in the house and they use their diaries for the same reason (Teacher A4).*

Letters of this type from participants tend to contain emotional outpourings of emotion generated by the challenges of the program itself or the tensions associated with living in close proximity to co-participants.

A remarkable and widespread phenomenon reported at all programs imposing 'communication isolation', where phone calls and other electronic forms of communication are not permitted, is what might be termed 'mail-lag'. This describes the time gap between the point at which the letter is written, and the point at which it is received by its intended recipient, and the participant's differential emotional states corresponding to these two points in time.

While something of a necessity for those programs founded in the pre-internet age, mail-lag reflects one by-product of participant isolation described in an earlier chapter. The participant may use the letter to share a problem and seek assistance from an outside party, but by the time the letter has been received, the root cause of the unhappiness has often been resolved or forgotten:

> *Often I get a call from a parent who has received a letter from so and so and they sound really upset. I don't know what it's about, so I say I will get back to them when I know more. By that time, they have received another letter saying everything is good (Teacher A4).*

Participants learn that due to mail-lag the letter home is not a source of immediate succour in a crisis. As a result, they must develop inner resilience to cope independently, or acquire emotional support through social connections in the immediate setting: both are intentional outcomes of experiential program design.

An interesting variant on the written letter is a deliberate form of contrived, predictive, self-evaluation that we might call the 'letter to self'. This form of reflection in use at two schools studied requires participants write a letter to their future selves, setting goals and anticipating what the experience might have been like. During the final reflection, participants open their own letter. It is a 'bookending' device that provides participants with an appreciation of their changed perspective – a 'before' and 'after' view of themselves.

One program that did not practice formal reflection did, however, require participants to produce written and visual records of learning at various points in the program. These written and visual records of the participant experience could also be interpreted as a form of self-guided reflection.

Of course, one of the obvious challenges associated with any genre of written reflection, especially when used to demonstrate evidence of understanding, is the extent to which participants have the requisite skills to reflect in writing. A recurring theme at all campuses employing written reflection was the perceived need to develop stronger written skills to permit a more sophisticated level of reflection.

Accordingly, one of the skills developed throughout each program requiring participants to produce written reflection is more effective written communication. In fact, many of the programs studied also acted as writers' workshops at times, particularly at the beginning of programs. Whether documenting their own experiences through a visual diary, or writing to parents about their experiences, a participant's ability to express ideas or communicate complex and novel concepts through the written word is a highly valued competency in 21st century education, but one which is perhaps given insufficient emphasis in mainstream schooling:

> *Understandably some of the participants have never written letters before they come here and they are used to electronic communication (which is not offered here). They are used to getting information across instantly. We try to teach them the skills of how to **show** not **tell** – that's a big thing in writing – to try and show in their writing (Program Manager A).*

Where participants are wrestling with novel experiences in unfamiliar settings, they sometimes lack the vocabulary to express their responses with any accuracy. The home school may also not understand the need for developing a richer lexicon or more robust approach to certain more personalised genres of writing, because the context and conduct of the experiential program is not clear, or not part of the home school world.

Written reflection in the form of a daily journal is an obligatory part of the daily routine in some programs. Even with prior preparation and an adequate vocabulary, some participants reportedly just dislike journal writing. One teacher commented on an apparent gender disparity in motivation to maintain a personal journal during a program:

We encourage them to keep a journal. Most participants hated it, but you would get some participants that would keep the most magnificent journals and they will have them in ten/twenty years from now to look back on them and you will have some that wished they had. It's very difficult to encourage, particularly fourteen year-old boys (Teacher F3).

For this age group, the appeal of writing for posterity is somewhat limited.

Spoken Reflection

Spoken reflection across the programs studied showed similar diversity, both in terms of mode and purpose. For some teachers, spoken reflection is used to open up participants to share their feelings and responses in a very conversational manner. It is a mode of reflection that is particularly well suited to cohorts of somewhat cynical participants, weary of formal reflective writing tasks aimed at manufacturing responses to unremarkable events.

One teacher, accustomed to dealing with negative participant attitudes to experiential activities and formal written reflections, noted that informal, spoken sharing after an activity, possibly in an unexpected setting, often produced surprising reactions:

In my experience of doing it, nearly every participant is quite negative beforehand: "What are we doing here, it's boring." And some are apprehensive. Then we go for a coffee afterwards and debrief. Without exception…they just love the experience so much and I think the reason that they love it is that it's experiential. There's no written work involved. There is no reflection involved, beyond the conversation. (Program Manager C).

This approach does not work for all schools and all students, but it does offer an insight into the need for flexibility and creativity in choosing the mode, genre, and even the setting for reflection that is worthy of the name.

Not all spoken reflection is conversationally informal. Other programs used more formalised modes of spoken reflection, such as extempore performances, lectures, even street theatre, as a vehicle for reflection on the nature and meaning of an experience. These structured spoken activities are aimed at asking the participant to arrange their thoughts in response to an experience and communicate those thoughts to an audience. The process of sharing these thoughts with an audience may be iterative to an extent; through sharing and audience feedback, the thinking underlying the spoken reflection is shaped and reshaped to more closely conform to the participant's understanding of their experience.

One program offered in an urban setting invited participants at the conclusion of the program to assist with induction for the incoming group. For these participants, formal reflection occurred through sharing their experiences of learning with new participants. This was treated as a component of a formal induction and orientation activity for the following year's cohort of participants. The orientation activity was designed and run by the participants:

> *At the end of last year, we had two kids from the cohort take out a group of the incoming kids on a personalized tour, so they had to base the tour around what they thought was interesting. They had to create a map, they had to create a brochure about where they were going and why they were going there and they had to run the tour (School Manager C).*

A striking feature of this example of reflection in action is the implied disparity between the values and expectations of teachers and participants:

> *It was fascinating the places that they thought were interesting or important. They kept us out for about two to three hours and showed me places in the city that I didn't know. They explain things in different ways. Like they showed us where a little playground was because this was a fun place to come, they took us someplace to eat where the guy would give you free drinks if you bought food. You had a real sense of identity and ownership (School Manager C).*

This was one of the more unusual and educationally interesting forms of spoken reflection observed in the study. In closing the loop between successive cohorts of participants, it provides for a form of 'cross-generational' transfer of experience and knowledge. It is worthy of focus here because it is evidence of a learner's reflection surprising teachers with unexpected insights.

Another unusual form of spoken reflection saw the participants of a remote experiential program construct a mock-up of the dormitory living environment as a part of the concluding reflection in action at the home school. This form of reflective 'installation' is aimed at both parents and participants. As participants share with their parents about the realities of dormitory life, they are building a bridge between their remote experience and home life. This assists in the reintegration of participants back into the normal routines of school and home. This practice also highlights the close participant connection with the physical living space, which was noted by nearly all participants in the study.

The artefacts produced through spoken reflection are typically more interactive, but also more volatile than written artefacts, unless recorded in some way. In practice, where formal reflection is used as an intentional device to assist in memorisation and realisation of learning, both written and spoken modes of reflection are typically employed in various combinations.

Reflection: Self-Evaluation, Self-Actualisation

What do teachers and participants expect from reflection? The employment of reflection as a vehicle for learning is widespread, suggesting that educators believe in its value as either an explicit or implicit mechanism for learning. The role of reflection in experiential learning is explored in more detail in the following section. However, a small selection of the more interesting observations relating to the practice of reflection are shared below. These anecdotes point to the individual power of reflection for some participants.

One widely prevalent view of reflection among experiential educators is its perceived power to facilitate the articulation of participants' reactions to novel experiences. One house supervisor at a remote residential program commented on the capacity many participants display for using reflection to self-evaluate:

I think that kids are really challenged about what's OK. and what's not with their behaviour. The kids have got a lot of stuff inside them already and through this experience they explore the way that they deal with other people. They are going to find out: "Hey, wow, I didn't realise that I could be this patient", or "I didn't realise that I had this much resilience", or "I didn't realise that I actually need help". We have some great success stories. And also in those hard times as well, kids are directly involved in learning what's OK and what's not in questioning their own behaviour and their own thinking (Program Manager F).

For some of these participants, experiencing this type of direct and personal feedback to develop a deeper level of self-awareness is almost without precedent.

Confronting experiences may have unexpected consequences for participants when they think about them afterwards. The following excerpts from an interview with an experiential program manager chart the journey of one participant who underwent something of a personal transformation after reflecting on her contact with homeless people during an activity undertaken in an urban setting:

She was so taken with the homeless situation; she was so shocked by it and had no understanding to begin with that she suddenly wanted to have an out-of-uniform day to raise money to give to the homeless. She helped in the soup kitchen with the homeless people, in her own time (Program Manager C).

In this case, after a disturbing initial contact, reflection in action then led into written reflection in the form of personal narrative:

She then actually started to write stories based on the homeless person's perspective.

This participant's journey from experience to discovery to reflection to action continued throughout the year, as she then took a step further with a series of spoken presentations to other learners:

She started at the beginning of the year with no knowledge, just thinking that this is really wrong, (growing) to the understanding she had at the end, where she could talk from that age group to the next group about statistics, about the research that she had done, about interviews that she had had with homeless organizations and homeless people.

At the conclusion of the program, the participant had developed a changed perspective on her world:

She grew as a person because of that project and she used that as a tool to explore her own relationship with the world around it and herself.

This illustration would not be complete without a final comment from the program manager on the status of this participant with respect to her more academically capable peers:

She was a 'special needs' kid as well. She wasn't a high achiever.

Reflection is potentially a powerful learning tool that works for learners of diverse ability.

In the earlier chapter on social interaction, the phenomenon of social 'levelling' was discussed. In experiential learning, the highly hierarchical pecking order of academic attainment among student cohorts in mainstream schools may also be levelled or overturned completely. Learners who struggle with the often narrow and content-focused demands of more conventional learning assessments conducted in classroom settings may find hidden or underdeveloped strengths in experiential settings.

This phenomenon is illustrated in another short anecdote from a program manager concerning a disengaged participant who experienced a dramatic improvement in attitude and attainment in an experiential setting:

A good example is a boy that we have just had recently, who had all sorts of learning attitudes, being disengaged from the program. He has just conducted an interview with the parents, who came in and did the interview with him, and he just got a glowing report. I mean what happened to him?

218

The mechanism of reflection illuminates some potential reasons for the change:

Somehow, at some point along the way, over the last few months he changed. Is it things that the teacher said? Or how they dealt with him? What he has actually understood for the first time in his life is the reward that he gets out of it is what he puts in (Program Manager C).

Across all of the programs studied, many of the teachers interviewed reflected on the nature of the change in some participants and the reasons behind it. While speculative ideas were in abundant supply, the most common and perhaps insightful response was the *power of the experience.*

Institutional Learning and Reflection

This chapter on reflection has largely focused on the implementation of reflective practices among learners. What of practitioners and institutions? Do they reflect and learn from experience in the same way expected of participants? While not a strong focus in the studies undertaken in researching this book, the extent to which schools successfully integrate their experiential and mainstream programs to harness and mutually reinforce the benefits flowing from these modes of learning might be one measure of the degree of institutional learning that has taken place. For a range of reasons, the evidence of institutional learning to connect experiential and mainstream learning programs is disappointingly slim.

Among experiential educators, there were different views on what happens to the participants after the conclusion of the experiential program. For some teachers, this was the greatest area in need of attention from a whole school perspective:

There's not much of a follow up afterwards. It does bother me a bit. You are all of a sudden removed from all normal school structure and home life to a different situation, and then go back to a more strict academic type program again (Teacher 3).

Most of the teachers interviewed reported some degree of post-program correspondence with at least some of their former students. The post-program experiences of many participants point to the powerful transformational impact of the program and the possible failure of the home school to recognise and adjust to the prior learning of their students:

Their values have changed. They are frustrated that they can't build the same relationship with the teachers (at the home school) that they did here and they all of a sudden have to wear a school uniform and comply to rules and expectations that they see as superficial and not important anymore (Teacher F4).

The frequency of reporting of post-program frustration among participants by teachers was high.

Participants are subjected to two sharp discontinuities in their learning: one transitioning into the experiential setting and the second transitioning back to 'real life' in school. It is a disorientating experience that has some parallels with *The Wizard of Oz* or perhaps *Pygmalion*: learners find it difficult to adjust to the realities of the new setting and then find the return to their former lives just as challenging. Most lacking is the learner sense of continuity of experience. They have changed, but the world to which they return has not.

One campus manager took another view on the contrasting behaviours and attitudes of participants, during and after the experiential program. She speculated that the participants were somewhat at fault:

> *They played lip service to the values and ideas of the program in order to make it through, but they quickly dropped all of that when they got back to the main school (Campus Manager F).*

This view does tend to support the notion of learner adaptation to a new setting and set of learning challenges, followed by reversion to an earlier and successful approach, when the original setting is restored.

Consolidating the experiential gains and growth, therefore, does depend to an extent on the degree to which mainstream learning programs and institutions can adapt to the transformed learners they welcome back.

In fairness to larger institutions offering experiential programs at remote sites with limited accommodation capacity, practical, and particularly financial, considerations often dictated the implementation of the program by way of a rotation of classes through the campus site during an academic year. This organisational structure meant that different classes would participate in the experiential program at different times of the school year.

The integration of mixed groups of participants, some of whom had not undertaken the experiential program, worked against the effective integration of participant groups back into the parent school and created difficulties for those wanting to exploit the skills and experience of the experiential program in the classroom:

> *Just the organization of experiential learning at the remote site, you had to have one class away at any given time. So you had kids coming back into class and*

you had a whole lot of other kids who hadn't had the experience. So they were on a completely different level. So it was very difficult to integrate them back properly and smoothly into the program (Campus Manager F)

For institutions and learners alike, experiential learning programs are innovative, intense, rewarding, but also disruptive events, both administratively and educationally. Deep and sustained reflection by teachers and leaders is an essential part of a school's institutional responsibility in planning, implementing, and reviewing experiential programs. Harnessing the accrued benefits of an experiential program to ensure experiential continuity in the Deweyan sense stands as a major challenge, somewhat unmet, by many of the schools examined in this study.

Analysis of Modes of Reflection

The two different major approaches to reflection encountered during the study are emergent-implicit and guided-explicit. The former is participant-centred, implicit reflection-in-action in which the learner engages in the process in a highly individualised manner, allowing the experience to speak for itself. The latter is teacher-centred and structured as a discrete post-activity cognitive process in its own right. The teacher-centred approach reflects the Vygotskian notion of the mature outer social state conquering the immature inner dialogue of youth (Vygotsky, 1986 [1934]). The participant-centred approach reflects a more Piagetian pattern of inner cognition constructing an assimilation of the novel experience over time (Bruner, 1997; Piaget, 1952).

The conduct and content of reflection is heavily influenced by the purpose of the reflective activity and its intended audience, if any. A reflection undertaken in private for the benefit of the participant alone will be quite different to a reflection that is intended to be shared with a large audience. The form or genre of reflection is also important, because it does suggest those aspects of an experience to which a learner may need to pay greater attention, possibly at the expense of others. Personal narratives and field reports tend to focus on different things.

The following table contains a list of the more common forms or genres of reflection observed during the study. The column marked 'orientation/ audience' lists the orientation of the learner when undertaking reflection. For those forms of reflection identified as 'private', the product of reflection is not intended for sharing with others. For the 'public' forms of reflection, the influence of the intended audience on the learner during the reflection is an important consideration.

Reflection genre	Purpose	Orientation/Audience
'pre-flection' Letter	Anticipatory reflection on likely nature and impact of the experience	Private
Journal	Daily recording personal milestones and dormitory experiences	Private (unchecked) or public (monitored by teacher)
Visual diary	Stress management: associated with visual arts program and academic assessment	Public: Visual Arts teacher and dormitory head
Spiritual reflection	Verbal reflection on experience	Public: peers/teachers
Extempore performance	Impromptu role play or performance to express or explore elements of the experience or activity	Public: teachers, peers, public
Student Meeting	Spoken reflection on recent events	Public: peers and leading teacher
Scrapbook	Record of personal journey and images of experiences	Public: pastoral care teacher
Webpage website	Visual and written record of experiences uploaded to a public website	Public: peers, parents, teachers, public
Interviews	Formal account of progress in program for student assessment	Public: Head of Program or Campus and parents
Feedback sheets	Structured written reflection on activities and teacher performance for staff and student assessment	Public: activity teacher and campus management
Lecture	Formal spoken address given by a student to an audience	Public: teachers, peers, parents
Activity Report	Formal written report of student learning on a specific activity	Public: teachers and parents
Formative Self Appraisal	Assessment of personal performance in program activities and projects	Public: teachers
Installation	Physical recreation of an aspect of the program setting in the home school setting to share experience with parents and peers	Public: parents, friends, teachers
Solo meditation	Extended reflection of whole experience in isolation from other participants	Private
Summary Self Appraisal	Formal report of learning on program for assessment	Public: teachers and parents

Table 2: *Formal Modes of Reflection*

A first glance, there appears to be a stark polarisation in the study on reflection. For some, an experience either only teaches for the *second* it lasts, therefore requiring immediate structured and socially mediated reflection to provide a form of cognitive scaffolding. For others, reflection is most *lasting* when it occurs implicitly, long after the experience is over. This dichotomy is further refined in the two value statements about reflection: either *integrity* is lost, if reflection is *guided*; or learners cannot *make meaning* unless they are guided.

The following three figures (figures 19, 20, and 21) illustrate three different ways of practicing reflection observed in programs of experiential learning.

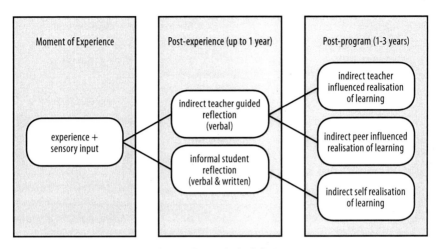

Figure 19: *Emergent-Implicit Reflection*

The structure depicted in Figure 19 shows reflection occurring in an unguided and informal way in the months and years following the experience. It is a learner-centred, *indirect* reflective process in that the purpose of the reflection is an inner assimilation or accommodation of a specific novel experience, activity, or problem. Experiences are allowed to build up, layer upon layer, without any overarching reflective structure to articulate the links between the experiences and the broader context of the learner's journey. There is an individualised randomness to this structure that allows learners to reflect in a highly subjective, yet personal, way on the experiences they believe to be relevant and at an appropriate time. The learner experiences a form of *reflection-in-action* and draws the explicit connections at a later date, exploring the impact of these highly personal experiences free of any school orchestrated structure or agenda (Estes, 2004; Schön, 1983). This structure does allow others to influence reflection implicitly, through social interaction that does not have as its primary purpose the processing of a particular event or experience.

The emergent-implicit approach reflects an institutional and professional confidence that reflection occurs, with or without intervention, as it is a function of the cognition of the individual, not the group. The subjective reflection thus generated is believed to speak clearly enough to achieve the intended learning outcomes of the experience. There is a strong underlying belief implicit in this approach that the individual's experience of the setting, social interaction and problem solving results in learning that achieves the intended range of outcomes, but not in any easily foreseeable time frame.

The indirect approach does reflect a philosophical commitment to the individuality of each learner's experience. At a cognitive level, each learner constructs a unique analogue or model of the experience, regardless of the programmed structuring of the experience through post-activity reflection. There is an assumption implicit in this approach, therefore, that accepts the fact that each learner's memory of an experience will reflect a wide range of random and unique elements. Allowing the reflection to occur over an extended period of time, and in an unstructured way, demonstrates an institutional conviction or faith that reflection will happen, with or without facilitation, and that it will be right for the individual learner. The reflective 'pathway' is unique for each learner.

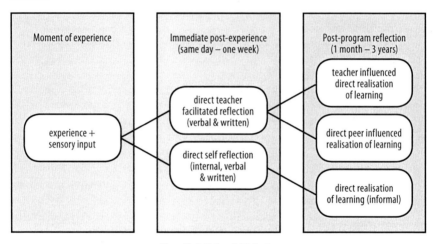

Figure 20: *Guided-explicit Reflection*

The approach to reflection depicted in Figure 20 is direct, teacher-guided and explicit. This approach is based on the belief that an experience has a highly transitory impact on the learner and that the experiential stimulation must be woven into a socially mediated and interconnected network of formalised thoughts, impressions, and ideas as quickly as possible. Social interaction is seen as critically important to the process of knowledge creation post-experience (Wells, 1999).

The reflective process is one of creating a personal narrative through interaction, retelling the story from an individual perspective, one that is coloured by the subjective impressions left behind by the experience. The personal narrative thus created becomes the memory thread that connects the different experiences for the individual and aids in later recall. Teachers and peers both contribute to the intra-mental processing of the experience in an explicit way. Direct reflection has a chronological structure that is generated by a facilitating teacher, where events are recalled soon after occurring, typically on the same day. The outermost structure is therefore similar for all learners, but their own construction of the detail of the narrative is subjective.

The guided-explicit model of reflection is potentially problematic, due to the possibility that guided aspect of the reflective process itself might shape, taint or contaminate the learners' memories of the experience (Estes, 2004). Guided reflection may influence reported memories in situations where learner experiences are subjectively assigned value and meaning by another agency (teacher) or summarised to suit an audience (teacher or parent). A complex range of emotions and memories collected during an experience may be expressed as indifference or negativity, depending on subjective learner perceptions of the intended audience. Where a complex experience informs a purpose-driven reflective process, there is a risk of trivialising the experience through excessive distillation: learners are somewhat at risk of turning months of experience into a sentence to meet an expectation of process-driven reporting.

The recording and encoding of experiences as memories emerge as critical factors in how the memory of the experience is processed, stored, or even *coloured* for future recall and reflection. There is an implicit contradiction in the different ways in which reflection is practiced. On the one hand, *the experience* only teaches for the *second* it lasts; it is cognitively perishable, requiring some form of teacher scaffolding or intervention to assist the learner to capture and structure the experience into a meaningful narrative. On the other hand, the experience teaches for *years,* and the learner is left to await a suitable moment after the experience to engage in reflection-in-action, where what has been learned emerges in the form of action (Schön, 1983, pp. 54-55), or a more discrete and considered form of cognitive processing, independent of teacher scaffolding.

One of the central influences on the practice and outcomes of reflection is learner retention and recall of the experience. The narrative developed through facilitation is likely to be different to the narrative developed by a learner in isolation, some months or years after the experience. While both may be cognitively rich with connections to the experience, the aim of immediate processing through facilitation is to capture the stimulation of the experience itself and channel this into enduring memories. By contrast, allowing the experience to lie fallow for a period of time suggests that only the most enduring residual stimulation remains for the individual learner to shape the narrative created through reflection.

In the latter case, the process of *reflection-in-action* becomes *knowing-in-action* and the passage of time potentially acts as a filter in which only those enduring memories that are significant to the individual, proven by testing in action, remain to create the long-term story of the experience (Argyris & Schön, 1974; Schön, 1983). These memories are more enduring because they have already withstood a preliminary test of time, reinforced through application in action.

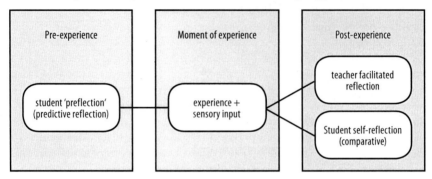

Figure 21: *Predictive Reflection*

A minor variation on the guided-explicit reflection approach is one where it is assumed that reflection will be informed by the sum of all previous experiences to a greater or lesser extent. In anticipation of later reflection, a predictive reflection (or *preflection*) is intended to create anticipation of future experience in the learner (Figure 21). This is intended to foreshadow the coming learning experience and the formal reflective process to follow. The purpose of *preflection* is to assist in creating an awareness of learning opportunities in the learner and to perhaps prepare the learner for the anticipated cognitive dissonance associated with the experience. This practice is an explicit manifestation of the Deweyan notion that educational experience is informed by past experience and, in turn, informs, shapes, and directs future experience (Dewey, 1997 [1938]). In a chronological sense, this model of predictive reflection and post-activity reflection forms a kind of metacognitive primer, or a *bookend*, to scaffold to the experience.

In practice, reflection, both explicit and implicit, is the mechanism by which an experience is turned into meaning, where sensory stimuli become knowledge. Reflection itself facilitates the process of learning from experience and is undertaken in both written and oral modes and by means of many different genres. Learning can also take place at many different chronological points along the timeline, from the initial occurrence of the experience through to the considered reflection years later. Reflection provides evidence of experience becoming learning, but there is no immediate, visible *causal* link between the experience and the reflection that facilitates the learning. However, learners do experience both immediate learning (in action) and delayed learning or insight, realised at a much later date.

The phenomenon of deferred *realisation* of learning, which is the manifestation of experientially acquired skills and knowledge at a much later date, sometimes years later, reflects the notion that learners *know more than they can say* (Schön, 1983, p. 51). The mechanism or trigger by which learners become aware of learning or through which learning is realised is reflection leading to action or reflection in action (Schön, 1983). This highlights the importance of the act of reflection when transforming an experience into knowledge, skills, or attitudes. Through reflection, these experiences may continue to 'teach' for years beyond their initial impact, regardless of the specific mode of reflection (Dewey, 1997 [1938]).

The foregoing shows that there are two fundamentally different approaches to the *management* of the relationship between experience and learning as facilitated through the mechanism of reflection. One view is that the learning must take place immediately, as without the scaffold of reflection, the experience may be lost through forgetfulness. The other perspective is that the experience is about doing and that reflection follows at a later time and is largely tacit. Both approaches report that learning follows reflection, whether immediate or delayed, explicit or tacit, thereby supporting the notion that reflection is critically important in the learning process, no matter the duration of the delay between the experience itself and the realisation of learning.

The two different approaches to reflection – immediate guided-explicit and deferred emergent-implicit – are therefore reconciled through what the experience eventually becomes: action. The *directed, explicit* interpretation of experience and the participant-centred implicit reflection on experience both translate into learner action. Whether teacher directed or self-directed, the shape of the experience afterwards, and the ultimate structure and detail of the individual stories recorded as memories, are profoundly affected by the reflective process, as are the resultant actions that reflect changed behaviour and new knowledge.

Chapter Summary: Reflection on Reflection

The enduring impact of experiential learning is built upon the construction of a cognitive connection between experience, reflection, and episodic memory. The extent to which an experience might result in enduring learning depends on meaning constructed by the learner after the event. By reconstructing, reorganising, and transforming the experience, reflection plays an essential role as the mechanism for the making of meaning from it, enabling it to influence behaviour and future experience.

There is a sharp dichotomy, however, in the practice of reflection in experiential learning programs, between teacher-facilitated reflection immediately after the experience, and participant initiated self-reflection taking place at some later point. Reflection is critically important to the learning process, but there is no consensus among practitioners on the extent to which a third-party must be involved in the reflective process. Experiential educators tend to plan around a timeframe of years for experiential learning to be processed and realised in more concrete outcomes, albeit through different mechanisms and practices. Action through making meaning and changed behaviour is the universally expected outcome.

Reflection is practised in both written and spoken modes and in many different genres, all of which provide the structures in which language is used to reconstruct the experience. In reflection, as Halliday suggests, language, as the essential condition of knowing, provides the means by which experience becomes knowledge (1993, p. 94). Language acts as the carrier, the vessel in which experience is transported from a collection of sensory stimulation to a rich, interconnected set of impressions, feelings, and ideas that become associated with the original experience. As such, the way in which language as a social artefact is used, both formally and informally, through peer-to-peer and teacher to peer interaction after the experience, is of pivotal importance in shaping the process by which the experience is translated into meaning for the participant.

In summary, participants make sense of their experiences through reflection: *reflection is learning*. Reflection itself may be either self-guided or teacher facilitated, and is effected through oral or written genres, both formal and informal. Participants, whether under guidance or independent of adult intervention, recall events from memory during the reflective process and subsequently construct narratives linked to these memories. Reflection therefore acts as the mechanism by which experience is reconstructed or reorganised and converted into action.

Key Questions

1. What role does reflection play in learning?
2. What form does reflection take?

3. Is reflection a private or public process?
4. What level of importance is placed on learner agency in reflection?
5. What is the role of the teacher in the reflective process?
6. Should time for reflection be scheduled?
7. What is the ideal time frame in which reflection should take place?
8. What are the products of reflection?
9. With whom should the products reflection (if any) be shared?
10. How is reflection linked with future learning?

Part III: Experiential Learning and its Educational Implications

Chapter 12: Education and Experience

We have now considered in a little more detail what the essential elements of experiential learning look like from the perspective of practitioners – teachers and program managers – all of whom express passionate advocacy for this mode of learning. For readers with an interest in establishing or enhancing a formal program of experiential learning in a dedicated or remote setting, there may be some ideas of practical value in the preceding chapters. For those readers who lack the resources or opportunity to offer experiential learning programs of this scale and complexity in a school, the reaction may be the polite equivalent of "So what?" The optimist in me would encourage the addition of just one more word: "So what now?"

The notion that we learn deeply and memorably from experience and reflection is the central idea explored in this book. Its absence as a widespread and explicit practice in most formal programs of education is something the book seeks to address. Adopting or adapting elements of this approach to learning in any context may have a lasting and positive impact on the experience of learners anywhere and everywhere. While there are risks, the ways in which we learn from and remember personal experiences are too powerful to be neglected.

At this point, it is perhaps worth revisiting some of the theoretical concepts associated with learning in general and from this perspective, examine the possibilities for changing the way we see some of the fundamental aspects of learning in any context. Our schools are uniquely designed and situated (setting), fundamentally and intensively social, contrarily risk-driven and risk-averse, and are often inconsistently reflective in practice. To be sure, these are key findings from the research undertaken, but they are also essential characteristics of human learning.

Settings, Social Groupings, and Skills

Based on the discussions in the first two sections of this book, it is suggested here that it is possible to create new patterns of social interaction or reshape existing ones through the thoughtful design of setting, interaction, task allocation, risk management, and reflection. With the possible exception of home schooling, we do isolate our learners each day from their parents in schools and so create a small window of social separation from the influences of home for a short while. There are challenges inherent in coping with the settings of formal learning anywhere, whether urban or remote. Learning tasks and routines with a strong collective, collaborative focus may act to shape groups structures and impact on the construction of meaning. Individuals cannot *know* or *be* in isolation (Leontiev, 1981; Vygotsky & Luria, 1993 [1930]); they form their identities and construct their understanding of the world within a social context, relative to the understandings of other members of a social group. What an individual knows or does is fundamentally dependent on the particular social dynamic, the flow of interaction, between members of the group. One of the factors shaping this macro-level, social dynamic is setting.

The specific social pressures and circumstances associated with a particular setting have a clear impact on the formation of social structures and individual social identity within that setting. Extending the notion of settings and artefacts affording or inviting certain kinds of action, pre-existing peer groups formed under the influence of the prevailing physical, social, and cultural setting of the home school are modified under the circumstances present in a different setting. The interplay between the setting and the individual in the experiential program affords the possibility of displaying or deploying a different set of skills and knowledge, which in turn unsettles the social order.

Individuals occupy positions of higher or lower peer group status relative to other members of a group, on the basis of contextual need or merit, within a pre-existing social context, such as the school setting. When this setting is changed, the social dynamic is disturbed, and different implicit forces emerge to influence and perhaps alter the social standing of individuals within the overall structure of the group. Participants of social standing in one context do not automatically enjoy a similar status in a different setting. Each participant goes through a process of social reinvention that is often marked initially by the phenomenon of *levelling*, in which there is a dismantling of pre-existing social structures followed by a re-ordering of social status. The impetus for this social dynamic is generated by the properties of the specific setting and the associated challenges, needs and circumstances arising in the setting.

The relative social standing of any individual is determined by the capacity of that individual to contribute to the needs of the collective whole, but in a way that is informed by the setting in which the group and individual needs are framed and generated. It is the community in a specific setting, and with specific group and individual needs arising from conditions prevailing in that setting, that *affords* the learner the opportunity to deploy or display individual attributes to benefit the whole (E. J. Gibson & Pick, 2003; Greeno, 1994). If the needs of a social group, say a class, are changed by design, a new force has been introduced into the social dynamic. With thoughtful intention, this can be used to sculpt social structures in ways that may allow hidden or underutilised skills in the group to emerge.

This constructed or facilitated social interaction also illustrates the Vygotskian notion of external social forces overcoming the internal, egocentric voice (Vygotsky, 1978). Social forces lead to the re-evaluation of the social status of some individuals, with some of high status in the home school setting finding themselves placed in a lower position and *vice versa*. The needs of the group and the affordances of the setting (J. J. Gibson, 1986) are the driving forces behind this peer group re-evaluation and reconfiguration. Ultimately, these novel social forces act in a Vygotskian manner, that is, with the external forces overcoming individual egocentricity to challenge and change the social masks that learners have previously developed to cope with the prevailing social order in the home or school setting.

In light of this reconsideration of the role of social interaction within the experiential learning transaction model, Figure 22 shows the relationship of learners interacting with each other and the learning problem, all within the learning setting. In line with the revised theoretical model, the new knowledge and modified behaviours are depicted as attributes of the group, rather than the individual.

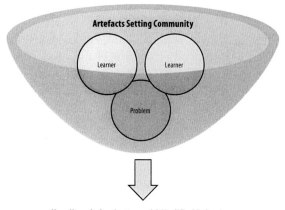

New Knowledge (autonoetic) Modified Behaviour

Figure 22: *Socially Mediated Learning Within An Experiential Setting*

A way of illustrating the hierarchy of relationships between the components of the modified experiential learning model is depicted in Figure 23. This figure takes a learner-centric view of constructed social interaction within an experiential learning setting. The learners interact with each other, 'nested' within the setting, and the problem is activated or manifested through interaction between the learners and the setting.

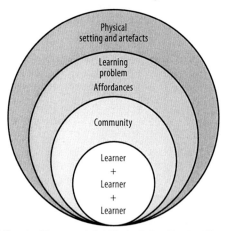

Figure 23: *Hierarchy of Components in Social/Setting Mediated Experiential Learning Model*

As each setting affords specific and potentially unique learning opportunities, one implication for the comprehensive development of individual learners as social beings is the need to consider the desirability of learner exposure to multiple settings. In mainstream schools, participant contribution, merit, and achievement reflect a particular set of explicit and implicit values that shape peer social structures and determine the nature of success. This system reflects the needs and functions of the community, institutional and individual, and develops within a specific educational and social setting, a setting that affords the potential for certain types of learning to take place.

If learner peer group structures, individual social status and role, and even academic success, are dependent at least in part on the particular challenges and social needs afforded by a specific setting, then exposure to multiple settings would allow the development and deployment of different social roles, personas, and abilities. A range of different settings and challenges may be needed to allow the development of different skills in individual participants, something that may not be possible in an educational 'mono-setting'.

A further implication of this is the need to examine the type of problems and problem solving skills that are favoured by each choice of setting and what is perhaps neglected or underemphasised as a result.

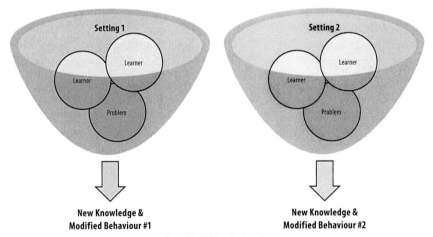

Figure 24: Multi-setting Learning

Ideally, education designed around the concept of a 'multi-setting' approach, illustrated in Figure 24 could create the potential for learners to experience multiple peer group structures, encouraging individuals to explore different social roles and personas within those settings. This could afford opportunities for learners to deploy and develop different skills and create different knowledge through the experience of a multiplicity of settings and challenges.

235

In summary, the setting for learning exerts a strong influence over a learner peer group, shaping social interaction and individual group status. The interaction between the setting and learner(s) affords the deployment of different types of skill or patterns of behaviour, both of which are a shared property of both the setting and the learner. The comprehensive development of the individual as a social being may rely on exposure to multiple settings with different affordances and challenges. Social status and role, along with academic success, are dependent on the properties afforded by learning settings, the implication of which is that the development and deployment of different social roles, personas, and abilities in all learners may depend on exposure to and immersion in a range of different settings and challenges: educational *multi-setting*.

Optimising Risk in Learning: Pain and Gain

How well do we understand the role of risk in formal education beyond the obvious dangers posed by the metaphorical and actual canyons and crevasses of learning in the wilderness? For many learners in the 21st century, the risks associated with failure to 'succeed' in competitive, examination-centric systems pit student against student and school against school for the purposes of rare asset allocation (selective school and college entry, government funding, league table rankings, etc.). Increasingly, we are seeking to pit teacher against teacher to allocate financial rewards based on student testing performance. Competition is seen as universally virtuous. There are also many risks deeply embedded in these competitive dichotomies.

Award driven competition rewards certain behaviours and punishes others. A hidden risk in the 'virtuous competition' model is that we may not necessarily understand completely what we are losing; virtues also have attendant vices. Teaching, for example, is widely understood as an inherently social and collaborative process. To reward highly individualistic competitive behaviour that limits collaboration on the basis of rational self-interest is self-defeating. Similarly, rewarding individual student performance can also be counter-productive when preparing for a life in highly collaborative, team centred professions. We need to consider risk and its management from a great many perspectives.

In fact, taking another look at what we might consider to be 'virtues' from an educational perspective, none are unipolar; all exist in dichotomous pairs. Where we emphasize one attribute, there is a concomitant de-emphasis of something else. If we extol competition, we suppress collaboration; if we advocate for absolute safety, we reduce hazard recognition and risk management skills; if we privilege content mastery, we impoverish imagination and creativity.

The presence of risk as an indispensable element of the experiential learning transaction lies in the inherent uncertainty over the learner's reaction to novelty and any outcomes arising from any cognitive dissonance thus generated. For the learner, what is unknown, or has not yet been experienced, forms the cognitive dissonance – the knowledge gap – that is the genesis of the learning process (Piaget, 1952). Logically, there is an unavoidable element of risk or uncertainty associated with learning that is beyond the demonstrated level of experience of a learner. The potential for error and hence risk, therefore, cannot be eliminated in experiential, or, in fact, any form of learning.

The types of risk to which learners are exposed in experiential learning programs reflect the affordances of the setting and the ways in which experiential learning problems are constructed and posed to the learner. The imposition of institutional limits on the degree of risk permissible in a learning problem is an observable phenomenon in all schools examined during the study, pointing to a potential conflict between the educational limit of learning risk and the institutional limit of learning risk. The theoretical role of risk, however, and particularly its relationship, if any, to other theories of learning and development, such as Vygotsky's zone of proximal development (Vygotsky, 1978), is not clear in the relevant theoretical writings.

At the level of the learner, the way in which risk is understood and managed should be a core concern of teachers in all educational settings. The unavoidable uncertainty of outcome in a novel or untried situation dictates that more attention should be paid to managing unexpected or incorrect outcomes. The learner's detection or awareness of their own mistakes, and the subsequent handling and recovery from those mistakes, give rise to questions that are powerful in guiding learning (Scardamalia & Bereiter, 1992). The learning strategies used to detect and resolve mistakes with maximal independence are not typically found in approaches to learning that seek to minimise or eliminate errors. In fact, where errors are reduced, there is a reduced potential for learning (Seiffert & Hutchins, 1992). In one sense, by increasing the 'margin for error', the potential for learning increases. In settings that are authentic and unpredictable, the existence of uncertainty itself introduces a heightened element of risk to experiential learning that is largely absent in the mainstream learning environment that is seen as more controlled and synthetic (Hoberman & Mailick, 1994).

The experiential learning programs studied are structured to varying degrees around the principle that learners should be given problems or tasks to complete with limited outside intervention in order to maximise opportunities for learner problem solving. As discussed above, the nature of the learning problem or task is facilitated by both the setting, and the structure of the social interaction within the setting. These problems arise out of the interaction or relationship between the learner and setting and are the core of the experiential curriculum (Scardamalia & Bereiter, 1994).

As the learner encounters novel situations, their learning moves incrementally, from areas of competence and certainty, into a zone that is beyond their existing set of skills, knowledge, and attitudes (Vygotsky, 1978). In typical experiential learning settings, these novel situations tend to reflect a more uncontrolled and unpredictable *reality* that is in contrast to the more ordered and controllable environment of the classroom. Both learners and teachers may be unaccustomed to a realistic learning setting in which the answer to a given problem may not be known.

One of the unpredictable elements that gives rise to risk is that the reaction of the learner to a novel situation is essentially unknowable prior to the experience. An authentic setting may also present problems that lie outside of the immediate experience of the supervising teacher. Even when teachers do have a solution, the culture prevailing at all experiential learning programs participating in the study is that teachers don't solve learner problems, or at least not immediately.

Risk is an inherent property of all learning. In experiential learning, risk lies at the centre of the interaction between setting, learner and problem. Where setting, learner, and problem interact, there is an element of uncertainty and hence risk.

In considering risk globally, the problems or questions we set for learners to answer are of particular interest, as they determine to an extent the nature and extent of the risk posed. Understanding how to frame and enact learning problems in experiential learning contexts is certainly of critical importance when managing learner risk, particularly in challenging or unfamiliar settings. From the research undertaken, the properties of the experiential learning problems observed are reflected in the following eight basic characteristics, each of which carries an attendant risk or uncertainty:

a. Experiential learning problems are *authentic;* authenticity is a quality derived from real world, uncontrolled settings; authenticity implies a degree of unpredictability that is beyond the control of the learner and teacher;

b. Learning problems are *challenging* in a way that goes beyond the learner's current experiential competency into their ZPD; risk derives from the unpredictability of outcome when meeting a new challenge and uncertainty over the teacher intervention point;

c. Learning problems or tasks are learner-centric and as such are identified or *defined* by the learner and require only minimal if any outside definition to be understood; learner inexperience may result in an ill-defined or misidentified learning problem;

d. Learning problems require learner participation or *intervention* (e.g., directions, actions, finding food, shelter, information), so there is little room for a learner to opt-out under normal circumstances; learner action to meet the perceived need is based on trial and error and may result in mistakes;

e. Learning problems are closely connected to a learner's *basic needs* and interests, they are non-trivial or contrived, so that learner motivation to engage in the problem or task is high; if basic needs are not met, however, teachers may need a set of remedial strategies or interventions;

f. Learning problems require learner *organisation* and planned *resource allocation* to be handled properly, thereby posing social risks and mistakes associated with the misallocation of resources to handle a problem;

g. Learning problems require some form of *negotiation* and *social interaction* with other learners for resolution – also a social risk; and

h. Learning problems, if unresolved, or mistakes if they are made, involve *real consequences*, that impact on the learner personally, thereby posing a range of risks from social, through physical, to cultural consequences.

These eight properties of experiential learning problems reflect the essential elements of experiential learning: the setting and its affordances determine the nature of the problem handled; learners are placed in a challenging, yet managed environment where assistance or support is tightly controlled; peer social interaction is designed to be unavoidable through imposed immersion in isolated or socially insular settings; and risk is an ever-present factor, arising from the realism of the setting, the unpredictability of learner action and reaction, and the potential for consequences arising from mistakes.

From a learner perspective, these problems should be framed in such a way as to stimulate curiosity, interest, or awareness of need. The framing of learning questions in contexts beyond remote experiential learning programs is an area of potential inquiry for mainstream educators. It begs the question: *do educators spend sufficient time and effort in posing provocative, interesting, inspiring, challenging, and purposeful questions to generate learning responses from their students?*

In response, we should understand that we learn best when we are *seeking answers to our own questions*. Learning problems are most effective when they are highly personalised.

Risk is inseparably linked to novel experience and the degree of risk is directly proportional to the level of challenge or difficulty in a learning activity. As learners move beyond their level of competence, they enter a mode of experiential learning where some assistance or scaffolding is needed to complete a learning activity (Vygotsky, 1978): the higher the degree of challenge, the greater the risk to the learner. Therefore, *the extent to which risk is tolerated* within a program or learning transaction is a measure of the *operationalisation* of the Zone of Proximal Development within the program.

The ZPD is interpreted in theoretical models of learning in at least two different ways. One interpretation asserts that the ZPD is a *state*, rather than a *zone*, where there is no explicit differentiation between types of learning activity or levels of learner competence: a learner is either learning in the zone or not (Chaiklin, 2003). Another way of viewing the ZPD is that it has the properties of a virtual zone rather than a pure state and as such it possesses boundaries and therefore allows for the possibility of differentiation within the zone boundaries. This implies that there is an implied property of the ZPD that allows for some variation in both the extent and type of adult or competent support provided, and the degree of achievement a learner might attain with that support.

The extent to which a learner is operating within ZPD therefore be might be qualified, depending on the specific circumstances of the learning task. Learners might be operating on the 'fringe' of ZPD, receiving minimal support, or may be at the very limit of their capacity to undertake a task with maximum assistance.

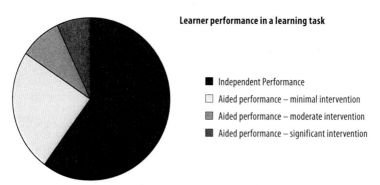

Learner performance in a learning task

- ■ Independent Performance
- ☐ Aided performance – minimal intervention
- ▦ Aided performance – moderate intervention
- ■ Aided performance – significant intervention

Figure 25: *ZPD as Variable Zone: Learner Performance in a Learning Task*

240

Figure 25 shows learner performance in a complex task that requires different levels of scaffolding intervention by a competent adult or peer. The black zone reflects what the learner is able to undertake without support. The areas depicted by the three shades of grey reflect task performance with increasing levels of assistance or intervention.

Whether the ZPD is seen as a *state* or *zone*, there is a strong element of institutional volition exercised in the provision or denial of scaffolding support (state) or the progressive introduction of scaffolding depending on the subjective difficulty of the task with respect to the learner (zone). In either case, it is the institution and ultimately the teacher who must manage the exposure of the learner to a learning problem beyond demonstrated competence and the provision of scaffolding (if any).

In experiential learning, the learner is exposed to problems that reflect authentic difficulties and risks. The existence of risk in these experiential learning tasks provides a form of *real world* practicum. These real world risks, however, are managed by experienced educators, who are expected to use their judgement to manage and control risk to ensure optimised conditions for learning without undue risk (Schön, 1987). For the participant learning experientially, therefore, there is a boundary between learning related risk and individual safety that must be managed.

Institutional tolerance of risk, or institutional risk 'appetite', in experiential learning reflects the extent to which the learner is permitted to work beyond a notional degree of competency in a given learning problem, and the degree and scope of competent intervention that is available to aid learners working beyond their competency. Through observation of risk tolerance in a school, it may be possible to examine the institutional culture that determines or influences how far participants are permitted to operate beyond their actual level of competence, and how much scaffolding is likely to be given in situations before a teacher intervenes or terminates the learning activity.

The professional intervention point, whether institutionally or individually determined, does not necessarily align with the notion of the ZPD as a purely individual phenomenon that identifies the gap at a learner's level between independent task competence and aided or facilitated task competence. Individuals will of course have different learning needs and differing levels of competency, hence the property of any individual child's ZPD is subject to many influences and factors. The way in which a school, program, or teacher works with a learner to provide some form of support, guidance, or scaffolding is subject to institutional policies, practices, and to the teacher's personal experience.

At what point does intervention take the locus of control over a learning experience away from the learner and for what reason? This reflects an aspect of *tolerance* of risk related to learning challenge that influences the *size* of the ZPD (Chaiklin, 2003), which has been sketched out in the study data, but not fully mapped from an individual-institutional perspective.

The ZPD relates to the type and detail of supporting instructions given, the provision of a more competent peer or adult, or the provision of other forms of scaffolding. These forms of intervention become operational at the point beyond which a learner is not able to work independently on a problem. In theory, the point at which a learner is no longer able to access or benefit from scaffolding or collaboration to undertake a task is the theoretical outer limit of that individual's ZPD as determined by the learner. In reality, it is the institution, through its policies and practices, which typically determines the limit at which there is intervention or a task is further modified or concluded.

Figure 26 provides an illustration of the difference between the risk tolerance of a hypothetical school and the ZPD limit of a notional learner. The 'x' axis (tasks 1-5) reflects a progression of increasing levels of difficulty for the learner across a series of tasks, with an increasing likelihood of unpredictable and erroneous outcomes, including risk to the learner of an emotional, cultural, or physical nature. The 'y' axis reflects the percentage of task completion. These are set at arbitrary levels for the purposes of illustration only.

The lowest of the three zones depicted in Figure 26 reflects the capacity of the learner to undertake elements of a task independently. The middle zone reflects the risk tolerance of the school with respect to scaffolding and supporting a learner in handling the task and the point at which the school will intervene to terminate an activity. The upper zone is the area beyond the school's tolerance of risk that the learner might still successfully undertake the task, given scaffolding. The 100% mark is the limit beyond which the learner is unable to undertake the task with or without scaffolding. The higher the risk inherent in the learning task, the earlier the institution requires intervention to protect the learner from potential or actual harm.

The gradient of the intervention point may vary from school to school according to differences at an institutional level and even individual teachers within the same program may set different standards for intervention. This risk tolerance reflects a complex mix of parental expectations, institutional philosophy, program history, legal precedent, and the nature of the setting itself. Programs with a longer history in the study demonstrated a higher risk tolerance in actual practice. This may be due to a higher level of parent trust in long-standing institutions and experienced teachers.

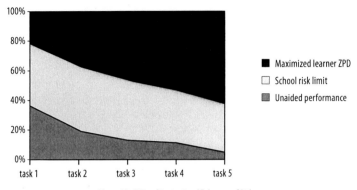

Figure 26: *ZPD and Institutional Tolerance of Risk*

The gap between the actual extent of ZPD and the institutionally imposed limitations driven by risk for a hypothetical program and teacher is depicted in Figure 27. This figure shows a 'radar' plot view, where the plot points reflect the completion level of a hypothetical task undertaken by a learner independently, expressed as a percentage. The inner plot shows the percentage of task completion by the learner unaided; the outer plot shows the completion level of the same task if scaffolded by a teacher, taking into account the risk appetite of the institution; the 100% limit for each task shows the theoretical level of completion if fully supported by a teacher, regardless of risk, thereby reflecting the full extent of an individual's ZPD. Again, the intervention points are shown for the purposes of illustration only, depicting a set of tasks with an escalating level of difficulty.

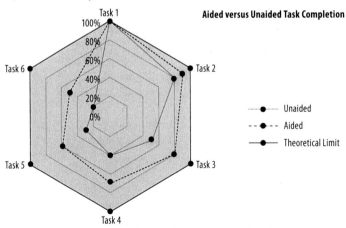

Figure 27: *Aided versus unaided task completion*

243

This depiction of a hypothetical learner undertaking a set of hypothetical experiential learning tasks illustrates one of the difficulties of operationalising the ZPD to its full extent in an institutional setting. Scaffolding is provided to assist the learner to achieve a higher level of accomplishment in a given task than would be possible through individual effort. The conflict between what is practicable in terms of time and resources and acceptably safe for an institution may not align with an individual teacher's view and may not be attuned to the potential of the learner to cope with risk in a novel situation.

In all forms of learning, taking measured risks is seen as both a need that is met experientially and a learned skill that must be practised and honed through testing theories and new ideas. Similarly, coping with adversity and failure requires mechanisms that are not necessarily innate to the learner. Experiential learning presents problems that are authentic and therefore subject to uncertainties and risks that provide a way of meeting the need for learned risk taking. It abandons the safety of the mainstream classroom; the problems encountered entail risk for learners, because to make the challenges meaningful, there must be freedom, responsibility, and difficulty; and the possibility of mistakes and failure is an unavoidable concomitant of challenge.

Challenge and therefore risk vary according to the learning setting and its affordances, the nature of the challenges and problems faced, and the extent to which intervention is exercised to resolve problems, reduce challenge, and thereby ameliorate risk. Learners are constantly challenged with the possibility or probability that previously learned coping strategies and problem solving skills are not reliable or effective in every new situation. Therefore, experimentation and risk taking need to be adopted in order to resolve them, with minimal adult intervention. The lesson we need to learn and absorb from experiential learning is that ideally teachers and other adults scaffold learner inquiry, risk-taking, and problem solving: they don't solve learner problems.

This approach to learning serves an unmet need: younger learners are still developing problem solving strengths and when adults habitually intervene to solve learner problems, a learning opportunity is lost. We can acknowledge that the need to intervene is often a by-product of efficiency-driven practices in mainstream education. Content coverage and accountability for achieving performance benchmarks are crucially important and teachers need to prioritise getting correct answers, rather than ceding a degree of control and agency to the learner, accommodating delays and mistakes in the search for solutions to problems.

Experiential teachers tend not to point out mistakes, unless the risk to the learner exceeds the potential benefit of perseverance with primary learner agency. They let participants discover mistakes for themselves. At most, leading questions may be asked at the critical juncture to encourage the learner to inquire more deeply about a course of action, direction, or solution being pursued. Learning experientially, participants take risks, they test a theory thoroughly and properly, and they challenge themselves. While acknowledging the potential risks, experiential teachers believe that the freedom to make mistakes is part of growing up.

So deeply valued is this opportunity to experiment and take risks that experiential teachers may deliberately withhold opinions during activities to ensure that decisions are actually made by learners. As a result, learners may initially become frustrated because they cannot find out the teacher's opinion.

Within the common appreciation of the value of risk and error, the nature and timing of teacher invention in learner-centred problem solving are important influences on the learner experience. At the extreme ends of the continuum ranging from total control to total freedom, this leads to very different experiences for learners. Learners may be permitted to struggle with problems, because their teachers know when to intervene, they are in control. At the other end of the spectrum, teachers with a low tolerance of risk, ambiguity or uncertainty emphasize control and certainty, both in terms of the time expended and the outcomes achieved. For some teachers who lack confidence or professional experience, the intervention point is not clear and so they may err on the side of caution. Thus, in any learning activity, the teacher intervention point is somewhat a function of teacher experience and judgement, but may also reflect institutional values and policies.

The tension between challenge and consequence can be summarised as a dichotomy between suffering and protection; they are the two end points of the risk spectrum present in education. Risk arises from difficult and demanding challenges and confronting experiences potentially leading to suffering; protection is offered to learners to varying degrees through a supportive scaffold of teacher intervention.

Program content is inextricably tied to the range of activities and experiences possible within the immediate setting chosen by the school. Settings range from urban streets to farms and remote mountaintops, each affording an opportunity for a specific type of experience that is unique to the setting, but each of which performs a similar theoretical function in experiential learning transactions. Schools, therefore, shape the thematic content of their programs through selection of setting and *vice versa*.

While risk is an essential element of experiential learning, the *degree* of risk tolerated in program design and implementation may vary considerably. This variation is based on school and teacher choices, such as the properties of the setting itself, institutional risk appetite reflected in the type and degree of challenge in experiential activities, and the level of teacher experience and confidence. Some settings are, by the nature of the challenge offered, or the operational complexities associated with the specific location, more inherently risky than others. Schools may moderate risk by adjusting the degree of contrast, or the physical, social or cultural *distance*, between the experiential and mainstream settings. The range of challenges and activities offered also reflects institutional choices regarding risk. Finally, individual teachers may also exercise choice in the level of risk tolerated in their own programs and activities.

Little has been said in the preceding chapters about ideal program duration. This is not an oversight. More so than any other element of program design, the duration of a program is a highly individual choice relating to the needs, resources, aspirations, and desired outcomes of the home institution. As we have seen earlier, an experience teaches for an instant and is still a source of learning years later. Program duration offers choice unique to each school.

The experiential programs participating in this study range from a month to a year. Experiential programs in the form of school excursions may run over just a few hours. The expected outcomes can be scaled up or down, depending on the time available or allocated. For those programs studied here, it is not strongly evident that the programs of one year's duration are experientially superior to the shorter programs of one month or more. Whether this holds true for even shorter programs of one week's duration or less is not evident in the data, as a comparative analysis of the impact of program duration on learning was not a specific aim of the study. However, it could be asserted that many of the experiential phenomena observed would be hard to replicate, except in embryonic form, in a week or less.

One consequence of program duration is that the longer the program, the greater the need for a parallel academic program to be offered concurrently. Schools offering longer programs are still held accountable for student progress in mainstream academic subjects and these are offered as a parallel curriculum. This bifurcated curricular structure introduces some intra-institutional tension and results in compromise for both the experiential and academic programs. The shorter programs all demonstrate a greater degree of integration between the experiential and academic elements of their respective programs and home school curricula are typically suspended for the duration of these programs.

The role of setting in learning requires greater attention from educators. For schools the implication is that the design of all types of learning spaces should reflect and incorporate the experiential principle of learning that setting is a *co-participant* in the experiential learning transaction. The higher the degree of experientiality in the learning activity in the mainstream, the more important the contribution to learning made by the affordances of the setting. To an extent, this principle of learner interaction with contrasting micro-settings has been adopted in the *Reggio Emilia* Approach (Gandini, 1998), but its application is limited to early childhood learning. What could be realised is that setting is significant in *any* learning that either explicitly or implicitly involves autonoesis, as this is, by the definition developed in this study, *experiential*. Thus, experiential learning transactions may take place in any educational setting.

At the start of this study it was noted that schools tend to select specialized, and often remote, settings for their experiential learning programs, each offering a strong contrast to the mainstream learning environment. To bring these challenging settings to the classroom in a literal sense would therefore logically require the translocation of the setting itself. This is both impractical and undesirable. The certainty of the controlled classroom setting is needed by other modes of learning conducted in the classroom. Furthermore, the strength of the contrast between the daily safety and certainty of the classroom and the novel risk and authenticity of the experiential setting lends power to the latter. To make what is novel routine would remove some of its power to challenge learners and shape memories into enduring learning.

The use of multiple settings and affordances in the way that the Reggio approach practices is an avenue for further exploration, both theoretically and practically. There appears to be some justification for the incorporation of multiple settings into mainstream learning programs, to ensure that learners experience learning in a diverse range of settings which may allow the construction of different social dynamics and allow the development of different skills and understandings. Social roles and structures require a range of settings to approach a higher state of development. Higher cognitive functions, and specifically language, are developed through social interaction, which often occur in settings that are not formally educational in structure or purpose (Wells, 1999), but which *afford* opportunities to learn in many different ways. A multi-setting richness may facilitate the development of more complex systems of social and linguistic interaction. Indeed, the homogenising isolation of learning in the safe, dedicated settings of mainstream education may be counter-productive: the *segregation* of learning environments from everyday life has been seen as the principal reason for the perceived failures of mainstream education for many decades (Dewey, 1997 [1938]).

Experiential learning emphasises teamwork, joint goals, shared resources, shared success and consequences, and reflection, elements that are often less important in mainstream learning, with its stronger focus on hard evidence of individual performance (Neill, 2006; Scardamalia & Bereiter, 1994). This individual and evidence-based approach typically adopted in mainstream schools is seen to create inert or irrelevant learning by some critics, lacking immediate or even mid-term practical, real-world applications (Breunig, 2005, pp. 112-116; Hyslop-Margison & Strobel, 2008; Scardamalia & Bereiter, 1994, p. 268). Learning must lead to the creation of new knowledge and modified behaviour that is not just measured or manifested individually, but must also be directly relevant to the learner. The contrast between the enduring, episodic memories of experiential learning and the context-free semantic learning of academic curricula is measured in its *autonoeticity*: the extent to which learning is cognitively linked to a learner's *self-awareness* of their experience of the world. This suggests that experientially enriching mainstream learning might be achieved through a greater focus on learner autonoesis as a highly durable and personally relevant form of cognitive process within an overarching framework of learning.

Autonoesis and reflection are linked through the post-experiential cognitive and metacognitive processing of experiential stimuli that facilitates the realisation of learning. Reflection also exists in mainstream education. In some curricular frameworks, for example, the International Baccalaureate Organisation's Learner Profile (International Baccalaureate Organisation, 2008, 2013), there is an explicit acknowledgement of the need for reflection in all learning. However, the extent to which reflection, both formal and informal, is a widespread practice in all schools or educational settings is unclear. The clear link between reflection and experience evident in this study suggests the need for reflection in some form to be incorporated into *all* learning, both experiential and semantic.

In the context of this discussion on what elements of experiential learning might be incorporated into mainstream education, the broader educational challenge remains unchanged from Dewey's time: how to make learning more effective, more authentic, and ultimately, more relevant to life beyond school (Dewey, 1997 [1938]). The lessons of the experiential learning model point to the need to reconsider how *where* we learn affects *what* we learn. It shows that *risks* are necessary for learning to take place, and that *mistakes* arise in the process of learning. Finally, *pausing* and *reflecting* are integral to the cognition of learning.

Across the millennia-long sweep of recorded human history, experiential learning has been the dominant mode of learning. It is only relatively recently, when economic imperatives have driven the need for an educated, literate workforce that we have witnessed the birth of almost universal institutional education. We are still wrestling with the social, cultural and educational implications of this historical development.

We know that learners construct their understanding of the physical world through personal, direct experience. Epistemologically, experiential learning is pragmatic: we deal with the world as we experience it, drawing on previously constructed experiential knowledge to make meaning of novel experiences so as to shape and connect with future experience (Dewey, 1997 [1938]). Experiential learning is fundamentally social in nature and relies on authentic settings and realistic problem-solving exercises (Dewey, 1997 [1938]). Experiential learning involves both a reactive and a reflective response: reaction to the stimulation of the sensory dimension, followed by reflection that leads to knowledge construction and further development and growth in the individual (Dewey, 1997 [1938]). Experiential learning is distinguished from semantic learning by the strong presence of learner self-awareness.

Comparison of Semantic and Experiential Learning Principles and Practice

At the conclusion of this exploration of experiential learning, by way of summary, the following table offers some thoughts on the relative merits and drawbacks associated with classroom or 'semantic' learning and experiential learning. There are no absolutes in this table. The parameters used for comparison are fairly broad and general in nature; the 'pros' and 'cons' of each parameter are described briefly.

Clearly, some comparisons are absurd: it would be impossible to compare a classroom lesson describing abseiling, perhaps augmented with audio-visual aids, with the physical act of descending a cliff face attached to a rope. The domains are therefore simplified to permit some direct in-principle comparison. However, some domains of learning do bear a degree of direct comparison, such as cultural understanding and language competence. These are considered from both perspectives on an equal basis.

The ultimate purpose of the table is certainly not to prove the superiority of either mode of learning, but rather to encourage teachers to explore the potential advantages of adopting one approach over another.

249

Classroom/Semantic Learning		Experiential Learning	
Pro	**Con**	**Pro**	**Con**
Setting			
Teacher-controlled setting; highly predictable as a venue; entry controlled; low risk; efficient in time usage; outcomes more predictable	Setting is contrived and too predictable = less memorable and impactful on student learning	Unstructured and real-world = highly memorable; more flexible; complex affordances permit a much greater range of possibilities; wide range of social interaction beyond school relationships possible	Inherently risky; setting may not be interesting to some students; access not easily controlled in some settings; duration of learning activities requires flexibility and may take more time than estimated; difficult to timetable.
Safe and predictable environment that only allows permitted participants; fittings, fixtures, equipment, devices, etc. are all subject to educationally appropriate regulation or building codes.	Very limited range of social interaction possible and duration of interaction determined by class length and student to teacher ratio.	Emergent design and outcomes driven by opportunity and student interest/need = challenging and stimulating; opportunistic = learning can take advantage of fixtures, fittings, equipment, or facilities not available in schools.	No certainty that students will not be exposed to challenging situations; controlling a public learning environment is usually beyond the scope of teacher training and experience; ensuring that devices or facilities accessed meet educational standards can be difficult.
Teaching Materials			
Rich, polished, teacher selected, peer reviewed, structured, content controlled, and purpose designed to meet the objectives of subjects or lessons.	Curated to meet the practical needs of teaching and learning in an institutional context; focus may be narrowed to exclude considerations and explorations that overflow the boundaries of subject or curricula; pre-processed and pre-digested to an extent, the learner challenge is limited to the extent permitted by the author(s).	Rich and authentic, reflecting the real world context in which the learning activity is offered; may extend students beyond the limits of classroom taught subjects; providing excellent grounding in the informational interactions of the adult world.	Uncontrolled by the teacher; may touch on adult themes beyond the level considered appropriate for the age-level; may include irrelevancies or be unfocused; not tailored to the particular needs of an activity or lesson; may require teacher interpretation; may require higher level research and analytical skills to extract the required information; may be confusing, unclear, or illogical to younger learners.

Language or cultural materials prepared ahead of time in accordance with a structured curriculum; finely honed to meet the needs of a specific activity; predictable sequence of learning materials, levelled to ability.	Materials reflect an intended program of language acquisition that may not accord with the needs of the learners and may demotivate if lacking intrinsic interest: fails to answer the student question: learning for what?	Rich authentic language and cultural environment that is open-ended; cultural materials are authentic and up to date; language artefacts are rich and genuine; cultural and language materials and artefacts are current, reflecting how native speakers use the language.	Cultural materials and artefacts are difficult to filter for content, currency, and quality; difficult to constrain range of language to which students are exposed and may be unpredictably advanced; native speakers may lose patience; native speakers may speak in dialect, slang, or with a heavy accent; quality control very difficult.
Outcomes			
Greater certainty in setting expected learning outcomes; sequenced outcomes build sequentially in accordance with allocated time in class; finely calibrated outcomes planned within curriculum framework; gradual, intelligent progression from one skill to the next possible.	Outcomes must be tailored to the overall progression of the class, according to the time allocated and reasonable expectations of progress for the bulk of students; outcomes aligned with what is possible or afforded by the classroom setting; outcomes generally reflect planned, intentional, but narrow benchmarks in accordance with subject assessment plan.	Outcomes determined by student engagement, ability, interest, and opportunity; outcomes suggested in part by the affordances of the setting; outcomes co-constructed by learners; outcomes are authentic and aligned with learner constructed objectives and met according to learner needs; learners may advance very quickly; learners take the time needed to achieve an outcome; the outcome and process used to achieve the outcome are broadly applicable in other real world contexts.	Learners may experience a sense of failure if they cannot complete a task; outcomes may not be achieved within an expected timeframe; outcomes may require teacher intervention that is finely tuned to the ZPD of the learner(s); learners may feel inadequate or anxious dealing with real world contexts to achieve outcomes.

Costs			
Predictable costs set according to the financial standing of the school; educational costs well known within the community; clear connection with cost and defined benefit.	Intensive skill development or access to authentic experiences may be expensive; some forms of equivalent learning (language learning) require smaller classes and specially trained teachers; staffing issues may impact on specialist subject continuity (culture, language, specialist skills or knowledge).	Costs vary according to proximity of activity site to school; costs vary according to the duration of the program, staffing levels, cost of accommodation (if offered), cost of catering (if offered); intensive one-to-one interaction is highly cost effective if travel costs are not prohibitive; huge gains possible in a relatively short period of time, hence efficiency can be high.	Distance, ease of access, and time/cost involved in designing and executing experiential programs may pose financial challenges to families; unfamiliar operating environment may increase costs; crisis or incident management may be costly; some costs may be difficult to predict; additional costs such as insurance may be expensive; more difficult to establish a direct cost-benefit relationship.
Cultural, Linguistic, or Activity Setting			
Classrooms are culturally familiar and operationally easy for students and teachers; predictable, controllable setting.	Lack of contrast or notable features; efforts to import L1 culture may appear clumsy and contrived; no challenges to learners' cultural frame of reference.	Culturally distinct and disruptive = memorable and challenging; students may see a change in their worldview; great empathy for target language and its people; greater affective domain reinforcement for the adventurous.	Culturally challenging and may place some learners in distress due to rupture of contact and disorientation or separation anxiety; learner affective domain support needs may be extensive.

Learning Activities and Problems			
Learning problems structured and progressive; problem solving skills may be developed sequentially; teacher controlled and defined; outcomes achievable within a limited amount of time; intentionally linked to preceding and subsequent learning; easily assessed; performance more easily quantified and compared to previous performance and peer performance.	Problems set lack real world urgency and authenticity; lack of connection between learners' own needs and the problems set in the classroom; limited development of character and personal attributes; assessment scope and focus limited to what is permissible and practicable in a classroom setting; summative assessment limited to quantifiable outcomes that are artificial or constructed for use within an institutional context.	Open-ended potential for problem solving in a range of social and cultural contexts; emergent design allows greater tailoring of activities to meet the needs and interests of learners in context; greater relevancy to learner interests at the time of the activity; inquiry focus may take learning down pathways that are identified and negotiated with the learners; activities with physical, cognitive, social, or cultural challenges may develop a wider range of personal attributes such as character, resilience, courage, patience, cooperation, insight, and leadership.	Potential for problems to overwhelm students or escalate beyond the capacity of the learner or the teacher to manage easily; problems are emergent and therefore hard to predict; unpredictable engagement by learners as problems may be based on learner discovery and interest; immediate setting or context may not allow the pursuit of particular lines of inquiry at the time needed.
Reflection			
Reflection on learning aligned closely with lesson or unit objectives; reflection may be structured or even taught as a discrete skill; reflections may be integrated into the progression from one lesson to another; reflection and feedback managed in smaller and more easily managed sessions.	Reflection tends to be more a review of mistakes and applied learning from the lesson under review; limited personal engagement; lack of direct connection to the formation of personal and cultural identity due to the lack of real-world connection; institutions may not prioritize or schedule time for reflection; curricular pressures may squeeze out time for reflection; results of reflection may not be easily integrated into further learning.	Reflection may be rich, extensive, and intensive; reflection may be undertaken over a very extended timeframe, mainly due to the intensive nature of the experience; reflection connects the experience to learning in a direct, meaningful way; teachers may facilitate reflection to ensure it has taken place and direct its implementation to an extent; teachers may assist learners with interpretation of reflections on experience or learning in general.	Uneven capacity for students to reflect; lack of skills in forming a reflection and accessing its outcomes; differential experiences lead to different reflections and therefore different outcomes; some reflection may take years to complete; teacher intervention may contaminate reflection; forced reflection for an audience may colour the learner's memories and understandings developed from an experience.

Risk			
Low risk, high reliability; risks carefully managed; consequences controlled and limited by institutional policies and practices; learning risk controlled by teacher and institution.	Range of challenges limited to controlled settings and institutional values; strong dependency on adults to make decisions; risk aversion may limit challenge and opportunity for learning; risk aversion may stunt development of problem solving skills and personal resilience; school setting not necessarily ideal preparation for life beyond school.	High risk, high return in experiential learning; real world experience = readiness for real world challenges; teacher safety net to manage immediate risks; strong development of learner skills and coping strategies; confidence building; independence enhanced.	Higher risk of unacceptable and unforeseen consequences; uncontrolled learning environment may present risks that are not foreseeable; individual learner reactions unpredictable; may result in 'too far, too soon' experiences that have negative consequences for some learners; more difficult to analyse and manage risk at the teacher and institutional level.

Table 3: *Comparison of semantic and experiential learning: pros and cons*

All genuine learning has the power to shape behaviour, change attitudes and generate new knowledge. Experiential learning, by virtue of its enduring, and highly personal nature extends its influence over many years in the lives of learners. Because experiential learning is autonoetic, it cannot be made obsolete by new experiences; each learning experience adds to existing cognitive structures or generates new ones, but all remain an integral element of the learners constructed reality. The experiences of others that are learned noetically can become obsolete.

While acknowledging the risks and limitations, by tapping into the enduring power of experience, there are many benefits and skills that may potentially accrue to the learner and the community. The following list is but a sample of these:

a. Memorable and enduring learning that is personally relevant and empowering, meeting individual needs and interests (individual);

b. More engaged, independent, resilient, and skilled learners become higher achieving learners in post-program learning at the home school (individual and institutional);

c. Learners develop real world applications for their knowledge and skills experientially and these flow through into post-school behaviours and attitudes (individual and community);

d. Direct transfer of culture and knowledge is facilitated through direct learner contact with the wider community that is cross-generational (individual and community);

e. Learners develop competence in facing real problems to develop real solutions (individual);

f. Experiential learners develop stronger leadership skills in a range of challenging settings (individual);

g. Experiential learners develop character traits that are strongly reflective of the host culture and community and thus contribute to community building and values (individual and community);

h. Emergent inquiry and discovery of experiences develops greater flexibility in learners (individual);

i. Experiential activities may be used as vehicles to develop highly specialized skills not available or applicable in schools, but which may have relevance in the community (individual and community);

j. Experiential programs in specific contexts and settings facilitate the direct transfer of sub-cultural knowledge – e.g., workplace culture (individual and community);

k. Experiential programs emphasize social interaction, collaboration, and personal development and as such offer a more focused targeting of some educational resources for these purposes (individual and institutional);

l. Experiential activities facilitate exposure to a wider range of social interactions, physical and cultural challenges that build tolerance and assimilation (individual);

m. Mistakes and errors are expected and welcome, thus building confidence and problem solving and recovery skills (individual);

n. Life-long learning skills are encouraged and developed through experience beyond school settings (individual);

o. Experiential learning encourages a more reflective approach to learning that emphasizes learner honesty and objectivity in self-appraisal (individual);

p. Schools and learners develop a stronger link between the classroom and the real world through participation in learning beyond school (individual, institutional, and community);

q. Institutions learn to accommodate and develop a wider range of individual learning styles and standards (institutional);

r. Institutions may achieve higher school retention through engagement arising from stronger personal relevance of learning experiences (individual and institutional);

s. Experiential programs, by virtue of their immersion in community settings beyond school, develop closer connections with community standards and expectations; and

t. Experiential learning offers a more authentic and reliable means of testing desirable character traits, such as independence, courage, and resilience, in a formative manner, thus contributing to school and community culture and values (individual, institutional, and community).

This list provides nothing more than a sketch of the potential benefits of adopting an experiential approach to learning. One of the reasons for this tentativeness is the highly individualized nature of experiential learning outcomes that reflect a unique interaction between the learner and the experience itself.

The question embedded in Dewey's principle regarding the continuity of past and present experience and its power to shape future experience assumes a greater importance at this juncture. There is a tension between these two modes of learning that reflects competing learning paradigms, socio-political agendas, and philosophies. To pass the Deweyan test, experiential learning program outcomes should serve to inform further educative experience to the benefit of learners and their communities. Building strong connections between these different modes of learning to ensure that they are mutually reinforcing remains a challenge that is to an extent unmet.

Chapter 13:
Learning Rites

Experience: it seems we cannot live without it. It shapes our earliest encounters with the world, guides our first wobbling steps, and leads us through the journey of life to its conclusion. What does it offer in response to the difficult questions posed in the prologue? If we don't understand the nature of experience and how it contributes to our development, then the answer might be disappointing. If we don't understand how to use the power of experience, then education will be all the poorer. While not without risk, our experiences appear to be highly memorable and directly linked to our capacity to learn and adapt; they build what we know as 'character', enhance adaptability, and develop resilience.

There are schools and educators who believe that experience offers a great deal to formal education, so much so that programs of experiential learning have proliferated in recent decades in certain parts of the world, without a strong, research-driven theoretical base. These programs are promoted by schools, and accepted by parents and participants, as innovative, progressive, and memorable. Without a clearly articulated theory of experiential learning on which to base promotion, schools with strong experiential programs attach importance to the intended learning outcomes, such as independence, leadership, resilience, courage, and maturity, as a way to secure parental and participant commitment to the programs. They are believed to be character building.

The belief in the power of experience runs deep in certain corners of the teaching profession. For parents and students, there is a degree of implicit trust and acceptance of the educational value of the programs to justify the cost and disruption to schooling. Access to these programs to date, however, remains limited, partly due to cost, but also due to some 'official' scepticism towards the capacity of experiential learning to contribute to outcomes associated with high-stakes examinations.

The most commonly targeted demographic for the type of program examined in this book is the middle years of schooling: teenagers. The belief in these programs cited above seems to suggest that they may serve other educational and social needs of the participants as perceived by parents, teachers, and the participants themselves. These other needs are not given explicit articulation in any school literature and are not even readily apparent as findings in the research presented in this book.

It is no secret that in mainstream school settings, students in the so-called 'middle years' of schooling, typically from 12 to 16 years of age, are often reported to be difficult to teach, disengaged, and disaffected (P. Cole, 2006; Office for Policy Research and Innovation, 2009). For schools with the resources and the philosophical commitment, the establishment of experiential programs in remote settings may be seen as a response to this issue of teenage disengagement in learning; their popularity is possibly a measure of their success in meeting the perceived special learning needs of the age group.

One relatively recent study of teenagers in school found that student motivation in learning declines steadily in all schooling sectors from the age of 10, with school disengagement and absenteeism peaking at the age of 14. The report suggested that mainstream learning environments are ill-suited to the educational needs of this latter group (P. Cole, 2006; P. Cole, Mahar, & Vindurampulle, 2006, pp. 2-3; Office for Policy Research and Innovation, 2009, p. 9). Another study also found a strong correlation between participant intentions and engagement in education at the age of 14, and the completion of a high school diploma or certificate (P. Cole et al., 2006, p. 3). During these teenage years, students are difficult to teach, but at the same time, they are heavily reliant on engaging learning to ensure later school retention and educational outcomes. It is a heady and volatile period of adolescent development, in which any innovation that enhances learner motivation and engagement may reap long-term rewards for learners, schools, and the wider community.

This study offers the basics of a unified model of education underpinned by experience. The experiential learning achieved in these programs conforms to a clear theoretical model with a high degree of congruence across the programs studied. While there are many variations in the manner of implementation across the programs studied, the experiential approach to education in certain contexts and settings reflects a single model.

The nature of the experiential learning transactions in the programs was found to be structurally different to that which might be expected of the Piagetian model of constructivist learning in a typical classroom. Blending engaging settings, social interaction, authentic problems, risk, and reflection, this mode of learning is qualitatively different to classroom learning and, in the programs studied, the model of learning developed from the study findings explains how enduring educational and developmental outcomes that are not possible in a mainstream school setting are achieved.

Educationally, it might be concluded, therefore, that the wider employment of experiential learning of the type examined in this study offers schools a means of addressing the disengagement and disaffection associated with the middle school years of education. The theoretical model explains how experiential learning works, and provides a set of principles by which programs in other settings might be designed and implemented. Access to this type of program, therefore, should and can be far more widespread than is presently the case; students across all schools should have access to experiential learning activities designed around the setting-based model theorised in this study.

Experience as a Rite of Passage

Is there more to this than just engaging and entertaining teenagers in isolation from the parents and school? Looking at ethno-social practices of education across nations and ages, these programs offer a distant but clear echo of a type of time-honoured ritual present in many communities around the world: a rite of passage into adulthood.

At a socio-cultural level, the residential experiential learning programs, in two different dimensions – *setting* and *socialisation* – appear to parallel very traditional, even ancient, ritualistic practices that are deeply rooted in the cultural observances of earlier civilisations (Andrews, 1999). These programs therefore may be seen to act as a form of social *initiation rite* for adolescents, a *rite of passage* (van Gennep, 2004 [1909]), marking their transition into adulthood, thereby meeting a social need that is perhaps frustrated by the widespread abandonment of such traditional rituals in the contemporary western world (J. Davis, 2003; Stokrocki, 1997).

As a form of initiation, the residential experiential programs prepare learners for their adult responsibilities in the wider community through a process of isolation, confrontation, risk, engagement, and reflection (Bell, 2003; Maddern, 1990; Neill, 2003). Through isolation and challenge, students are encouraged or compelled to take responsibility for themselves and others, and exercise courage in the face physical challenges. In particular, the strong emphasis on the natural environment in the wilderness or rural experiential learning programs may be interpreted as a form of initiation for environmental custodians, who are appreciative of the setting's natural beauty and protective of its flora and fauna (Boulet & Clabburn, 2003).

In the structure and challenges of these experiential programs there are discernible echoes of adolescent initiation rites from earlier ages and cultures. Traditional initiation rites comprise different stages: separation or isolation from society through a journey; preparation and instruction from adult elders; a transition or visioning process; participation and testing; and a reincorporation with a change in status and responsibility on return (Delaney, 1995; Maddern, 1990, pp. 29-30; Neill, 2003; van Gennep, 2004 [1909]). For example, the traditional initiation rites still practiced by Australian Indigenous cultures – known as *ceremony* – manifest strong parallels with some of the philosophical elements underpinning these experiential learning programs (Bourke & Bourke, 1995).

Indigenous *ceremonies* are conducted away from family and community, in settings that are deemed to be particularly significant because of their special qualities; the time of testing is confronting to the participants and can take many weeks to complete; on completion, *initiates* are welcomed back into their communities to assume adult responsibilities within their respective cultural group (Bourke & Bourke, 1995). They return changed, transformed by the experience.

Thus the initiation ritual itself consists of isolation and testing, and its purpose is to prepare initiates to construct special knowledge and accept adult responsibilities, both of which reflect deeply embedded cultural values. These rituals are not possible while embedded in the daily routines of the home community: they require special places and times.

These rituals mirror the type of experiential learning examined in this study in many ways: the isolation of special experiential settings, the leadership and instruction from teachers acting as *elders*, the testing through challenge, and the changed learner perceptions and status on return to the parent school. At both a philosophical and practical level, therefore, the parallels between traditional forms of initiation and the type of experiential learning examined in this study are clear and compelling.

As an initiation rite, the experiential learning program contributes to the socialisation of these adolescent learners, marking a critical milestone in their journey towards adult independence. It offers an alternative to the contemporary trend across the globe towards a steady, incremental creep into adulthood, where many of the traditional social events and ceremonies that marked the end of childhood and entry to adult circles in earlier times have been abandoned or rendered meaningless (Stokrocki, 1997). Experiential challenges offer the potential to act as rites of passage, providing visible and memorable social markers in the otherwise undistinguished contemporary journey towards adulthood from childhood (J. Davis, 2003; R. Garrison, 1998).

The settings examined in this study act in a way that is similar to those chosen for rites of initiation, as they afford the learner both *knowledge* and *testing*. Initiates and learners gain status and new responsibilities in their respective communities through their mastery of knowledge and testing in the ritual setting. Traditionally, these ritual settings are seen as special places with particular qualities that are needed to complete the rite successfully (Bourke & Bourke, 1995). Isolated settings offer rupture of social contact, particularly with immediate family members, testing independence, courage and character. Natural experiential learning settings in the study in particular are treated in a respectful, even reverential, way that is strongly congruent with traditional practices. There is a tension, possibly even a contradiction, implicit in this notion: on the one hand, from an environmental perspective, natural settings are held to be pristine, possessing a purity of spirit that can be known and appreciated – that speaks for itself – and demands our respect and protection; on the other hand, and at the same time, the untamed dimension of wilderness affords a test of character, challenging our courage, probing our fears, questioning our civilisation.

In the former view, appreciation of setting as a manifestation of natural edenic perfection is similar to that which inspires and motivates the environmental movement, where natural wilderness is seen as the last remnant of paradise lost, endangered and in need of protection (Merchant, 2004, p. 3). Learners learn to suppress their selfish inclinations towards the exploitation, or taming, of nature. Through direct experience, learners develop an appreciation of nature's aesthetic beauty and also its fragility. They experience a direct sensory connection with the setting through visual, aural, olfactory, and tactile stimulation that is constructed through the learning experience. This direct experience of one's surroundings is the *education of things* (Rousseau), with setting as both the object and agent of learning. The setting is treated as a precious and threatened heritage, given over in stewardship for future generations.

The latter view sees nature having the power to test of our *civilisation*, where the untamed, *hard* elements of nature, and our own fears and shortcomings, must be faced and overcome. The experiential programs in the study offer challenges that test skill, endurance, courage, and intelligence. This testing is physical, emotional, and even spiritual, for learners. With this testing, there is a risk, of mistakes, of consequences, and failure. Each generation of learners must face *risk* in this passage into adulthood, as challenge without risk, and particularly the risk of defeat, is meaningless from a ritual perspective. Risk makes the achievement of mastery more significant, more memorable, more enduring. Success in the testing serves as an important symbol of survival, of the reassertion of human supremacy over nature.

There is a potential contradiction implicit in associating both *nurturing* and *testing* with setting. This apparent contradiction is reconciled through the notion that both our reverence for, and our testing within, a setting are informed and constrained by our humanity and its attendant needs. We nurture and protect the environment, but it must also provide for us, and sustain us. We pit our skill and courage against the environment, but not to the point of mutual destruction. It is a metaphorical form of *sparring*, where competition and respect strike a dynamic balance that must be monitored and carefully managed. Testing and appreciation demand commitment and maturity from learners: both pose risks to learners and demand adult-like judgement. This metaphor of setting as both a worthy adversary and an object of admiration highlights further the extent to which the setting acts as an important *co-participant* in experiential learning.

The learners in these programs are taken to places in which the experience of learning reflects deep-seated, yet implicit, cultural beliefs that are largely hidden from view in the mainstream classroom. To their families, their schools, and perhaps the community, these experiences serve to replace forgotten rituals and abandoned socialisation ceremonies and mark their transition into the adult world. The myths of natural perfection and ritualistic mastery of the elements are not uncommon themes in western education, but essentially as objects of semantic inquiry, not direct experience. It is only when the relative safety and predictability of the classroom and the family home are forsaken, that these learners experience and remember, transforming their attitudes, knowledge, and identity in ways that resonate deeply and broadly in their future learning.

All learning is ultimately experiential, but not all experiences are educative. The intelligent design and implementation of experiential learning, when effectively and thoughtfully integrated into a wider programs of learning, has power disproportionate to the time, effort, and resources allocated to shape the ideas, behaviours, attitudes, the very lives of learners, and by extension, the communities in which they live. Human experiential learning has already changed the world; it has the power to remake and renew, if we are willing to take the risk.

Postface

So what is wrong with us and how do we fix it? There are perhaps no easy answers, but some helpful hints in the voices of those who contributed so richly and generously to the ideas explored in this book.

We might be more aware of our surroundings: our immediate environment shapes us in ways that we don't understand well.

We might examine our social interactions and understand that they are at least in part the product of our immediate environments; if we change the setting, we may change the social relationships that give shape to our lives.

We might pay attention to risk: it is not always bad, and is usually necessary to grow.

We might spend more time in introspective reflection, allowing the process to sift and shape the sensory flow in which we all exist from moment to moment, retaining that which is developmentally important.

Finally, we might embrace experience as a powerful and wise teacher that can guide every step in our learning journey.

References

Adkins, C., & Simmons, B. (2003). Outdoor, Experiential, and Environmental Education: Converging or Diverging Approaches? Retrieved from www.ericdigests.org/2003-2/outdoor.html

Amin, T. G., & Valsiner, J. (2004). Coordinating Operative and Figurative Knowledge: Piaget, Vygotsky, and Beyond. In I. M. Carpendale & U. Miller (Eds.), *Social Interaction and the Development of Knowledge* (pp. 87-109). Mahwah, NJ: Lawrence Erlbaum Associates.

Amsel, A. (1989). *Behaviorism, Neobehaviorism, and Cognitivism in Learning Theory: Historical and Contemporary Perspectives.* Hillsdale, NJ: Lawrence Erlbaum Associates.

Anderson, L., & Krathwohl, D. (2001). *A Taxonomy for Learning, Teaching and Assessing: A Revision of Bloom's Taxonomy of Educational Objectives.* New York: Longman.

Andrews, K. (1999). The Wilderness Expedition as a Rite of Passage: Meaning and Process in Experiential Education. *The Journal of Experiential Education, 22*(1), 35-43.

Argyris, C., & Schön, D. (1974). *Theory In Practice: Increasing Professional Effectiveness.* San Francisco: Jossey Bass Publishers.

Aristotle. (1908 [350BC]). The Nicomachean Ethics. Retrieved from classics.mit.edu/Aristotle/metaphysics.html

Association for Experiential Education. (2005). AEE Definition of Experiential Education. Retrieved from www.aee.org/faq/nfaq.htm

Bachelard, G. (2002 [1938]). *The Formation of the Scientific Mind: A Contribution to a Psychoanalysis of Objective Knowledge* (M. McAllester Jones, Trans.). Manchester: Clinamen Press Ltd.

Backtalk. (1999). A Challenge to Brain-Based Educators. *Phi Delta Kappan, 81*(3), 254.

Baer, R. (2003). Mindfulness Training as a Clinical Intervention: A Conceptual and Empirical Review. *Clinical Psychology: Science and Practice, 10*(2), 125-143.

Baines, L. A., & Stanley, G. (2001). Constructivism and the Role of the Teacher: We Still Want to See the Teacher. *Phi Delta Kappan, 82*(9), 695.

Baker, A., Jensen, P., & Kolb, D. A. (2002). Conversation as Experiential Learning. Retrieved from psol.gmu.edu/psol/perspectives2.nsf/0/420c26d74b4d72b88525696f001 2b605?OpenDocument

Barker, E. (1959). *The Political Thought of Plato and Aristotle*. New York: Dover.

Barnes, P. (2005). Resource Guide: Outdoor Education. March. Retrieved from www. hlst.ltsn.ac.uk/resources/outdoor.pdf

Bassok, M. (1997). Object-Based Reasoning. In D. Medin (Ed.), *The Psychology of Learning and Motivation: Advances in Research and Theory* (pp. 1-39). San Diego, CA: Academic Press.

Beard, C., & Wilson, J. (2002). *The Power of Experiential Learning: a handbook for trainers and educators*. London: Kogan Page Limited.

Beard, C., & Wilson, J. (2006). *Experiential Learning: A Best Practice Handbook for Trainers and Educators*. London: Kogan Page.

Bell, P. (2003). The Rites of Passage and Outdoor Education: Critical Concerns for Effective Programming. *The Journal of Experiential Education, 26*(1), 41-50.

Bereiter, C. (2000). Keeping the Brain in Mind. *Australian Journal of Education, 44*(3), 226-238.

Boom, J. (2004). Individualism and Collectivism: a Dynamic Systems Interpretation of Piaget's Interactionalism. In J. Carpendale & U. Miller (Eds.), *Social Interaction and the Development of Knowledge* (pp. 67-85). Mahwah, NJ: Lawrence Erlbaum Associates.

Bornstein, M. H., & Bruner, J. S. (1989). *Interaction in Human Development*. Hillsdale, NJ: Laurence Erlbaum Associates.

Boulet, M., & Clabburn, A. (2003). Retreat to Return: Reflections on group-based nature retreats. *Gatherings,* (8). Retrieved from www.ecopsychology.org/journal/gatherings8/ html/sacred/retreat_boulet&clabburn.html

Bourke, E., & Bourke, C. (1995). Aboriginal Families in Australia. In R. Hartley (Ed.), *Families and Cultural Diversity in Australia* (pp. 48-69). St. Leonards, NSW: Allen & Unwin.

Breunig, M. (2005). Turning Experiential Education Theory and Critical Pedagogy into Praxis. *Journal of Experiential Education, 28*(2), 106-122.

Bringuier, J. C. (1980). *Conversations with Jean Piaget* (B. M. Gulati, Trans.). Chicago, Illinois: University of Chicago Press.

Brown, J. (1988). *The Life of the Mind: Selected Papers*. Hillsdale, NJ: Lawrence Erlbaum Associates.

Bruer, J. T. (1999, 15 April 1999). In Search of . . . Brain-Based Education. Retrieved from www.pdkintl.org/kappan/kbru9905.htm

Bruner, J. S. (1966). *Toward a Theory of Instruction*. Cambridge, MA: Belknap Press.

Bruner, J. S. (1987). Prologue to the English Edition. In R. Rieber & A. Carton (Eds.), *The Collected Works of L.S. Vygotsky* (Vol. 1, pp. 1-18). New York: Plenum.

Bruner, J. S. (1992). The Narrative Construction of Reality. In H. P. Beilin, Peter (Ed.), *Piaget's Theory: prospects and possibilities* (pp. 348). Hillsdale, NJ: Lawrence Erlbaum.

Bruner, J. S. (1996). *The Culture of Education.* Cambridge, Massachusetts: Harvard University Press.

Bruner, J. S. (1997). Celebrating Divergence: Piaget and Vygotsky. *Human Development, 40*(2), 63-73.

Bruner, J. S. (2004). A Short History of Psychological Theories of Learning. *Daedalus, Vol. 133,* 13.

Bruner, J. S. (2006). The Act of Discovery *In Search of Pedagogy – Volume 1: The Selected Works of Jerome S. Bruner* (pp. 57-66). Abingdon: Routledge.

Caine, R., & Caine, G. (1994). *Making Connections: Teaching and the Human Brain.* New York: Addison-Wesley.

Casareno, A. (2002). Ed Ellis: Working to Improve Education for Adolescents with Learning Disabilities. *The Intervention School & Clinic, 37*(5), 292-297.

Cates, W., & Ohl, T. (2006). The Nature of Groups: Implications for Learning Design. *Journal of Interactive Learning Research, 17*(1), 71-89.

Chaiklin, S. (2003). The Zone of Proximal Development in Vygotsky's Analysis of Learning and Instruction. In A. Kozulin, B. Gindidis, V. Ageyev, & S. Miller (Eds.), *Vygotsky's Educational Theory in Cultural Context* (pp. 39-64). Cambridge: Cambridge University Press.

Chrenka, L. (2002). Constructivism and the Role of the Teacher: Misconstructing Constructivism. *Phi Delta Kappan, 82*(1), 694-695.

Cole, M., & Hatano, G. (2007). Cultural-Historical Activity Theory. In S. Kitayama & D. Cohen (Eds.), *Handbook of Cultural Psychology* (pp. 109-135). New York: Guildford Press.

Cole, M., & Wertsch, J. V. (1996). Beyond the Individual-Social Antimony in Discussions of Piaget and Vygotsky. *Human Development, 39*(5), 250-256.

Cole, P. (2006). Reforming Year 9: Propositions for school policy and practice. Retrieved from www.edstaff.com.au/docs/Peter Cole – Reforming Year 9.pdf

Cole, P., Mahar, S., & Vindurampulle, O. (2006). *Understanding Year 9 Students: A Theoretical Perspective.* Melbourne: Research and Innovation Division Office of Learning and Teaching.

Collins, A., Brown, J., & Newman, S. (1989). Cognitive Apprenticeship: Teaching the Crafts of Reading, Writing, and Mathematics. In B. Resnick (Ed.), *Knowing, learning, and instruction: Essays in honor of Robert Glaser* (pp. 453-494). New Jersey: Lawrence Erlbaum Associates.

Confrey, J. (1995). How Compatible Are Radical Constructivism, Sociocultural Approaches, and Social Constructivism? In J. Gale & L. Steffe (Eds.), *Constructivism in Education* (pp. 185-227). Hillsdale, NJ: Lawrence Erlbaum.

Confucius. (1983). The Analects (??). Retrieved from www.cnculture.net/ebook/jing/sishu/lunyu_en/07.html

Cook, P. (2006). The Project Approach: An Appreciation for the Constructivist Theory. *Forum on Public Policy: A Journal of the Oxford Round Table, 1*(Fall), 1-21.

Cooper, R. (1993). *Heidegger and Whitehead: A Phenomenological Examination into the Intelligibility of Experience*. Athens, OH: Ohio University Press.

Covington, M. (2000). Goal Theory, Motivation, and School Achievement: An Integrative Review. *Annual Review of Psychology*, 171.

Crutzen, P., & Stoemer, E. F. (2000). The 'Anthropocene'. *Global Change Newsletter, 41*, 17-18.

Daniels, H. (1996). *An introduction to Vygotsky*. London ; New York: Routledge.

Daniels, H. (2001). *Vygotsky and Pedagogy*. London: RoutledgeFalmer.

Davis, J. (2003, November). Wilderness Rites of Passage: Healing, Growth, and Initiation. Retrieved from www.johnvdavis.com/wild/wrop.htm

Davis, M. (2012). MRC Home: Aoccdrnig to a rscheearch at Cmabridge. Retrieved from www.mrc-cbu.cam.ac.uk/people/matt.davis/cmabridge/

De Sousa, R. (2004). Emotions: What I Know, What I'd Like to Think I know, and What I'd Like to Think. In R. C. Solomon (Ed.), *Thinking About Feeling: Contemporary Philosophers on Emotions* (pp. 61-75). Oxford: Oxford University Press.

Delaney, C. H. (1995). Rites of Passage in Adolescence. *Adolescence, 30*(120), 891-897.

Dennen, V. P. (2004). Cognitive Apprenticeship in Education Practice: Research on Scaffolding, Modeling, Mentoring, and Coaching as Instructional Strategies. In D. Jonassen (Ed.), *Handbook of Research on Educational Communications and Technology: A Project of the Association for Educational Communications and Technology* (pp. 813-828). Mahwah, NJ: Lawrence Erlbaum Associates.

Dewey, J. (1909). *Moral Principles in Education*. New York: Houghton Miffin.

Dewey, J. (1921). *Democracy and Education: An Introduction to the Philosophy of Education*. New York: MacMillan.

Dewey, J. (1929). *The Quest for Certainty: A Study of the Relation of Knowledge and Action*. New York: Minton, Balch & Company.

Dewey, J. (1997 [1910]). *How We Think*. Mineola, NY: Dover Publications Inc.

Dewey, J. (1997 [1938]). *Experience and Education*. New York: Touchstone.

Dewey, J. (1998 [1897]). My Pedagogic Creed. In L. Hickman & T. Alexander (Eds.), *The Essential John Dewey: Pragmatism, Education, Democracy* (Vol. 1, pp. 229-235). Bloomington: Indiana University Press.

Dewey, J. (1998 [1905]). The Postulate of Immediate Empiricism. In L. Hickman & T. Alexander (Eds.), *The Essential Dewey: Pragmatism, education, democracy* (Vol. 1, pp. 115-120). Bloomington, Indiana: Indiana University Press.

Dewey, J. (1998 [1916]). Natural Development and Social Efficiency as Aims. In L. Hickman & T. Alexander (Eds.), *The Essential Dewey, Volume 1: Pragmatism, Education, Democracy* (pp. 257-264). Bloomington, Indiana: Indiana University Press.

Duffy, T., & Cunningham, D. (2001). Constructivism: Implications for the Design and Delivery of Instruction *The Handbook of Research for Educational Communications and Technology*. Bloomington, Indiana: The Association for Educational Communications and Technology.

Duit, R. (1995). The Constructivist View: A Fashionable and Fruitful Paradigm for Science Education Research and Practice In J. Gale & L. Steffe (Eds.), *Constructivism in Education* (pp. 271-286). Hillsdale, NJ: Lawrence Erlbaum Associates.

Engeström, Y. (1993). Developmental studies of work as a testbench of activity theory: The case of primary care medical practice. In S. Chaiklin & J. Lave (Eds.), *Understanding Practice: Perspectives on Activity and Context* (pp. 64-103). Cambridge: Cambridge University Press.

Engeström, Y., & Miettinen, R. (1999). Introduction. In Y. Engeström, R. Miettinen, & R. Punamaki (Eds.), *Perspectives on Activity Theory* (pp. 1-18). Cambridge: Cambridge University Press.

Epstein, R., Kirshnit, C. E., Lanza, P., & Rubin, L. C. (1984). 'Insight' in the pigeon: antecedents and determinants of an intelligent performance. *Nature, 308*(1), 61-62.

Ernest, P. (1995). The One and the Many. In J. Gale & L. Steffe (Eds.), *Constructivism in Education* (pp. 459-488). Hillsdale, NJ: Lawrence Erlbaum Associates.

Estes, C. (2004). Promoting Student-centered Learning in Experiential Education. *Journal of Experiential Education, 27*(2), 141-161.

Fenwick, T. (2000). Experiential Learning in Adult Education: A Comparative Framework. Retrieved from www.ualberta.ca/~tfenwick/ext/pubs/aeq.htm

Flavell, J. H. (1963). *Developmental Psychology of Jean Piaget.* Princeton, New Jersey: D. Van Nostrand.

Floden, R., & Prawat, R. (1994). Philosophical Perspectives on Constructivist Views of Learning. *Educational Psychologist, 29*(1), 37-48.

Fodor, J. A. (1980). Fixation of belief and concept acquisition. In M. Piatelli-Palmerini (Ed.), *Language and Learning: The debate between Jean Piaget and Noam Chomsky* (pp. 142-149). Cambridge, MA: Harvard University Press.

Foos, P., & Sarno, A. (1998). Adult Age Differences in Semantic and Episodic Memory *Journal of Genetic Psychology, 159*(3), 297-311.

Fox, K. (2008). Rethinking Experience: What Do We Mean by This Word "experience"? *The Journal of Experiential Education, 31*(1), 36-54.

Freeman, M. (1987). Is infancy learning egocentric or duocentric? Was Piaget Wrong? *Pre- and Perinatal Psychology Journal, 2*(1), 25-42.

Freeman, P., Nelson, D., & Taniguchi, S. (2003). Philosophy and Practice of Wilderness-Based Experiential Learning *Journal of Physical Education, Recreation & Dance, 74*(8), 25-27.

Freire, P., & Giroux, H. (Eds.). (1992). *Cultural Pedagogy: Art, Education, Politics.* New York: Bergin & Garvey.

Furth, H. (1987). *Knowledge as Desire: An Essay on Freud and Piaget* (Vol. 10). New York: Columbia University Press.

Gallego, M. A. (2001). Is Experience the Best Teacher? *Journal of Teacher Education, 52*(4), 312.

Gandini, L. (1998). Educational and Caring Spaces. In C. Edwards, L. Gandini, & G. Forman (Eds.), *The Hundred Languages of Children: The Reggio Emilia Approach –*

Advanced Reflections (pp. 161-178). Greenwich: Ablex.

Garrison, R. (1998). Developmental Pathways as Rites of Passage. *Reaching Today's Youth, 3*(1), 33-36.

Garrison, W. (2003). Democracy, Experience, and Education: Promoting a Continued Capacity for Growth. *Phi Delta Kappan, 84*(7), 525. Retrieved from www.questia.com/ PM.qst?a=o&d=5001512002

Gibboney, R. (2006). Intelligence by Design: Thorndike versus Dewey. *Phi Delta Kappan, 88*(2), 170.

Gibson, E. J., & Pick, A. D. (2003). *An Ecological Approach to Perceptual Learning and Development.* Oxford: Oxford University Press.

Gibson, J. J. (1986). *The Ecological Approach to Visual Perception.* Hillsdale, NJ: Lawrence Erlbaum Associates.

Gladwell, M. (2008). *Outliers: The Story of Success.* New York, NY: Little, Brown and Company.

Glassman, M. (2001). Dewey and Vygotsky: Society, Experience, and Inquiry in Educational Practice. *Educational Researcher, 30*(4), 3-14.

Gordin, D., Hoadley, C., Means, B., Pea, R. D., & Roschelle, J. (2000). Changing How and What Children Learn in School with Computer-Based Technologies *The Future of Children, 10*(2), 76-101.

Grabowski, B., & Jonassen, D. (1993). *Handbook of Individual Differences, Learning and Instruction.* Hillsdale, NJ: Lawrence Erlbaum Associates.

Gredler, M. E., & Green, S. K. (2002). A Review and Analysis of Constructivism for School-Based Practice. *School Psychology Review, 31*(1), 53-70.

Gredler, M. E., & Shields, C. (2004). Does No One Read Vygotsky's Words? Commentary on Glassman. *Educational Researcher, 33*(2), pp. 21-25.

Greenaway, R. (2005). Experiential Learning articles and a critique of David Kolb's Theory. Retrieved 10 April 2005, from Roger Greenaway, Reviewing Skills Training reviewing.co.uk/research/experiential.learning.htm – top

Greeno, J. G. (1994). Gibson's Affordances. *Psychological Review, 101*(2), 336-342.

Guthrie, E. R., & Horton, G. P. (1946). *Cats in a Puzzle Box.* New York, NY: Rinehart & Company.

Hackmann, D. (2004). Constructivism and Block Scheduling: Making the Connection *Phi Delta Kappan, 85*(9), 697-702.

Hahn, K. (1960). Outward Bound: Address by Dr. Kurt Hahn at the Annual Meeting of Outward Bound Trust on 20th July, 1960. Retrieved from www.kurthahn.org/writings/ obt1960.pdf

Halliday, M. A. K. (1993). Towards a language-based theory of learning. *Linguistics and Education, 5*, 93-116.

Harlow, S., Cummings, R., & Abersturi, S. (2006). Karl Popper and Jean Piaget: a Rationale for Constructivism. *The Educational Forum, 71*(1), 41-48.

Hattie, J., Marsh, H. W., Neill, J., & Richards, G. (1997). Adventure Education and Outward Bound: Out-of-Class Experiences That Make a Lasting Difference. *Review of Educational Research, 67*(1), 43-87.

Hausfather, S. (2001). Where's the Content? The Role of Content in Constructivist Teacher Education. *Educational Horizons*(Fall), 15-19.

Hendricks, B. (1994). Improving Evaluation in Experiential Education. Retrieved from www.ericdigests.org/1995-2/improving.htm

Henry, J. (1989). Meaning and Practice in Experiential Learning. In S. Weil & I. McGill (Eds.), *Making Sense of Experiential Learning: Diversity in Theory and Practice* (pp. 29-33). Milton Keynes: Open University Press.

Henson, K. (2003). Foundations for Learner-Centered Education: A Knowledge Base *Education, 124*(1), 5-16.

Herbert, D. (1999). *What do students remember from lectures? The role of episodic memory on early learning.* Paper presented at the Australian Association for Research in Education – New Zealand Association for Research in Education Conference.

Herbert, D., & Burt, J. (2004). What do Students Remember? Episodic Memory and the Development of Schematization. *Applied Cognitive Psychology, 18*, 77-88.

Hickey, D. (1997). Motivation and Contemporary Socio-Constructivist Instructional Perspectives *Educational Psychologist, 32*(3), 175-193.

Hirsch, E. D. (2001). Romancing the Child: Progressivism's Romantic Roots. *Education Next, 1*(1), 34-39.

Hoberman, S., & Mailick, S. (1994). *Professional Education in the United States: Experiential Learning, Issues, and Prospects.* Wesport, CT: Praeger Publishers.

Hogan, D., & Tudge, J. (1999). Implications of Vygotsky's Theory for Peer Learning. In A. King & A. O'Donnell (Eds.), *Cognitive Perspectives on Peer Learning* (pp. 39-65). Hillsdale, NJ: Lawrence Erlbaum Associates.

Howard, R. (1995). *Learning and Memory: Major Ideas, Principles, Issues and Applications.* Westport, CT.: Praeger.

Husserl, E. (1983 [1913]-a). *Ideas Pertaining to a Pure Phenomenology and to a Phenomenological Philosophy: First Book* (F. Kersten, Trans. Vol. II). Dordrecht, The Netherlands: Kluwer Academic Publishers.

Husserl, E. (1983 [1913]-b). Introduction to Ideas Pertaining to a Pure Phenomenology and to a Phenomenological Philosophy (F. Kersten, Trans.). In E. Bernet (Ed.), *Ideas Pertaining to a Pure Phenomenology and to a Phenomenological Philosophy: First Book* (Vol. II, pp. XVII-XXIII). Dordrecht, The Netherlands: Kluwer Academic Publishers.

Hyslop-Margison, E., & Strobel, J. (2008). Constructivism and Education: Misunderstandings and Pedagogical Implications. *The Teacher Educator, 43*(1), 72-76.

Inhelder, B., & Piaget, J. (1958). *The Growth of Logical Thinking from Childhood to Adolescence* (S. Milgram & A. Parsons, Trans.). New York: Basic Books.

International Baccalaureate Organisation. (2008, 2009). IB Learner Profile Booklet. Retrieved from www.ibo.org/programmes/profile/documents/Learnerprofileguide.pdf

International Baccalaureate Organisation. (2013). IB Learner Profile. Retrieved from www.ibo.org/contentassets/fd82f70643ef4086b7d3f292cc214962/learner-profile-en.pdf

Itin, C. M. (1999). Reasserting the philosophy of experiential education as a vehicle for change in the 21st century. *Journal of Experiential Education, 22*(2), 91-98.

James, W. (1912). *Essays in Radical Empiricism.* New York: Longmans, Green and Co.

Jarvis, P., Holford, J., & Griffin, C. (2003). *The Theory & Practice of Learning.* London: Kogan Page.

Jonassen, D. (2009). Reconciling a Human Cognitive Architecture. In S. Tobias & T. Duffy (Eds.), *Constructivist Instruction: Success or Failure?* (pp. 13-33). New York: Routledge.

Jordan, S., Messner, M., & Becker, A. (2009). Reflection and Mindfulness in Organizations: Rationales and Possibilities for Integration. *Management Learning, 40*(4), 465-473.

Kant, I. (1996). *Critique of Pure Reason* (W. Pluhar, Trans.). Indianapolis: Hackett.

Karpov, Y. (2003). Vygotsky's Doctrine of Scientific Concepts: Its Role for Contemporary Education. In A. Kozulin, B. Gindidis, V. Ageyev, & S. M. Miller (Eds.), *Vygotsky's Educational Theory in Cultural Context* (pp. 65-82). Cambridge: Cambridge University Press.

Khalil, E. (2004). *Dewey, Pragmatism and Economic Methodology.* New York: Routledge.

Kirschner, P. A., Sweller, J., & Clark, R. E. (2006). Why minimal guidance during instruction does not work: An analysis of the failure of constructivist, discovery, problem-based, experiential, and inquiry based teaching. *Educational Psychologist, 41*(2), 75-86.

Kitcher, P. (1996). Prefaces and Introduction: Kant's Central Problem *Critique of Pure Reason* (pp. xxv-lx). Indianapolis: Hackett.

Knapp, D. (2000). Memorable Experiences of a Science Field Trip. *School Science and Mathematics, 100,* 65.

Knopf, M. (1995). Memory for Action Events: Structure and Development in Adulthood. In W. Schneider & F. E. Weinert (Eds.), *Memory Performance and Competencies: Issues in Growth and Development* (pp. 127-140). Mahwah, NJ: Lawrence Erlbaum.

Köhler, W. (1930). Some Tasks of Gestalt Psychology. In C. Murchison (Ed.), *The Psychologies of 1930* (pp. 143-161). Worcester, MA: Clark University Press.

Kolb, A., & Kolb, D. (2008). Experiential Learning Theory: A Dynamic, Holistic Approach to Management Learning, Education and Development. Retrieved from Learning From Experience website: learningfromexperience.com/media/2010/08/ELT-Hbk-MLED-LFE-website-2-10-08.pdf

Kolb, D. A. (1984). The Process of Experiential Learning. Retrieved from www.learningfromexperience.com/images/uploads/process-of-experiential-learning.pdf

Kozulin, A. (1986). Vygotsky in Context. In A. Kozulin (Ed.), *Thought and Language* (pp. xi-lvi). Cambridge, Massachusetts: MIT Press.

Kraft, R., & Sakofs, M. (Eds.). (1989). *The Theory of Experiential Education* (2nd ed.). Boulder, CO: Association for Experiential Education.

Kuhn, T. S. (1996). *The Structure of Scientific Revolutions* (3rd ed.). Chicago: University of Chicago Press.

Land, S., & Hannafin, M. (2000). Student-Centred Learning Environments. In D. Jonassen & S. Land (Eds.), *Theoretical Foundations of Learning Environments* (pp. 1-23). Hillsdale, NJ: Lawrence Erlbaum Associates.

Laubscher, M. (1994). *Encounters with Difference: Student Perceptions of the Role of Out-of-Class Experiences in Education Abroad.* Westport, CT: Greenwood Press.

Lave, J. (1997). The Culture of Acquisition and the Practice of Understanding. In D. Kirshner & J. Whitson (Eds.), *Situated Cognition: Social, Semiotic, and Psychological Perspectives* (pp. 17-36). New Jersey: Lawrence Erlbaum Associates.

Leontiev, A. N. (1981). *Problems of the Development of the Mind.* Moscow: Progress Press.

Liu, C., & Matthews, R. (2005). Vygotsky's philosophy: Constructivism and its criticisms examined. *International Education Journal, 6*(3), 386-399.

Locke, J. (1952 [1689]). An Essay Concerning Human Understanding. In R. M. Hutchins (Ed.), *Locke Berkley Hume* (Vol. 35, pp. 318). Chicago: Encyclopedia Britannica Inc. .

Loyens, S., & Gijbels, D. (2008). Understanding the effects of constructivist learning environments: introducing a multi-directional approach.*2008*(36), 351-357. Retrieved from publishing.eur.nl/ir/repub/asset/14906/2008120300307.pdf

Luckner, J., & Nadler, R. (1997). *Processing the Experience: Strategies to Enhance and Generalize Learning* (2nd ed.). Dubuque, Iowa: Kendall/Hunt.

Lutterman-Aguilar, A., & Gingerich, O. (2002). Experiential Pedagogy for Study Abroad: Educating for Global Citizenship. Winter. Retrieved from www.frontiersjournal.com/issues/vol8/vol8-07_luttermanaguilargingerich.htm

Maddern, E. (1990). What Is It Fifteen Year Olds Need? Notes on developing initiations appropriate to our times. *Adventure Education, 17*(1), 29-32.

Mahoney, M. J. (2003). *Constructive Psychotherapy: A Practical Guide.* New York, NY: The Guildford Press.

Marsh, C. (2004). *Key Concepts for Understanding Curriculum.* London: RoutledgeFalmer.

Martin, B., Cashel, C., Wagstaff, M., & Breunig, M. (2006). *Outdoor Leadership: Theory and Practice.* Champaign, IL: Human Kinetics.

Martin, J. (1993). Episodic Memory: a Neglected Phenomenon in the Psychology of Education. *Educational Psychologist, 28*(2), 169-183.

Mayer, F. (1960). *A History of Educational Thought.* Columbus, OH: Charles E. Merrill Books.

Mayer, R. (2004). Should There Be a Three-Strikes Rule Against Pure Discovery Learning? The Case for Guided Methods of Instruction. *American Psychologist, 59*(1), 14-19.

Mayer, R. (2005). Introduction to Multimedia Learning. In R. Mayer (Ed.), *The Cambridge Handbook of Multimedia Learning* (pp. 1-16). New York: Cambridge University Press.

McDermid, D. (2015). Pragmatism. *Internet Encyclopedia of Philosophy.* Retrieved from www.iep.utm.edu/pragmati/

McKenzie, M. (2000). How are Adventure Education Program Outcomes Achieved?: A review of the literature. *Australian Journal of Outdoor Education, 5*(1), 19-28.

McKenzie, M. (2003). Beyond "The Outward Bound Process:" Rethinking Student Learning. *The Journal of Experiential Education, 26*(1), 8-23.

Merchant, C. (2004). *Reinventing Eden: The Fate of Nature in Western Culture.* New York: Routledge.

Miettinen, R. (2006). The concept of experiential learning and John Dewey's theory of reflective thought and action. In P. Jarvis (Ed.), *From Adult Education to the Learning Society: 21 Years of the International Journal of Lifelong Education* (pp. 243-266). London: Routledge.

Miller, N., & Boud, D. (1996). Animating learning from experience. In D. Boud & N. Miller (Eds.), *Working with Experience: Animating Learning* (pp. 3-13). New York: Routledge.

Mok, I. (2003). *A "Teacher-Dominating" Lesson in Shanghai: The teacher's and the learner's perspectives.* Paper presented at the Learner's Perspective Study, University of Melbourne. extranet.edfac.unimelb.edu.au/DSME/lps/assets/lpswebupdates/Teacherdominating.pdf

Montgomery, E. H., & Darling, J. R. (1967). *Timbertop. an Innovation in Australian Education.* Melbourne: F.W. Cheshire.

Moore, A. (2000). *Teaching and Learning: Pedagogy, Curriculum, and Culture.* London: Routledge.

Mowrer, R., & Klein, S. (2001). The Transitive Nature of Contemporary Learning Theory. In R. Mowrer & S. Klein (Eds.), *Handbook of Contemporary Learning Theories* (pp. 1-22). Mahwah, NJ: Lawrence Erlbaum Associates.

Neill, J. (2003, 6 December 2003). Rites of Passage: Van Gennep 3-Stage Model & Outdoor Education – Commentary on Bell (2003). Retrieved from wilderdom.com/rites/RitesOfPassageCommentaryBell2003.html – Recommendations

Neill, J. (2004, 12 Feb 2004). Outdoor Education in the Schools: What Can It Achieve? Retrieved from www.wilderdom.com/html/OutdoorEducationInSchoolsWhatCanItAchieve.html

Neill, J. (2006, 10 May 2006). Experiential Learning & Experiential Education. Retrieved from wilderdom.com/experiential/

O'Brien, L. (2002). A Response to "Dewey and Vygotsky: Society, Experience, and Inquiry in Educational Practice". *Educational Researcher, 31*(5), 21-23.

OECD. (2014). The Learning Environment and Organisation of Schools. In OECD (Ed.), Education at a Glance 2014: OECD Indicators: OECD Publishing. Retrieved from dx.doi.org/10.1787/eag-2014-en.

Office for Policy Research and Innovation. (2009). *Understanding Year 9 Students Forum Report.* Melbourne: Education Policy and Research Division.

Oliver, K., & Hannafin, M. (2001). Developing and Refining Mental Models in Open-Ended Learning Environments: A Case Study. *Educational Technology Research and Design, 49*(4), 5-32.

Outward Bound International. (2004). Kurt Hahn – The Founder's Story. Retrieved from www.outwardbound.net/about/history/kurt-hahn.html

Owen-Smith, P. (2004). What is Cognitive-Affective Learning (CAL)? *Journal of Cognitive Affective Learning, 1*(1), 11.

Oxendine, C., Robinson, J., & Willson, G. (2004). Experiential Learning. *Emerging Perspectives on Learning, Teaching, and Technology*. Retrieved from www.coe.uga.edu/epltt/elt.htm

Panofsky, C., John-Steiner, V., & Blackwell, P. (1990). The development of scientific concepts and discourse. In L. Moll (Ed.), *Vygotsky and education: instructional implications and applications of sociohistorical psychology* (pp. 251-270). Cambridge: Cambridge University Press.

Parkinson, J. (2003). *Improving Secondary Science Teaching*. New York: RoutledgeFalmer.

Pea, R. (1993). Practices of distributed intelligence and designs for education. In G. Salomon (Ed.), *Distributed Cognitions* (pp. 47-87). New York: Cambridge University Press.

Pegues, H. (2007). Of Paradigm Wars: Constructivism, Objectivism, and Postmodern Stratagem. *The Educational Forum, 71*(4), 316-330.

Perkinson, H. (1984). *Learning from Our Mistakes: A Reinterpretation of Twentieth-Century Educational Theory*. Westport, CT: Greenwood Press.

Phillips, D. C. (1995). The Good, the Bad, and the Ugly: The Many Faces of Constructivism. *Educational Researcher, 24*(7), 5-12.

Piaget, J. (1952). *The Origins of Intelligence in Children* (M. Cook, Trans.). New York: International Universities Press.

Piaget, J. (1962). Comments on Vygotsky's critical remarks concerning *The Language and Thought of the Child,* and *Judgement and Reasoning in the Child*. Retrieved from www.marxists.org/archive/vygotsky/works/comment/piaget.htm

Piaget, J. (2002 [1923]). *The Language and Thought of the Child* (M. Gabain & R. Gabain, Trans.). London: Routledge.

Piaget, J., & Garcia, R. (1991). Logic and Genetic Epistemology In P. Davidson & J. Easley (Eds.), *Towards a Logic of Meanings*.

Plato. (1952). *The Republic* (B. Jowett, Trans. Vol. 7). Chicago: Encyclopedia Britannica.

Plato. (2002). *Phaedo* (G. Grube, Trans.). Indianapolis: Hackett.

Poag, C., Goodnight, J., & Cohen, R. (1985). The Environments of Children: From Home to School. In R. Cohen (Ed.), *The Development of Spatial Cognition* (pp. 71-113). Hillsdale, NJ: Lawrence Erlbaum Associates.

Popper, K., & Eccles, J. C. (1997). *The Self and Its Brain*. Berlin: Springer-Verlag.

Pritchard, M. (2010). *Experiential Learning Programs in Australian Secondary Schools.* (PhD Thesis), University of Melbourne, Melbourne, Australia. Retrieved from hdl.handle.net/11343/35988

Quay, J. (2003). Experience and Participation. *The Journal of Experiential Education, 26*(2), 105-112.

Readdick, C., & Bartlett, P. (1995). Vertical Learning Environments. *Childhood Education, 71*(2), 86-90.

Richardson, K. (2000). *The Making of Intelligence.* New York: Columbia University Press.

Rickinson, M., Dillon, J., Teamey, K., Morris, M., Choi, M. Y., Sanders, D., & Benefield, P. (2004, 3 September 2004). A Review of Research on Outdoor Learning. Retrieved from www.peecworks.org/PEEC/PEEC_Research/S000F79A7

Rittel, H., & Webber, M. (1973). Dilemmas in a General Theory of Planning. *Policy Sciences, 4*, 155-169.

Roberts, P. (2000). *Education, Literacy, and Humanization: Exploring the Work of Paulo Freire.* Westport, CT: Bergin and Garvey.

Rogers, C. (1969). *Freedom to Learn.* Columbus, OH: Charles E. Merrill.

Rogers, C. (1983). *Freedom To Learn for the 80's.* Columbus, OH: Charles E. Merrill.

Rogoff, B. (2003). *The Cultural Nature of Human Development.* New York: Oxford University Press.

Round Square. (2010). Round Square. Retrieved from www.roundsquare.org/index.php?id=11

Rousseau, J. J. (1957 [1762]). *Emile* (B. Foxley, Trans.). New York: Dutton.

Santayana, G. (1980 [1905]). *The Life of Reason: Reason in Common Sense* (Vol. 1). New York, NY: Dover Publications.

Scardamalia, M., & Bereiter, C. (1992). Text-based and Knowledge-based Questioning by Children. *Cognition and Instruction, 9*(3), 177-199.

Scardamalia, M., & Bereiter, C. (1994). Computer support for knowledge-building communities. *The Journal of the Learning Sciences, 3*(3), 265-283.

Schön, D. (1983). *The Reflective Practitioner: How Professionals Think in Action*: Basic Books.

Schön, D. (1987). *Educating the Reflective Practitioner: Toward a New Design for Teaching Learning in the Professions.* San Francisco: Jossey-Bass.

Scrutton, R., & Beames, S. (2015). Measuring the Unmeasurable: Upholding Rigor in Quantitative Studies of Personal and Social Development in Outdoor Adventure Education. *Journal of Experiential Education, 38*(1), 8-25.

Seiffert, C., & Hutchins, E. (1992). Error as Opportunity: Learning in a Cooperative Task. *Human-Computer Interaction, 7*(4), 409-436.

Skinner, B. F. (1950). Are Theories of Learning Necessary? Retrieved from psychclassics.yorku.ca/Skinner/Theories/

Smith, J. P., diSessa, A. A., & Roschelle, J. (1993). Misconceptions Reconceived: A Constructivist Analysis of Knowledge in Transition. *The Journal of Learning Sciences, 3*(2), 115-163.

Smith, M. (2003). Summary: Off-site Educational Visits and the Impact on Attainment. Retrieved from www.collegest.org.uk/SHOE/Outdoor Ed/documents/Summary.doc

Snodgrass, J. (1989). How Many Memory Systems Are There Really?: Some Evidence From the Picture Fragment Completion Task In C. Izawa (Ed.), *Current Issues in Cognitive Processes* (pp. 135-171). Hillsdale, NJ: Lawrence Erlbaum Associates.

Steffe, L. (1995). Alternative Epistemologies: An Educator's Perspective. In J. Gale & L. Steffe (Eds.), *Constructivism in Education* (pp. 489-523). Hillsdale, NJ: Lawrence Erlbaum Associates.

Stokrocki, M. (1997). Rites of Passage for Middle School Students. *Art Education, 50*(3), 48-55.

Styles, E. A. (2005). *Attention, Perception, and Memory: An Integrated Introduction.* Hove, England: Psychology Press.

Sutton, J. (2004, 10 May 2004). Memory. *The Stanford Encyclopedia of Philosophy (Summer 2004 Edition).* Summer 2004. Retrieved from plato.stanford.edu/archives/sum2004/entries/memory

Swann, A. (2008). Children, Objects, and Relations: Constructivist Foundations in the Reggio Emilia Approach. *Studies in Art Education, 50*(1), 36-.

Tappan, M. (1998). Sociocultural Psychology and Caring Pedagogy: Exploring Vygotsky's "Hidden Curriculum". *Educational Psychologist, 33*(1), 23-34.

Tharp, R., & Gallimore, R. (1988). *Rousing Minds to Life: Teaching, learning, and schooling in social context.* Cambridge: Cambridge University Press.

The Duke of Edinburgh's Award. (2011). The Duke of Edinburgh's Award.

Theobald, P., & Tolbert, L. (2006). Finding Their Place in the Community: Urban Education outside the Classroom. *Childhood Education, 82*(5), 271-274. Retrieved from

Tobias, S., & Duffy, T. (2009). The Success or Failure of Constructivist Instruction: An Introduction. In S. Tobias & T. Duffy (Eds.), *Constructivist Instruction: Success or Failure?* (pp. 3-10). New York: Routledge.

Tobin, K., & Tippins, D. (1993). Constructivism as a Referent for Teaching and Learning. In K. Tobin (Ed.), *The Practice of Constructivism in Science Education* (pp. 3-21). Hillsdale, NJ: Lawrence Erlbaum Associates.

Tudge, J., & Rogoff, B. (1989). Peer Influences on Cognitive Development: Piagetian and Vygotskian Perspectives. In M. H. Bornstein & J. S. Bruner (Eds.), *Interaction in Human Development.* Hillsdale, NJ: Lawrence Erlbaum Associates.

Tulving, E. (1972). Episodic and Semantic Memory. In E. Tulving & W. Donaldson (Eds.), *Organization of Memory* (pp. 381-403). New York: Academic Press.

Tulving, E. (2002). Episodic Memory: from mind to brain. *Annual Review of Psychology,* xvi.

Tulving, E. (2004). Episodic Memory and Autonoesis: Uniquely Human? In H. S. Terrace & J. Metcalfe (Eds.), *The Missing Link in Cognition: Origins of Self-Reflective Consciousness* (pp. 1-56). New York: Oxford University Press.

Uljens, M. (1997). *School Didactics and Learning: A School Didactic Model Framing an Analysis of Pedagogical Implications of Learning Theory.* Hove, UK: Psychology Press.

UWC International. (2015). UWC Guiding Principles. Retrieved from www.uwc.org/uwc_education/guiding_principles.aspx

van Gennep, A. (2004 [1909]). *The Rites of Passage* (M. Vizedom & G. Caffee, Trans.). London: Routledge.

Van Note Chism, N., & Bickford, J. (2002). *The Importance of Physical Space in Creating Supportive Learning Environments* (Vol. 92). San Francisco: Jossey-Bass.

Vandenbroucke, S., Crombez, G., Van Ryckeghem, D. M. L., Brass, M., Van Damme, S., & Goubert, L. (2013). Vicarious pain while observing another in pain: an experimental approach. *Frontiers in Human Neuroscience, 7*(2013), 265. doi:dx.doi.org/10.3389%2Ffnhum.2013.00265

von Foerster, H. (1973). On Constructing Reality. *Principia Cybvernetic Web.* Retrieved from pespmc1.vub.ac.be/books/Foerster-constructingreality.pdf

von Glasersfeld, E. (1995). A Constructivist Approach to Teaching. In J. Gale & L. Steffe (Eds.), *Constructivism in Education* (pp. 3-16). Hillsdale, NJ: Lawrence Erlbaum Associates.

von Glasersfeld, E. (1996). *Radical Constructivism: A Way of Knowing and Learning.* London: Falmer Press.

Vygotsky, L. S. (1978). *Mind in Society : The Development of Higher Psychological Processes* (M. Cole, Trans.). Cambridge, MA: Harvard University Press.

Vygotsky, L. S. (1986 [1934]). *Thought and Language* (A. Kozulin, Trans.). Cambridge, MA: MIT Press.

Vygotsky, L. S. (1987). The Genesis of Higher Mental Functions. In R. Reiber (Ed.), *The History of the Development of Higher Mental Functions* (Vol. 4, pp. 97-120). New York: Plenum.

Vygotsky, L. S. (1994 [1934]). The Problem of the Environment. In R. van de Veer & J. Valsiner (Eds.), *The Vygotsky Reader* (pp. 338-354). Leiden: Blackwell.

Vygotsky, L. S., & Luria, A. R. (1993 [1930]). *Studies on the History of Behavior: Ape, Primitive, and Child* (J. E. Knox & V. I. Golod, Trans.). Hillsdale, NJ: Lawrence Erlbaum Associates.

Walsh, V., & Golins, G. (1976). The Exploration of the Outward Bound Process. Retrieved from wilderdom.com/pdf/Walsh&Golins1976ExplorationOBProcess.pdf

Webb, M. (1980). *A Definitive Critique of Experiential Learning Theory.* (doctoral qualifying thesis), Cape Western Reserve University, Cleveland, OH. Retrieved from cc.ysu.edu/~mnwebb/critique/TheCritique_final2_wtp.pdf

Wells, G. (1994). *Learning and Teaching "Scientific Concepts": Vygotsky's Ideas Revisited.* Paper presented at the Vygotsky and the Human Sciences, Moscow. people.ucsc.edu/~gwells/Files/Papers_Folder/ScientificConcepts.pdf

Wells, G. (1999). *Dialogic Inquiry: Towards a Sociocultural Practice and Theory of Education*. Cambridge: Cambridge University Press.

Wertsch, J. (1991). *Voices of the Mind: A Sociocultural Approach to Mediated Action*. Cambridge, MA: Harvard University Press.

Wertsch, J. V. (1985). *Vygotsky and the Social Formation of Mind*. Cambridge, Massachusetts: Harvard University Press.

Wertsch, J. V., Toma, C., & Hiatt, F. L. (1995). Discourse and Learning in the Classroom: A Sociocultural Approach In J. Gale & L. Steffe (Eds.), *Constructivism in Education* (pp. 159-176). Hillsdale, NJ: Lawrence Erlbaum Associates.

Williams, I. (2005). Creating a Capacity for Relatedness Through Discontinuous Experiences. *Journal of Cognitive Affective Learning, 1*(2), 13-19.

Willingham, D. B., & Preuss, L. (1995). The Death of Implicit Memory. 2(15). Retrieved from psyche.cs.monash.edu.au/v2/psyche-2-15-willingham.html

Wood, D., Bruner, J. S., & Ross, G. (1976). The Role of Tutoring in Problem-Solving. *Journal of Child Psychology and Child Psychiatry, 17*, 89-100.

Yeganeh, B., & Kolb, D. (2009). Mindfulness and Experiential Learning. *OD Practitioner, 41*(3), 13-18.

Zernike, K. (2015, 24 October 2015). Obama Administration Calls for Limits on Testing in Schools. *The New York Times*. Retrieved from www.nytimes.com/2015/10/25/us/obama-administration-calls-for-limits-on-testing-in-schools.html?hp&action=click&pgtype=Homepage&module=first-column-region&region=top-news&WT.nav=top-news&_r=0

Zhang, J. J., & Patel, V. (2006). Distributed Cognition, Representation, and Affordance. *Cognition & Pragmatics, 14*(2), 333-341.